*	Signifies an ungrammatical combination of words
( )	Signifies optional element(s)
{ }	Signifies a choice between elements
X^+	Signifies that the element X can be repeated
→	"Consists of"
⟹	"Is transformed as follows"
∅	The null symbol; signifies either the deletion of an element or an uninflected (infinitive) verb form
CAPITALS	Capital letters signify a deep-structure concept (not words spoken in the surface structure)

Discovering English Grammar

Discovering English Grammar

Richard Veit
University of North Carolina at Wilmington

HOUGHTON MIFFLIN COMPANY   BOSTON
Dallas   Geneva, Illinois   Lawrenceville, New Jersey   Palo Alto

Printed in the U.S.A.

Library of Congress Catalog Card Number: 85-81189

ISBN: 0-395-40316-2

ABCDEFGHIJ-VB-898765·

*This book is dedicated
to anyone who ever drew a tree diagram
and found that a little elf within the brain
was kicking up its heels and exclaiming,
"Hey, this is fun!"*

Contents

To the Instructor

Discovering English Grammar is a textbook for college courses in the structure of the English language. I had several goals in mind as I wrote it.

To Teach a Transformational Approach to Syntax   Transformational grammar is unquestionably the dominant school of modern linguistics. No other approach provides equivalent insights into the structure and workings of our language, nor does any other approach lend itself so successfully to undergraduate teaching.

To Provide Broad Coverage of the Major Constructions of the English Language   Many textbooks, particularly those that teach transformational syntax, focus principally on the methodology of their approach, while examining a relatively few "interesting" constructions. In contrast, my purpose in this book is to offer a genuine survey of English grammatical structures. Methodological considerations have been made secondary to the goal of providing an understanding of the language itself.

To Offer Instruction That Is Clear to Undergraduates in the Liberal Arts and in Education   Many students who lack technical facility have difficulty understanding advanced syntactic analysis, which can be quite complex and abstract. Accordingly, I have provided a "broad," rather than a "narrow," coverage of transformational syntax. When confronted with a conflict between complexity and clarity, I have always opted for clarity. I have eliminated many formalisms that are not necessary for students' understanding of the language, and I have frequently chosen simpler, "classical" transformational analyses over more recent but more difficult ones.

To Teach Grammar as a Process of Discovery   As its name implies, *Discovering English Grammar* does not teach grammatical information as received truth. Instead, it engages students as participants in an inductive search for the structure of the language. Students are asked to help discover the grammar of English by examining sentences and supplying hypotheses to account for them. In addition, the method of discovering grammar without relying on previous assumptions makes this book accessible to students who lack previous training in grammar.

To Arrange Material in a Pedagogically Useful Way   Topics are not arranged according to a classification of constructions or parts of speech; instead, they are arranged in a practical teaching sequence. Simpler and more easily understood concepts precede more complicated ones. Concepts in later chapters build upon those in earlier chapters.

To Offer Frequent, Useful Exercises   Exercises are frequent and located throughout the text, not just at the ends of chapters. They provide experiences that reinforce lessons taught in preceding sections, and they challenge students to make their own discoveries about English grammar. Students are impelled not just to know grammar but to *do* grammar.

To Stimulate Students   I have treated grammar with the same attitude of intellectual excitement that I feel for the subject. I have attempted to treat my readers with respect and to make my writing clear, straightforward, and interesting.

To Prepare Future Teachers of Grammar   For those users of this book who will teach grammar in the schools, the best preparation is a thorough understanding of the English language. Although the approach of this book is transformational, readers will be prepared to teach with whatever materials and methods are mandated by their school systems. I use widely accepted terminology throughout and include a chapter on teaching grammar in the schools.

To Prepare Students for More Advanced Syntactic Study   For students who go on to more advanced work in linguistics, *Discovering English Grammar* offers the best preparation of all—a thorough familiarity with the structure of the language. Furthermore, the inductive method of this book instills a spirit of scientific inquiry that trains students to challenge hypotheses and to form new ones. Students who use this book will be well prepared to accommodate additional data and new theories and methods.

I would like to thank those who helped me, directly and indirectly, with this book. First, I owe a debt to the nuns of St. Joseph School who taught me grammar, these many years ago, with such energy and thoroughness. They gave me my first love for the subject, and they prepared me well for my subsequent linguistic study. Thanks, too, to David Hacker and Larry Martin, who initiated me into the joys of transformational grammar at the University of Iowa. I would also like to thank the friends and colleagues who gave invaluable advice and aid with this book, including Elizabeth Pearsall and John Clifford, University of North Carolina at Wilmington; Michael Knotts, East China Petroleum Institute (Dongying, People's Republic); Stephen H. Goldman, University of Kansas; Gordon J. Loberger, Murray State University, Kentucky; and Barbara Weaver, Ball State University, Indiana. To them all, my abiding thanks.

And with that sentence fragment, let the book begin.

Richard Veit

Discovering English Grammar

1 Introduction

A writer's greatest pleasure is revealing to people things they knew but did not know they knew.
—Andy Rooney

The purpose of this book is to reveal to you something you already know. In fact, you not only know the subject, but you are an expert in it. If these sound like preposterous statements, I will give you one that will sound even more so: You, the reader of this book, know the grammar of English better than I know it—better, even, than any English teacher or professor of linguistics knows the grammar of English.

Those seemingly impossible statements are nevertheless completely true. Let me explain.

The word *grammar* is used in many different senses. Most people are familiar with *grammar* both as a subject they studied in grammar school ("A noun is the name of a person, place, or thing") and as a kind of language etiquette ("Don't say *ain't*; it's bad grammar"). Linguists use the word in a somewhat different sense, and that is the sense in which you are a grammar expert.

Grammar as we mean it is simply your language knowledge. Whatever your brain knows that allows you to use language we will call your grammar. Your grammar is what enables you to understand the very words you are now reading as well as to speak and write words and sentences of your own. You have had a grammar of English for as long as you have known English. This collected language knowledge is not a physical thing exactly. No surgeon can cut open the brain and say, "Aha! There's the grammar!" Nevertheless, we sometimes find it helpful to think of a grammar as if it were a thing, perhaps a compartment in the mind where language knowledge is stored or even, if we want to compare the brain to a computer, as a program that runs language for us.

Your English grammar is certainly well developed. Most likely you have been using English for many years. Every day you produce and understand thousands of English sentences, and you do so effortlessly. You understand what others say to you, and they understand you. Clearly, you are an expert in English grammar.

Just as *grammar* is used in several senses, the word *know* can be used in different ways as well, and that is what allowed me to say that you "know" grammar better than I "know" it. Our brains have both conscious and subconscious knowledge, and I meant that you know grammar *subconsciously* better than I, or any other linguistics or English professor, know it *consciously*. Discovering consciously what we already know subconsciously about language is, in fact, the goal of this book and of all linguistic study.

Why Study Grammar?

The main reason we study grammar is that we human beings are curious and want to learn more about ourselves. Curiosity about what we are and what kind of world we inhabit has led humans to study such fields as psychology, biology, history, and linguistics. The study of how we create language can provide important insights into the nature of our minds and the way we think. It can help us understand better what it means to be human. In particular the discovery of how complex and yet elegant our grammars are will give us an appreciation of humanity's achievement in creating this marvelous instrument. We can also appreciate our own individual achievements (which we accomplished rather effortlessly as small children) in mastering so formidable a task as learning the English language.

Grammar study also has some more immediately practical benefits, but I would discourage you from spending time on the subject if practical gain is your only goal, because you may be disappointed. People who decide to study grammar because they want to be better writers or because they want to speak a more standard dialect or because they have trouble with punctuation will find some—but not complete—help here. Because our language knowledge is mostly subconscious, not conscious, the best way to become a good writer or speaker is to read widely and practice often. A writing or speech course is likely to be at least as important as a grammar course for these purposes.

On the other hand, grammar study is not without practical benefits. We use some conscious knowledge about language when we speak and write, and conscious grammatical knowledge can help us to understand what we are doing and allow us to make some enlightened choices. Knowledge of grammar can also give us a tool for analyzing our writing and a vocabulary for discussing it.

Another practical goal that at least some readers of this book will have is to gain a background for teaching grammar in the schools. Chapter 18 considers questions concerning the goals and methods of teaching grammar to elementary and secondary students.

There is still one final reason for studying grammar, and that is that it can be a very exciting and even pleasurable activity. In each class I teach in the structure of the English language there are students (I hope a majority) who, like me, find it downright fun to study grammar. These include some students who had found grammar anything but fun in grade and high school where it was taught "the old way." I hope you are one of those who will share the joy this very exciting subject can bring.

Conscious and Subconscious Knowledge

English grammar is just one of many things you know subconsciously far better than you know consciously. When you walk up a flight of stairs, for example, you can do so without having to think about how to do it. You can climb stairs while carrying on a conversation, while composing a love sonnet, even while walking in your sleep. Although many hundreds of muscles are finely coordinated in the task of climbing stairs, you perform it errorlessly and even gracefully, and without any apparent mental effort. Yet if you or I were asked to describe how we climb stairs we would do it very inaccurately at best: "Let's see," we might say. "First you bring the right leg up and bend the knee. You point the toe up, shift your weight forward, and bring the sole down on the next step. Then...." Of course you would not have begun to describe which muscles you use when you bend the knee. Your description is a long way from capturing the directions your brain gives to your body as you move. The fact is that unless you are a highly trained physiologist, you do not "know" much about how you climb stairs. And yet in another sense you "know" how to do it quite well, since you do it all the time. Your conscious knowledge of the task cannot come close to matching what you know subconsciously.

Unfortunately no easy way has been discovered to move knowledge from the subconscious to the conscious part of the mind. If we want to know consciously how we climb stairs or regulate our heartbeats or create language or do any of a thousand other things we know subconsciously how to do, we have to work hard to discover them from the outside. If, for example, we wanted to know about stair-climbing, we would have to conduct meticulous studies of people climbing stairs. We would study slow-motion movies of the action, examine and perhaps dissect the human leg, and perform tests—and even then we would need to make guesses about how stair-climbing is accomplished.

Learning about language is even more difficult because there are no language muscles to examine. We cannot simply look within the brain to see how its works operate. We can't see the insides of the mind at all. What we have to go on in our study is almost entirely on the outside. The best we can do is examine the language that we produce and then try to draw conclusions about how we produced it. Of course we can consult our intuitions and gut feelings about our language use, but intuitions are not always reliable guides to language, and we are wise to regard them skeptically.

Another obstacle to learning about language is that language is so much more complex than stair-climbing. Trying to describe just the structure of English (ignoring such other aspects of language as speech sounds and the creation of meaning) will take up this entire book, and even that will only introduce us to the subject. Linguists agree that we are just beginning to discover what language is about and that we will be learning more and more for centuries to come. Because we can gain conscious knowledge about our grammars only by examining what they produce (since we can't examine the grammars in our minds directly), it is at best a kind of enlightened speculation. Not all linguists make the same speculations, and there is much disagreement about what it is that we "know." You can easily see why you and I are far more expert in the subconscious knowledge of grammar than anyone is in the conscious knowledge of it.

How Does the Grammar Work?

Among the things that people disagree on is what the study of English grammar can show us. Surely it can examine the sentences we produce and classify their parts, calling this a noun, that a verb, and so on. But most modern linguists have a more ambitious goal than just describing the language we produce. They hope also to describe the way we produce it. In addition to showing you how the English language is constructed, this book will also consider how we *do* the constructing. It will try to gain some insights into what goes on in the mind when we create and understand English sentences. What is it that we know when we know language?

You can make a start at discovering what it is you know by considering your answers to some questions. Begin with this one:

How many English words do you know?

Although no one can give an exact answer, that is still a reasonable question. The words you either use or can recognize probably number in the tens of thousands. But what about this question:

How many English sentences do you know?

This one seems much less reasonable. You can't count the number of sentences you know because you hear and create new ones all the time. For example, there are many sentences on this page that you have never encountered before, and yet you have no difficulty understanding them. It may surprise you to know that you frequently create entirely original sentences, sentences that are brand new to the English language. You could pause right now if you wanted and easily invent a perfectly clear English sentence that no human being living or dead has ever spoken or written or even thought of before. Even though there are a limited number of words that you know, you can put them together in an unlimited variety of ways.

The answer to the second question is that there are potentially an infinite number of sentences that we can know. Since our finite minds cannot store an infinite number of sentences, clearly we must have some means of creating sentences other than by pulling out the ones we want from a storage vault in the brain. We must have a way of creating them afresh by putting together their parts. The question this book is interested in is how we do it.

Clearly we don't throw words together at random. We would recognize only one of the following combinations of words as an English sentence:

He who laughs last laughs best.

Best laughs last laughs who he.

Best he last laughs laughs who.

Laughs who last best laughs he.

All but the first of these combinations are nonsentences. Since we are quite certain they are not products of our English grammar, we can label them as deviant or *ungrammatical*. The first sentence, on the other hand, is *grammatical*, and it surely didn't get that way by accident. How is it that we constantly create grammatical sentences like the first example and never produce gobbledygook like the other three?

The answer is that our subconscious knowledge must include some system, some set of principles for putting words together into sentences in a grammatical way. We can call these principles *grammatical rules* if we like, rules that we follow in order to create sentences, and these rules are an important component of our grammars. If our subconscious knowledge of English (which we are calling our English grammar) includes these rules, one goal in our quest for conscious knowledge about our language must be to discover what those rules might be.

This Book's Purpose

In this book we will try, then, to discover consciously the rules of our grammar, to create a model on paper of the grammar that exists in our minds. Although it is only a model of our grammar, we will use the term loosely enough to call it a *grammar* too. In that sense, this book aims to create a grammar of the English language.

How do we do it? Rather than guess what these rules are or accept on faith what others have said in the past, we can adopt a more scientific approach. A good start might be to try simply to describe some sentences that we produce. If we find some consistent feature in our descriptions, we can make a guess, or *hypothesis*, that the consistent feature represents a rule that speakers of English follow when they create sentences. We can then test the hypothesis on other sentences. If the rule works for them as well, we will say that our hypothesis is a good one, and we will keep the rule in our proposed grammar. If not, we will have to modify it or replace it with a better rule or abandon it altogether.

The procedure, then, that we will follow in this book is more like experimentation than the revelation of unquestioned facts. I intend the book to take you through a process of discovery. Rather than saying to you, "Behold the truth; accept and memorize it," I will say, "Let's see if this hypothesis accounts for what we do." This procedure will involve some trial and error. Each hypothesis we examine will be tentative, subject to later revision. Indeed, as we proceed in our investigation we will frequently revise some of the rules we proposed at an earlier stage.

You are invited to participate in this quest to understand the English language. Very likely you will think of some alternative explanations or better formulations of rules than I propose. Your instructor may provide additional hypotheses, and if you go on to take more advanced courses in syntax (the study of language structure), you will encounter still more alternatives for stating rules and still other theories about how language works.

Summary

To sum up these introductory remarks: A *grammar* is a person's subconscious language knowledge. You use your English grammar whenever you speak or write English or understand someone else's speech or writing. A grammar consists of principles or *rules* that allow you to create an infinite number of possible sentences out of a finite number of words. In this book the term *grammar* will also be used to describe the model on paper that we will construct of that mental grammar. That is the book's aim: to create a grammar or model of the rules we follow in using English. Actually, our investigation will be limited to one aspect of grammar, namely *syntax*, or the structure of language, the study of how words are put together in grammatical ways. Other aspects of language, such as how we form words or create sounds and meanings, are beyond the scope of this book.

2 Describing a Sentence

We humans are not the only species that engages in oral communication. Monkeys, like many other animals in the wild, communicate through a number of calls. A monkey community may have a dozen or more expressions for different communicative purposes—perhaps one call to signify danger on the ground (such as an approaching leopard), another to warn of danger from the air (a hawk), perhaps others to express anger or to attract a mate. One of many differences between their system of communication and ours, however, is that theirs consists of a limited set of fixed calls, while we can speak a limitless number of meaningful sentences. Monkeys cannot invent new expressions to suit their purposes the way we can.

Our language has this enormous range because it consists of parts that can be arranged in unlimited ways. The sentence that you are now reading is made up of two dozen familiar parts, or words, arranged in what is presumably a novel, original way. In the following list, four words are variously arranged to produce many different sentences:

1. No monkeys have words.

   Monkeys have no words.

   Have monkeys no words?

   Have no monkeys words?

   No words have monkeys.

   Have no words, monkeys!

Some of these combinations are unusual, some are perhaps even silly, but they are all grammatical sentences, nonetheless. You can probably think of still more combinations of these four words that would constitute English sentences, but not every possible combination is grammatical. The following, for example, is clearly not English:

2. *Words monkeys have no.

Notice the asterisk (*) in the example. We will adopt this commonly used symbol to designate combinations of words that are **ungrammatical***. That is, we do not* *recognize them as English sentences. Notice too that I have numbered the examples and other data in this and subsequent chapters. This will give us a handy way to refer to them in our discussion.*

Our ability to arrange words in different ways allows us to produce an infinity of grammatical sentences, but since not all arrangements are grammatical, our grammar must consist of principles or rules for arranging them. Violations of the rules result in ungrammatical sentences. An important part of our study will be a search for these rules.

Discovering the Parts of Sentences

Our beginning plan of action will be to analyze sentences and see what conclusions we can draw from them. Notice that I am already making an assumption: that the sentence is the unit of language we should examine. That choice is in a sense arbitrary. If we wished, we could start by examining larger units, such as paragraphs or longer verbal exchanges with one or more participants. But our intuitions tell us that sentences are units that are somehow basic—that have an integrity. They are the smallest units that can stand alone (a complete verbal exchange might consist of a single sentence), and all the larger units are composed of sentences. No smaller unit of language can exist with the same independence (except perhaps for exclamations such as "Drat!" and even these might be called sentences too). So unless our experimenting shows us otherwise, we will assume that the sentence is the unit we should study.

Let us begin with this one:

3 | The monkey saw a leopard.

If you were asked to divide sentence 3 into its parts, you would of course identify the five words that comprise it. But what if you were asked about larger units? Are there any groupings of words in the sentence that seem to "go together"? Your intuitions would probably lead you to identify *the monkey* and *a leopard* as units. They seem to belong together in a way that *monkey saw* or *saw a* clearly do not. Furthermore, *the monkey* and *a leopard* seem very similar, as if they are units of the same type. In fact we can substitute one for the other and still have a grammatical (although different) sentence:

4 | A leopard saw the monkey.

In contrast, if we switched *the monkey* with a different grouping such as *saw a*, the result would be ungrammatical:

5 | *Saw a the monkey leopard.

This corroborates our intuition that *the monkey* and *a leopard* act as units in sentence 3.

How important is this discovery? If we determine that sentences are constructed out of such units, we will have gained an important insight into the structure of the English language. From now on we will call all such units **constituents** of sentences (since the units are assumed to *constitute* the sentences). All subparts of sentences can be called constituents, from individual words like *monkey* to multiword phrases like *the monkey* to the entire sentence itself.

I said in the first chapter that our intuitions, while important, are not always reliable guides to language analysis, and it is wise to subject them to independent tests. Another test of the reality of a constituent like *the monkey* is whether other such constituents can be found that can substitute for it in a grammatical sentence. Are there other groupings of words that can fill the blank in 6?

6   ——————— saw a leopard.

In fact there is a limitless range of possible substitutes such as these:

7
The crocodile saw a leopard.

A leopard saw a leopard.

The wise, old, alert monkey saw a leopard.

Anita saw a leopard.

The man who had a scar above his right eye saw a leopard.

We saw a leopard.

Each of the underlined phrases works in our test, and each feels intuitively like a unit. We will conclude that all of these units are constituents of the same type. For convenience, let us arbitrarily give this type of constituent a name. We will call it a **noun phrase**, or **NP** for short. Actually the name is not so arbitrary, but I will wait until the next chapter to explain why.

Not every grouping is a noun phrase, however. None of the groupings in 8 can successfully fill the blank in 6:

8
*Ate saw a leopard.

*Ate a banana saw a leopard.

*Very happy saw a leopard.

*Fearfully saw a leopard.

*Over the river and through the woods saw a leopard.

According to our test procedure, none of the underlined groupings in 8 seems to be a noun phrase.

In addition to the two noun phrases, our sample sentence, *The monkey saw a leopard*, also contains the word *saw*, which, according to our test, is not a noun phrase. What can we discover about it? By performing the same substitution test that we conducted on noun phrases, we can find many other words that could take the place of *saw* in the sentence: *angers, tickled, resembles,* and *hypnotized*, to name a few. So *saw* belongs to another category of constituents; we will call it a *verb*, or **V**.

Our analysis of sentence 3 has shown us that it consists of a noun phrase followed by a verb and then another noun phrase. We could restate that in shorthand form (with **S** standing for *sentence* and **=** standing for *consists of*):

9 | S = NP + V + NP

We can analyze sentence 3 further. Two of the constituents appear to have constituents of their own, since the noun phrases each consist of two words. The words *the* and *a* can be interchanged, and we will call them **articles**, abbreviated **Art**. Likewise *monkey* and *leopard* belong to the category **noun** or **N**. Statement 10 can describe the noun phrases in 3:

10 | NP = Art + N

Finally, many people also have the intuitive feeling that just as *a leopard* is a constituent, so too is the longer phrase, *saw a leopard*. They call this supposed constituent a *verb phrase*, or **VP**. If so, it contains a verb and a noun phrase. That is,

11 | VP = V + NP

Although the existence of the verb-phrase category is less clearcut than that of the other constituents we have described, there seems to be evidence for accepting it, and most linguists do so. Some of the evidence relies on our intuitions about meaning. Sentences seem to consist of two parts, usually a doer and an action. These two parts are sometimes called the sentence's *subject* and its *predicate*. In this book, we will generally use the grammatical category names, noun phrase and verb phrase. Here are some examples:

12 |
NP (Subject) / VP (Predicate)

The monkey / saw a leopard.

The lima bean casserole / spoiled my appetite.

Jerry / fell asleep on the couch.

Knowing how to use a computer / got me a job as cashier in a movie theater.

NP (Subject) / VP (Predicate)

The playhouse that Nell and
Regis built in the backyard out
of lawnchairs and blankets / collapsed.

They / never knew what hit them.

We will adopt the hypothesis that the verb-phrase category exists and will proceed accordingly.

Exercises

Let us subject our last hypothesis to some further testing. Can you divide each of these sentences into subjects (noun phrases) and predicates (verb phrases)? If you can, draw a slash (/) between those two constituents. Are there any uncertainties? If so, make note of them and discuss them in class.

1. Vernon sneezed.
2. Lucille's husband's uncle told an off-color joke.
3. A day-old bacon-lettuce-and-tomato sandwich on rye bread sat forlornly on the shelf.
4. You always hurt the ones you love.
5. The time it took me each morning to drive from home to my job at the park seemed relatively insignificant.
6. Our ability to arrange words allows us to produce an infinity of grammatical sentences.

Since we are interested in all the word groupings that make up sentences, we will need to take the verb-phrase constituent into account. We can revise 9, our original description of sentence 3, as follows:

13   S = NP + VP

Both of the sentence's two constituents, in turn, have constituents of their own:

14   NP = Art + N

15   VP = V + NP

Note that statement 14 describes the noun phrase in 15 as well as the one in 13.

Labeled Brackets and Boxes

Many people find it useful to put their analyses into a visual form. Just as a map helps a geographer comprehend a large territory or a blueprint helps an engineer, a *diagram* can help a student of grammar to visualize and better understand the makeup of a sentence.

One kind of diagram consists of *brackets* placed around constituents. Each bracket can be labeled with a subscript to show the type of constituent it is. The following is labeled as a sentence:

16 [$_S$ The monkey saw a leopard]

Since the sentence consists of two constituents, a noun phrase and a verb phrase, we can put labeled brackets around them as well:

17 [$_S$ [$_{NP}$ The monkey] [$_{VP}$ saw a leopard]]

The verb phrase has a verb and a noun phrase as its constituents, as labeling can show:

18 [$_S$ [$_{NP}$ The monkey] [$_{VP}$ [$_V$ saw] [$_{NP}$ a leopard]]]

Finally, both of the noun phrases consist of two parts, an article and a noun:

19 [$_S$ [$_{NP}$ [$_{Art}$ The] [$_N$ monkey]] [$_{VP}$ [$_V$ saw] [$_{NP}$ [$_{Art}$ a] [$_N$ leopard]]]]

One limitation of labeled brackets is that after too many brackets are added they become confusing to look at—quite a drawback, since their purpose is to clarify the makeup of the sentence for us. Using *boxes* instead of brackets to show groupings of constituents can help somewhat:

20

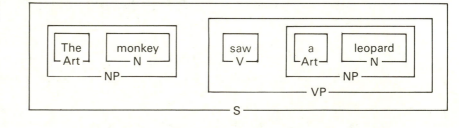

Exercises

1. Place labeled brackets around each of the constituents in these sentences:

   a.   The   soldier   spied   an   enemy

   b.   A   downpour   spoiled   the   picnic

2. Place labeled boxes around the constituents in these sentences:

   a.   The   ending   salvaged   the   movie

   b.   An   amateur   won   the   championship

Reed-Kellog Diagrams

Both brackets and boxes have a limited usefulness, particularly with long, complex sentences. A better way of showing the structure and makeup of sentences is needed. In the late nineteenth century two grammarians named Alonzo Reed and Brainerd Kellog invented a type of diagram which became widely adopted for grammar study in American schools. Here is a *Reed-Kellog diagram* of sentence 3:

21

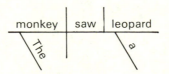

The longer vertical line separates the first noun phrase from the verb phrase, and the shorter one separates the two components in the verb phrase. Articles are placed on diagonal lines under the nouns.

Reed-Kellog diagrams show us much about the sentence's structure, but they too have limitations. Constituents are not labeled, the relationship of smaller constituents to larger ones is not always clear, and the diagrams do not always capture the sentence's word order.

Tree Diagrams

Since the 1950s, tree diagrams have become the most widely used way of displaying a sentence's makeup. In a *tree diagram*, the constituents of a category are shown branching out from it. For example, if a category A has constituents X, Y, and Z (that is, if we can describe it as A = X + Y + Z), then a tree diagram of A would look like this:

22

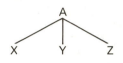

To draw a tree diagram of sentence 3, we can start by showing its major constituents, as we described them in statement 13:

23

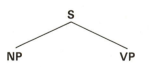

We can add to this tree by drawing in the constituents of the verb phrase, as in statement 15:

24

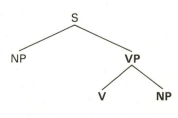

Next we can describe the two noun phrases, as in 14:

25

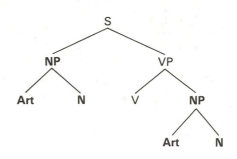

Finally we can complete the tree by attaching the words to the appropriate labels:

26

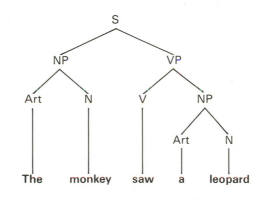

Look carefully at 26, our completed tree diagram of the sentence. It is important that you use tree diagrams to help you *see* the structure of sentences. Otherwise, drawing them becomes a useless exercise. Spend a few moments examining 26, trying to make its visual display meaningful to you. Notice that the tree is shaped somewhat like a triangle, with its apex on top at the sentence label S, and its base on the bottom with the words that comprise the sentence, arranged in left-to-right order. You will want to be able to look at any tree diagram and read the sentence across the bottom.

Look also at what 26 shows about how the sentence is constructed. Notice that it shows that the article *a* and the noun *leopard* together constitute a noun phrase. Notice too that that noun phrase (*a leopard*) together with the verb *saw* make up a verb phrase. And that verb phrase together with the noun phrase *the monkey* constitute the whole sentence. You can use a tree diagram as an aid to your understanding if you can look at it and actually *see* the sentence and the way it is made up.

Practice this important skill by skipping ahead a chapter or two and examining some of the trees you find. Can you look at the trees, read the sentences they diagram, and see how they are structured?

You will notice that when we drew tree 26, we began with the sentence label S and ended with the sentence's words. We could just as easily have proceeded in the other direction, beginning with the words, then labeling them, and finally grouping them as constituents. The result would have been an upside-down tree (or actually a right-side-up one, since the trees we are used to seeing in nature have a single trunk at the bottom and many branches at the top):

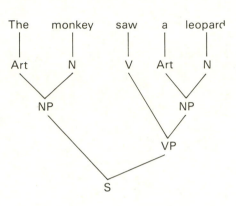

It is usual, however, to draw trees with the S on top, as in 26, and that is how we will draw them from now on in this book. You can practice diagramming in the following exercises:

Exercises

1. Draw tree diagrams of the sentences in exercise 1 on page 13. Your trees will have the same structure as tree 26.

2. Draw trees for the sentences in exercise 2 on page 13 without looking at trees in the book or at other trees you have drawn. Practice so you can do them entirely on your own.

Check your trees carefully. Make sure all the words are attached to their category labels with a line. (Note: The words are part of the tree.) Sloppy trees make the sentence's structure difficult to see. Have you drawn yours neatly? In studying grammar, a little artistic flair helps.

An Elementary Grammar of English

So far we have looked at ways of describing a sentence, but we have not yet addressed our real goal: discovering the nature of the grammar in our heads that allows us to construct the sentence. How do we go about putting together a sentence like 3?

A solution would be to recast the descriptions we made of it—abbreviated in statements 13, 14, and 15—in the form of *rules*. We can read these rules as directions for constructing a sentence:

28   a.   S → NP VP

       b. VP → V NP

       c. NP → Art N

Rules 28a–28c can be interpreted as follows: "Begin with the sentence category, and let it consist of two parts, a noun phrase and a verb phrase. Whenever you encounter a verb phrase, let it consist of a verb and a noun phrase. When you encounter a noun phrase, let it consist of an article and a noun."

I have replaced the equal sign in our earlier descriptions, such as 13, with an *arrow* (→) which can be read as "will have the following constituents" or simply as "consists of." I have also removed the plus sign between constituents. The rules 28a–28c are called *phrase-structure rules* or **PS rules**, because they show how phrases, or groups of words, are structured. That is, a phrase-structure rule shows what constituents make up the phrase in question.

With a set of phrase-structure rules and a list of the available words, which we will call a *lexicon* (a kind of dictionary), we will have a small grammar, a model that will allow us to produce our sample sentence 3:

29

AN ELEMENTARY GRAMMAR	
PS RULES	**LEXICON**
S → NP VP	Art: the, a
VP → V NP	N: monkey, leopard
NP → Art N	V: saw

By following the phrase-structure rules in 29 and then inserting words from the lexicon, we can produce tree 26. Actually, since there are two articles and two nouns in our lexicon, there is nothing to require us to insert them as we did. By making different choices about which articles and nouns to insert, we could also have produced a slightly different sentence:

30

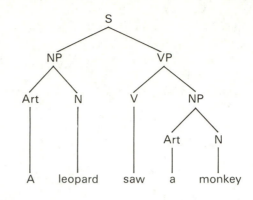

In fact our grammar can produce sixteen different sentences, including these:

31

The monkey saw a leopard.

A leopard saw the monkey.

The monkey saw a monkey.

The leopard saw the leopard.

This ability to produce multiple sentences is an advantage, since our long-term goal is to construct a grammar that will be able to produce all possible sentences of English. Grammar 29 has another valuable quality, in that it will not produce any ungrammatical combinations of the words in its lexicon such as this:

32

*Monkey leopard a saw monkey the the.

The phrase-structure rules of 29 simply do not allow it to produce nonsentences like 32.

There isn't much variety in the sentences that grammar 29 will produce, but we are only beginning. By adding to its lexicon, we can allow our grammar to produce many more grammatical English sentences. Consider this expanded grammar:

33

PS RULES	LEXICON
S → NP VP	Art: the, a
VP → V NP	N: monkey, leopard, hunter, missionary
NP → Art N	V: saw, befriended, frightened, ate, amused, captured

Grammar 33 will produce dozens of sentences such as this one:

34 A monkey amused the missionary.

Another way of saying that the grammar's rules produce sentences such as 34 is to say that the grammar *generates* them. For that reason, grammars such as 29 and 33 are called *generative grammars*.

Exercises

1. Draw tree diagrams to show how grammar 33 can generate the following English sentences. For each sentence, follow the phrase-structure rules to draw a tree. Notice that you will have to use the noun-phrase rule twice in order to complete the tree. Then select the appropriate words from the lexicon, and attach them to the tree. Draw a new tree for each sentence.

   a. A monkey amused the missionary.
   b. The hunter befriended a leopard.

2. Use the grammar to generate three additional sentences. For each draw the tree (following the phrase-structure rules) and insert vocabulary from the lexicon.

Grammar 33, while it can generate many different sentences, still cannot produce all the grammatical sentences of English. To do that, it will need to be expanded considerably. Our goal, I said, is to create a grammar on paper that does everything our mental grammars can do. That is, it should be capable of generating all of the grammatical sentences of English, but incapable of generating any combinations of words that are ungrammatical.

Our goal is ambitious—so ambitious that we will not accomplish it fully. Linguists still have much to learn about what our mental grammars "know." But we can discover a great deal. The next chapter will extend our process of discovery.

3 Nouns, Verbs, and Adjectives

In the previous chapter, we decided that if we wanted to learn about English grammar, the sentence was the proper unit of language for us to investigate. Using a sample sentence, *The monkey saw a leopard*, we proceeded to do so, and we were able to construct a grammar capable of generating that and a number of other English sentences. If you look carefully at what we did, however, you will notice that our investigation was based on at least one unexplained assumption.

Our assumption for investigating sentences was that we already knew what sentences were. Was this assumption valid? All of us create sentences whenever we talk or write, but in identifying them, our conscious knowledge does not always match what we know subconsciously. How do we know what a sentence is? When we read, it is easy to spot a sentence as a group of words that begins with a capital letter and ends with a period or question mark. But how do we know where to put the capital letters and punctuation when we write?

The traditional school-grammar definition of a sentence is not very much help: *A sentence is a group of words that expresses a complete thought*. This definition captures our understanding about a sentence's independence, but one person's idea of a complete thought may not be another's.

Some assumptions are unavoidable in scientific investigation, and one that will be basic to our study is that certain word groups that we believe to be sentences are indeed sentences. In this instance we must trust our intuitions, at least to start. Based on this assumption, we can try to construct a model of grammar, and if the model proves to be consistent with our intuitive feelings about sentences and if it proves capable of consistently generating groups of words that we recognize as grammatical English sentences, then we can be satisfied that our assumption was a valid one.

Starting with this and other assumptions, we have already provided a syntactic definition of a sentence, which took the form of a phrase-structure rule:

1. S → NP VP

In addition to giving directions for creating a sentence, the rule also explains what a sentence is. To put the definition in words:

2 A **sentence** is a group of words that consists of a noun phrase followed by a verb phrase.

This, we will assume for now, is what a sentence is. Our continuing investigation of sentences will tell us if this assumption is a good one.

Proper and Common Nouns

Definition 2 says that a sentence consists of two kinds of phrases. A *phrase* is any grouping of words that acts as a constituent. In addition to noun phrases and verb phrases, we will also encounter other kinds of phrases in upcoming chapters.

   A noun phrase, we discovered, is a group of words that can fill a slot like the one in 3:

3 _____ saw a leopard
       (NP)

The monkey is a noun phrase, and so are *a leopard, a missionary,* and *the hunter.* These noun phrases all consist of an article and a noun, and so we described a phrase-structure rule for noun phrases:

4 NP → Art N

As you can guess, it is the noun that gives its name to the phrase. The noun is in a sense the most important constituent of the noun phrase.

   Following rule 4, we identified *monkey* and *leopard* as nouns. That is, our classification was based on a word's ability to fill a slot like this one:

5 the _____
           (N)

Words like *headache, ocean, spinach,* and *romance* can also fill the slot and so are nouns. Meaning, you will notice, has not entered into our method of classifying nouns. Instead we have used the purely syntactic method of slot-filling. The study of grammar cannot ignore meaning, however, and we will have occasion to consider meaning as our inquiry continues. In traditional school grammar, a definition based on meaning is usually given, such as this one: *A noun is the name of a person, place, or thing.*

Rule 4 described a noun phrase as an article-noun combination, but a little investigating will show us that there are other kinds of noun phrases as well. In some cases, for example, a single word can fill the slot in 3:

6   <u>Tarzan</u> saw a leopard.

      <u>Rover</u> saw a leopard.

The names *Tarzan* and *Rover* must also be noun phrases, even though they do not consist of the two elements Art and N. Rule 4, then, is apparently inadequate since it does not describe all possible noun phrases. Let's try to improve it.

We will call all names like *Tarzan* and *Rover* **proper nouns** (abbreviated N_P). In writing it has become traditional to begin a proper noun with a capital letter. *Elizabeth, Tennessee, Westinghouse,* and *Harvard* are all proper nouns. In the examples of **6**, the underlined proper nouns act as noun phrases all by themselves, without any articles in front of them. We would need an additional noun-phrase rule to describe them:

7   NP $\rightarrow$ N_P

Notice that we now have two different noun-phrase rules, 4 and 7.

If *Tarzan* and *Tennessee* are proper nouns, let us call the other nouns, the ones that are not used as proper names and are not usually begun with capital letters, **common nouns** (abbreviated N_C). *Monkey, missionary, college,* and *car* are all common nouns. We will revise **4** accordingly:

8   NP $\rightarrow$ Art N_C

The presence of rules 7 and 8 causes our model grammar to expand, as follows:

9

PS RULES	LEXICON
S $\rightarrow$ NP VP	Art: a, an, the
NP $\rightarrow$ Art N_C	N_C: engineer, car, city, company, detective
NP $\rightarrow$ N_P	N_P: Sidney, Constance, Chicago, Monsanto
VP $\rightarrow$ V NP	V: startled, bought, loves, hired

When we construct a model of our grammar, we can include in the lexicon only a sample of the words available to us. Clearly we do not have room here to list all the nouns and verbs that speakers of English know.

Since there are now two noun-phrase rules, the grammar provides choices for generating sentences. In drawing trees based on these phrase-structure rules, you can follow either rule whenever you encounter a noun-phrase label. Here are two of the trees that grammar 9 can generate:

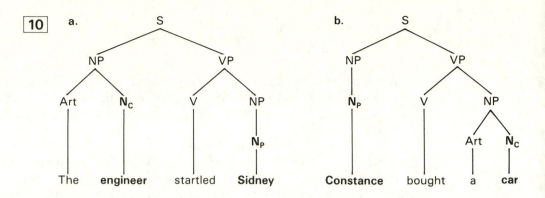

10

Until now all the phrases that we have seen have had precisely two constituents. In trees 10a and 10b, however, some of the NP labels branch into a single N$_P$. Categories, as we will continue to discover, can have one, two, three, or more constituents.

Exercises

1. Draw trees to show how grammar 9 can generate the following sentences. For each tree, follow the appropriate phrase-structure rules and insert words from the lexicon.

   a. Constance hired the detective.
   b. Sidney loves Chicago.

2. Draw trees for two additional sentences that the grammar can generate. Your trees should include both proper and common nouns. Use only words from the grammar's lexicon.

Transitive and Intransitive Verbs

Earlier we defined verb phrases as phrases that can fill a slot like this one:

11 The monkey _____ .

Among the verb phrases we could invent are *saw a leopard, imitated Francine, plays the cello,* and *attended Purdue.* We used the following phrase-structure rule to describe verb phrases:

12 VP → V NP

The slot in 11, however, can also be filled with other verb phrases that do not meet the description of 12:

13 The monkey <u>wheezed</u>.

The monkey <u>laughs</u>.

The monkey <u>died</u>.

Here the verb phrase seems to consist of a single word. Lone words that can fill the slot in 11 will be called *intransitive verbs* (abbreviated V_I). *Wheezed, laughs,* and *died* are all intransitive verbs. Another way of describing them is to say that an intransitive verb is a verb that is not followed by a noun phrase. In contrast, verbs like *saw, imitated,* and *resembles* are all *transitive verbs* (abbreviated V_T), since each is followed by a noun phrase. Some verbs can be used in either category:

14 The game *ended.*   **—Intransitive verb, not followed by an NP**

A riot *ended* the game.   **—Transitive verb, followed by an NP**

The similarity between transitive and intransitive verbs leads us to classify them in the same general category: *verbs.* We have considered verbs from a purely structural point of view. In traditional grammar, however, they are defined in terms of meaning: *A verb is a word that expresses action or being.*

The existence of both transitive and intransitive verbs will cause us to revise phrase-structure rule 12. Two rules will now be needed to account for verb phrases:

15 VP → V_I

VP → V_T NP

We can incorporate these revisions into our grammar:

16

PS RULES	LEXICON
S → NP VP	Art: a, the
NP → N_P	N_P: Paul, Lucy, Pierre, Bermuda, Canada
NP → Art N_C	N_C: rain, sailor, librarian, reptile, movie
VP → V_I	V_I: continued, wept, sneezed, objected, triumphed
VP → V_T NP	V_T: annoyed, threatened, dated, amused, admired, visited

Grammar 16 can generate sentences with both intransitive (17a) and transitive verbs (17b):

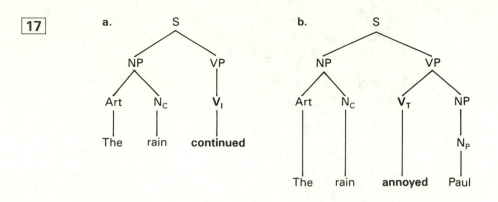

Exercises

1. Draw trees to show how grammar 16 can generate the following sentences. For each tree, follow the appropriate phrase-structure rules and insert words from the lexicon.

   a. Lucy threatened the librarian.
   b. A sailor sneezed.

2. Draw trees for four additional sentences that the grammar can generate. Your trees should include both transitive and intransitive verbs. If you wish, you may add words to the lexicon of 16.

Simplifying the Phrase-Structure Rules

Even with these revisions, our phrase-structure rules are still not adequate. Consider our rules for the noun-phrase category:

18 a. NP → Art N$_C$

b. NP → N$_P$

These rules can generate the italicized noun phrases in 19:

19 *Chevrolet* hired Ralph.

Ramona ordered *a pizza*.

But sometimes proper nouns are preceded by an article, and sometimes common nouns are not:

20 Ralph owns *a Chevrolet*.

Ramona loves *pizza*.

It would seem, then, that at least four different rules are needed for describing noun phrases:

21

a. NP → N$_C$ c. NP → N$_P$

b. NP → Art N$_C$ d. NP → Art N$_P$

The grammar is now getting unpleasantly complicated. Is there anything we can do about it? Fortunately, there is.

Because rules 21a and 21b are so similar to rules 21c and 21d, we can simplify the way we write the rules for noun phrases. We can replace the four rules 21a–21d with two general rules:

22 NP → N

NP → Art N

Although a distinction between proper and common nouns exists, we will no longer bother to note it in our rules. Henceforth we will classify every noun simply as N.

Of course not every noun can take an article (*Otto studied the linguistics, *Albert attended the Princeton*), nor can every noun exist without one (**Carl practiced longjump, *Frans visited Hague*). This knowledge about restrictions on the use of articles with nouns is part of our lexical knowledge (knowledge about words), and we will not aim for a full account of it here.

Even the two rules of **22** provide some unnecessary clutter, since the two of them can be summarized in a single statement: A noun phrase contains a noun, which may or may not be preceded by an article. In the writing of phrase-structure rules, *parentheses ( )* allow us to express *optional* elements. By placing parentheses around *Art*, we can compress the two rules into one:

23 NP → (Art) N

We can read rule 23 as follows: a noun phrase consists of an optional article and an obligatory noun. The rule allows us to draw two different trees:

24

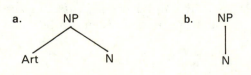

In the same manner, we will no longer note the distinction between transitive and intransitive verbs. From now on, we will write one rule 25 that is equivalent to the two rules of 15:

25   VP → V (NP)

That is, a verb phrase contains a verb, which may or may not be followed by a noun phrase.

Adjectives

Articles are not the only elements that can be optional in noun phrases. Consider the italicized noun phrases in these sentences:

26   *The tiresome monkey* saw a leopard.

The naive tourist bought *a defective camera*.

Good fences make *good neighbors*.

The words *tiresome, naive, defective,* and *good* are all **adjectives** (abbreviated **Adj**). In traditional grammar this category is defined as follows: *An adjective is a word that describes (or modifies) a noun.* All the following combinations of articles, adjectives, and nouns can occur in English noun phrases:

27   NP → N   (Clark)

NP → Art N   (the reporter)

NP → Adj N   (tall buildings)

NP → Art Adj N   (a single bound)

By using parentheses, we can write a single rule for noun phrases that will account for all four structures in 27:

28   NP → (Art) (Adj) N

Exercises

1. Note that in 28 *Art* and *Adj* are placed separately in parentheses. Is the following rule equivalent to 28?

   NP → (Art Adj) N

Are there any noun phrases in 27 that this rule would not be able to generate?

2. Imagine that in a grammar, all four of the following trees can exist. (Letters are used here in place of grammatical categories.) Write one phrase-structure rule capable of generating these four trees.

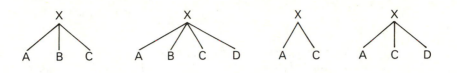

Is your rule able to generate any other trees besides these four? If so, can you revise it so that it can generate only these four trees?

3. How would you have to revise the rule so that, in addition to generating the four trees in exercise 2, it would also generate these trees?

Rule 28 is still not perfect, because sometimes more than one adjective can occur in a noun phrase:

29 *The old, gray mare* won the Derby.

Josette wore *expensive new red sneakers*.

A noun phrase can have any number of adjectives in a series (*the old, old, old, old, old, old philosopher*). We will place a raised plus sign (+) following an element in a phrase-structure rule to indicate that it may be repeated more than once. Our latest NP rule becomes:

30 NP → (Art) (Adj)+ N

That is, a noun phrase contains a noun, which may (but need not) be preceded by an article and may (but need not) also be preceded by one or more adjectives. Both the article and adjectives are optional. Notice how we have added to the power of our grammar. Even though the following grammar contains only three rules (compared with five in grammar 16), it is now capable of generating many more kinds of sentences.

PS RULES	LEXICON
S → NP VP	Art: an, the, a
NP → (Art) (Adj)⁺ N	Adj: adventurous, gaudy, purple, old,
VP → V (NP)	jaunty, sleepy, ugly, unreliable
	N: officer, soldier, shirt, actor,
	Amanda, Louis, professor, thief, car
	V: rewarded, embarrassed, performed,
	owns, insulted, charmed

Many linguists prefer to use a raised asterisk (*) instead of a plus sign to mark a repeatable element. I will use a plus sign to avoid confusion with the sign for an ungrammatical sentence or for a footnote.

Grammar 31 can generate sentences such as these:

32

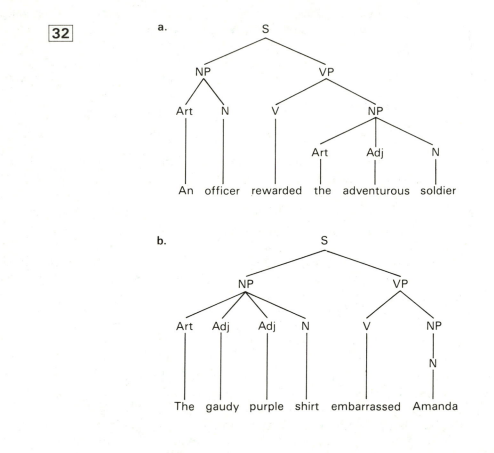

a.

An officer rewarded the adventurous soldier

b.

The gaudy purple shirt embarrassed Amanda

Exercises

1. Using grammar 31, draw trees for these sentences:

   a. The jaunty actor performed.
   b. Louis owns an ugly, unreliable old car.

2. Draw three additional trees for sentences with adjectives that can be generated by grammar 31.

A Further Note on Meaning

To this point we have been examining the English language from a largely structural viewpoint, attempting to construct a model of grammar as if meaning did not exist. Clearly, however, meaning is essential to language, since the very purpose of language is to communicate our meaning. Any attempt to construct a grammar that ignores meaning will fail. Grammar 31, for example, while it can generate many fine sentences, can also produce sentences that are certainly very odd, such as *The car performed Louis* and *The sleepy shirt owns a purple soldier*. While these sentences may not strictly be ungrammatical (if we exercise our imaginations, we might conceive of situations in which they could actually be said), they do violate our usual conceptions of appropriate meaning. Our grammatical knowledge surely includes certain notions of appropriateness that tell us, for example, that words like *perform* can occur with "animate" subjects like *actor*, but not with "inanimate" subjects like *car*. This knowledge about appropriate meaning (sometimes called **selectional restrictions** upon the lexicon) is a part of our mental grammar. We will not aim for a full account of it here, but if you take more advanced courses in syntax, you will encounter attempts to account more fully for meaning in the grammatical models you create.

Linking Verbs

According to the traditional definition of a verb ("a word that expresses action or being"), not all verbs are action words. The others, which "express being," are forms of the verb *be*. These verbs (such as *am, is, are, was,* and *were*), act as the verbal equivalent of an equal sign. They tell us that one thing is equivalent to another:

33 a. Brutus *is* an honorable man.

   b. The Titans *were* the winners.

   c. Millie *was* persistent.

Such verbs are distinguished from both transitive and intransitive verbs. They are usually called *linking* or *copulative verbs* (abbreviated V_L). In addition to the verb *be*, the following can also act as linking verbs: *appear, become, feel, look, remain, seem, smell, sound,* and *taste*. For example:

34 An unknown lawyer *became* the next governor.

The bread *smelled* delicious.

Unlike other verbs, a linking verb can be followed by either a noun phrase or an adjective. We can add these rules to our grammar:

35 VP → V_L NP

VP → V_L Adj

The rules of **35** allow us to generate sentences like these:

36

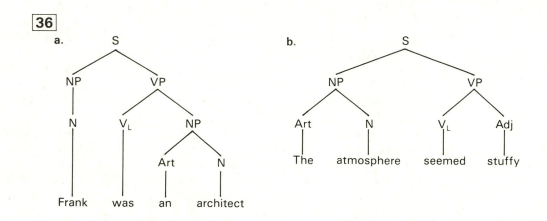

a.

S
- NP
  - N
    - Frank
- VP
  - V_L
    - was
  - NP
    - Art
      - an
    - N
      - architect

b.

S
- NP
  - Art
    - The
  - N
    - atmosphere
- VP
  - V_L
    - seemed
  - Adj
    - stuffy

Some of the words that act as linking verbs can also act as non-linking (transitive or intransitive) verbs in other sentences. Notice the difference between these sentences:

37 a. The turkey *smelled* delicious.   —*Linking verb*

b. The turkey *smelled* the fox.   —*Transitive verb*

38 a. Darlene *remained* the treasurer.   —*Linking verb*

b. Others left. Darlene *remained*.   —*Intransitive verb*

A test for whether a verb is a linking verb is whether a form of *be* can be substituted for it without substantially altering meaning: *The turkey was deli-*

cious, and *Darlene was (still) the treasurer,* but not *The turkey was the fox* (different meaning from **37b**) or *Darlene was.*

Exercises

1. Forms of the linking verb *be* can be followed either by a noun phrase—as in sentences **33a** and **33b**—or by an adjective—as in **33c**. Is the same true for all linking verbs? Use your lexical knowledge to decide whether each of the following linking verbs can take a noun phrase as well as an adjective: *appear, become, feel, grow, look, remain, seem, smell, sound, taste, wax.*

2. For each of those verbs, write a sentence in which the verb is followed by an adjective. Where possible, write another where it is followed by a noun phrase. (Note: Be certain that when it is followed by a noun phrase it still functions as a linking verb.)

In **35**, we wrote two rules to describe the possibilities for verb phrases that contain linking verbs. We always value simplicity in our grammar, however, and it would be better if those possibilities could be stated in a single rule. A single rule seems appropriate because we can recast the rules of **35** in a single statement: "A verb phrase can consist of a linking verb that is followed by either a noun phrase or an adjective." Fortunately a convenient rule-writing device allows us to express an either/or relation. Items that can be chosen as alternatives can be placed, one above the other, within **braces** { }. Using braces, we can now restate the rules of **35** as a single rule:

$$\boxed{39} \quad VP \rightarrow V_L \left\{ \begin{array}{c} NP \\ Adj \end{array} \right\}$$

In following this rule to generate a verb phrase, the grammar selects a linking verb, and then it must select either a noun phrase or an adjective. Notice how braces differ from parentheses. When two items are in braces, the grammar must select one or the other of them. It may not select both, and it may not select neither.

The Parts of Speech

Each of the word categories that we have seen so far (Art, Adj, N, and V) can be called a **part of speech**. In traditional grammar, eight parts of speech are usually identified: *noun, pronoun, adjective, verb, adverb, preposition, con-*

junction, and *interjection*. We will encounter and explore these categories in upcoming chapters, but our classification will identify some additional parts of speech as well.

As one example of the difference between modern (generative) and traditional grammar, we have already introduced the *article* as an independent part of speech. In traditional grammar, *article* is classified as a subtype of *adjective* because, like adjectives, articles usually precede (or "modify") nouns. Nevertheless, there is good reason for separating the two categories. Besides serving different purposes, articles and adjectives fill different syntactic slots. They are not interchangeable. When both occur within the same noun phrase, the article precedes the adjective. We can have *a miserable time* but not **miserable a time*. And whereas a noun phrase can have multiple adjectives (*happy, happy olden days*), it can have no more than one article (**the the an owl*). In order for our grammar to generate grammatical sentences, it is necessary for it to distinguish these two parts of speech.

Our grammar now looks like this:

40

PS RULES	LEXICON
S → NP VP	Art: an, the
NP → (Art) (Adj)⁺ N	Adj: enthusiastic, nonprofit, classical, velvet, decadent, former, long, hot, unbearable
VP → V (NP)	N: Sarah, skier, station, music, earmuffs, professor, class, summers
VP → V$_L$ $\begin{Bmatrix} NP \\ Adj \end{Bmatrix}$	V: played, lacks
	V$_L$: was, felt, become

Exercises

1. Show how grammar 40 is capable of generating a variety of English sentences. By following its phrase-structure rules and using its lexicon, draw tree diagrams of the following sentences:

    a. Sarah was an enthusiastic skier.
    b. The nonprofit station played classical music.
    c. The velvet earmuffs felt decadent.
    d. The former professor lacks class.
    e. Long, hot summers become unbearable.

2. The following three trees are among those that grammar 40 can generate. Complete the trees by supplying appropriate words. You are encouraged to add your own words to the lexicon of 40.

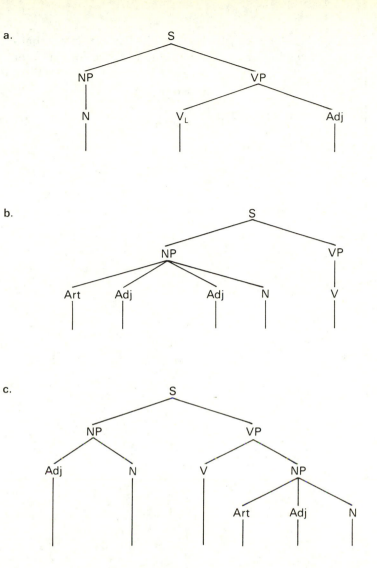

a.

b.

c.

3. Use the grammar to draw trees for four additional sentences. Add whatever words are needed to the lexicon. Your trees should represent a variety of structures; that is, be certain to choose a variety of options within the phrase-structure rules when you construct them.

4. The article *the* is called a ***definite article***, whereas *a* and *an* are called ***indefinite articles***. Under what circumstances do we choose to use one or

the other—or no article at all? For example, what are the differences in meaning or implication among these four different noun phrases?

$$\text{He disliked} \begin{cases} \text{the woman.} \\ \text{a woman.} \\ \text{the women.} \\ \text{women.} \end{cases}$$

4 Prepositions and Personal Pronouns

Our grammar-making is moving along nicely, and the model grammar that we have discovered can now generate many different kinds of sentences. Still, it cannot generate all of them, and you have probably spotted some of its inadequacies. You may already have your own suggestions for augmenting the grammar. Perhaps you have thought of better alternatives to some of our existing proposals. If so, by all means offer them in class. Remember that what we are engaged in is cooperative speculation about our subconscious knowledge. The more minds that participate in the speculation, the more successful our search for conscious knowledge will be.

Prepositions

One lack in our grammar is the ability to account for the italicized phrases in these sentences:

1 Mort scrambled *over the barricade*.

The smugglers sneaked the contraband *past the guards*.

The genetic researchers crossed a tiger *with a lion*.

Each of these phrases has the intuitive feel of a unit, and each consists of a noun phrase preceded by a word such as *over, past,* or *with*. We will call words of this kind *prepositions* (abbreviated **Prep**), since they are placed before (or "pre-posed" in relation to) noun phrases. The word *over* is a preposition, and the entire constituent *over the barricade* can be called a *prepositional phrase* or **PP**. A prepositional phrase consists of a preposition followed by a noun phrase. We can state our analysis as a phrase-structure rule:

2 PP → Prep NP

In the three examples of 1, prepositional phrases seem to occur at the end of sentences. But is the prepositional phrase part of the verb phrase, or is it a separate major constituent of the sentence? These two options for writing phrase-structure rules involving prepositional phrases are given below in 3 and 4, along with different trees they can generate. Examine them and see if you can decide which option is preferable. Either:

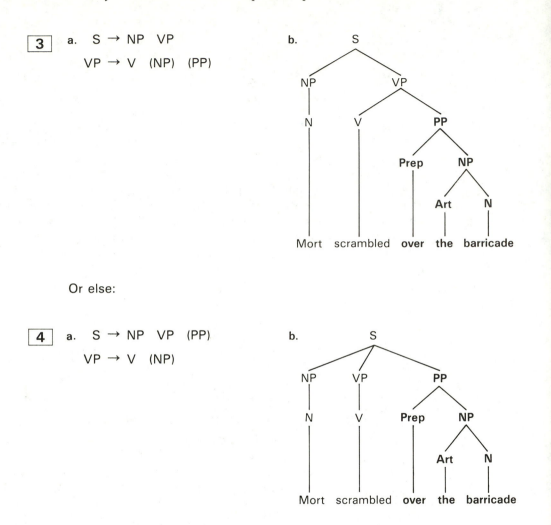

3 a. S → NP VP

VP → V (NP) (PP)

Or else:

4 a. S → NP VP (PP)

VP → V (NP)

Both options "work" in the sense that both can generate the desired sentence, but does one tree better reflect the structure of the sentence? Most linguists prefer option 3 with the prepositional phrase as a constituent of the verb phrase. Part of their reasoning is based on meaning: *over the barricade* is considered to be part of the verb phrase or predicate, because it completes the verb *scrambled*. That is, it describes where the scrambling took place. Most people have the intuitive sense that, in the sample sentences of 1, *scram-*

bled over the barricade, sneaked the contraband past the guards, and *crossed a tiger with a lion* are units or constituents. Accordingly, we will adopt analysis **3**.

When I was in the fifth grade, my class was assigned to memorize a list of the most common prepositions. The teacher said we would never forget them, and strangely enough she was right, at least in my case. Here is the list:

5

COMMON PREPOSITIONS				
about	behind	except	off	to
above	below	for	on	toward
across	beneath	from	out	under
after	beside	in	outside	until
against	between	inside	over	up
among	beyond	into	past	upon
around	by	like	since	with
at	down	near	through	without
before	during	of	throughout	

It probably isn't necessary for you to memorize the list too, but you should be able to recognize a preposition when you see one. With the adoption of rules 2 and 3a, our grammar now contains provisions for generating prepositional phrases:

6

PS RULES	LEXICON	
S → NP VP	Art:	the, a
NP → (Art) (Adj)⁺ N	Adj:	hapless, interminable
VP → V (NP) (PP)	N:	Beth, trapeze, Larry, oyster, shoehorn, wastrel, bar, Milo, grease, axle, colonel, corporal, private, Jones, Tibet, Wanda, smile, ceremony
PP → Prep NP	V:	jumped, opened, stumbled, cleaned, demoted, flew, maintained
	Prep:	from, with, into, to, across, throughout

Notice that the VP rule allows prepositional phrases to occur following both transitive and intransitive verbs. You may wonder why I left out the rule for linking verbs. I haven't forgotten it, but I have chosen to ignore it for now in order to simplify the grammar. From now on, as our grammars get more and more complex, we will omit certain rules when they are not relevant to the current discussion. You should still be aware that they exist, however, and would be listed in a complete, unabridged grammar.

Grammar 6 generates sentences like the following:

7

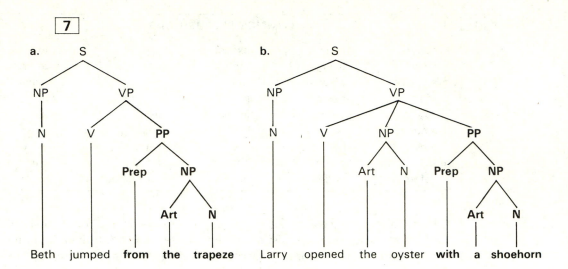

a. Beth jumped **from the trapeze**

b. Larry opened the oyster **with a shoehorn**

Notice that the prepositional phrase in 7a follows an intransitive verb (*jumped*), while the prepositional phrase in 7b follows a transitive verb (*opened*) and a noun phrase (*the oyster*).

Exercises

1. Use grammar 6 to draw trees for these sentences:

   a. The wastrel stumbled into a bar.
   b. Milo cleaned the grease from the axle.
   c. A colonel demoted the hapless corporal to private.
   d. Jones flew across Tibet.
   e. Wanda maintained a smile throughout the interminable ceremony.

2. Draw trees for four additional sentences. Add words to the lexicon as needed.

Prepositional Phrases within Noun Phrases

Not every prepositional phrase occurs within a verb phrase. Consider the following sentences:

8

The house *on the hill* overlooked the valley.

The cover *of the book* attracted attention.

The old man *with the moustache* won the award *for best poem*.

Each of the italicized prepositional phrases tells us something about the noun it follows and so seems to be part of a noun phrase. We can revise our noun-phrase rule accordingly:

9   NP → (Art) (Adj)+ N (PP)

The rule says that a prepositional phrase is an optional constituent at the end of a noun phrase. It allows the grammar to generate sentences like 10:

10

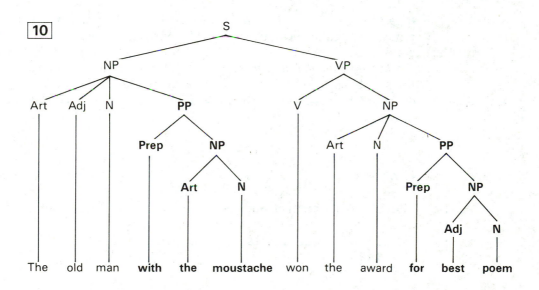

One interesting feature of rules 2 and 9 is that a prepositional phrase can contain a noun phrase and a noun phrase can contain a prepositional phrase. This allows us to have one prepositional phrase within another, as in sentence 11:

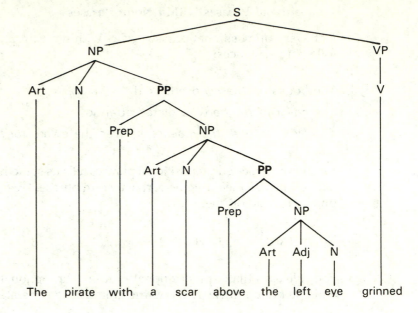

In fact, there is no reason why you would have to stop at two prepositional phrases. You could have any number of them, one inside the other. You could easily speak *of the size of the lettering on the top of the cover of the book about the decline of the Roman Empire,* to give an example with a series of seven prepositional phrases. This property of a grammar that allows it to generate constituents that recur again and again (as often as you choose) is called ***recursion***.

Exercises

The following grammar updates our discussion of prepositional phrases:

PS RULES	LEXICON	
S → NP VP	Art:	
NP → (Art) (Adj)$^+$ N (PP)	Adj:	
VP → V (NP) (PP)	N:	
PP → Prep NP	V:	
	Prep:	of, against, about, during, in, on, with, between, over, past

Except for the prepositions, I have left it for you to fill in the lexicon needed for generating the sentences in this exercise.

The following sentences have prepositional phrases as constituents of noun phrases. Use the grammar to draw trees for these sentences.

1. The contents of the box puzzled Cassandra.
2. The fight against pollution continues.
3. Mother read a story about a runaway locomotive.
4. The commotion during the exam caused a lapse in concentration.

A Case of Ambiguity

We have no trouble understanding what the sentences of 1 or 8 mean, but not all sentences are so clear. Consider sentence 12, for example. Is it possible to interpret it in more than one way?

12 Miranda saw the boy with a telescope.

Depending on your interpretation, sentence 12 could be equivalent to either of the following two sentences:

13 a. Miranda saw the boy by looking through a telescope.
b. Miranda saw the boy who had a telescope.

A sentence like 12 with two or more possible interpretations or "readings" is said to be *ambiguous*. In conversation or writing, the intended interpretation of such a sentence is usually clear from the context in which it occurs. But when it occurs in isolation, as 12 does, there is no way to decide whether the meaning of 13a or of 13b is intended.

The cause of the sentence's ambiguity is the uncertain role of the prepositional phrase, *with a telescope*. Since a prepositional phrase can occur either within a verb phrase—as in the second rule of 3a—or within a noun phrase—as in rule 9—both of the following two trees are possible. Study them, and notice which phrase-structure rules are used to construct them. Finally, decide which tree corresponds with the meaning of 13a and which with the meaning of 13b.

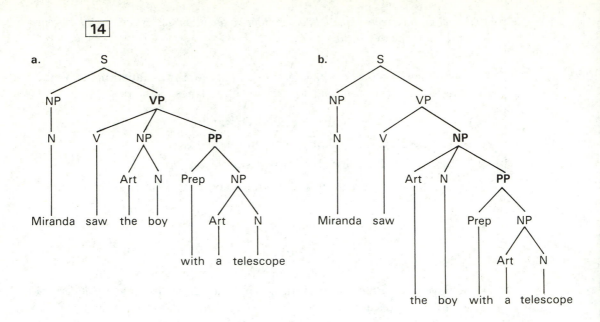

In 14a, the prepositional phrase *with a telescope* is a constituent of the verb phrase. As such, it is a partner of the verb *saw* and describes how Miranda did the seeing. It corresponds in meaning with 13a. In 14b, on the other hand, the prepositional phrase is a constituent of the noun phrase. It is a partner of the noun *boy* and describes which boy Miranda saw. It corresponds in meaning with 13b.

Let us review what our examination of sentence 12 has shown us. While 12 is ambiguous, the two trees 14a and 14b are not. The application of different phrase-structure rules has resulted in two trees with different internal structure. When words are inserted from the lexicon, however, it so happens that the wording of the two different sentences is identical. We will see that whenever two different trees can diagram the same sentence (actually two different sentences with the same words), the result is a case of ambiguity.

It is essential that you understand the difference in structure between 14a and 14b and can see why these trees correspond with 13a and 13b, respectively. The purpose of a tree diagram, as I said earlier, is to display a sentence's internal makeup. By looking at a tree, you should be able to see what the constituents are and how they relate to each other. Study trees 14a and 14b until the structure of each and the difference between them are clear to you. The concepts will become still clearer as you work through the following exercises. If you still have trouble, however, reread this chapter and ask your instructor to help you. Do not allow yourself to remain confused or you will have increasing difficulty as additional concepts are introduced.

Exercises

1. For each of the following sentences, decide whether the prepositional phrase is a constituent of a verb phrase, is a constituent of a noun phrase, or could be a constituent of either (that is, the sentence is ambiguous). Use the grammar from the exercise on page 42 to draw the appropriate tree(s) for each sentence.

   a. Rose noticed the chair in the den.
   b. Rose placed the chair in the den.
   c. Rose upholstered the chair in the den.

2. Underline all the prepositional phrases in the following sentences. Label each as a constituent of either a verb phrase or a noun phrase. Finally, draw a tree diagram of each sentence.

   a. Joe hit the ball with a bat.
   b. Joe admired the girl with a hat.
   c. Sandra rode a bus between the cities.
   d. Phyllis photographed the bridge over the river with an old camera.

   The following may not present clearcut choices. Be prepared to argue whether each prepositional phrase is a constituent of the verb phrase or the noun phrase. Draw the appropriate trees.

   e. The gambler placed a bet against the favorites.

      Does against the favorites *tell us how the bet-placing was done or what kind of bet was placed?*

   f. Jim saw a ghost in the mirror.

      Did he see *it in the mirror, or was it a* ghost *in the mirror?*

3. The following sentences contain recursive prepositional phrases (where one prepositional phrase occurs inside another). Draw trees to show their structure.

   a. The car skidded past the end of the pavement.
   b. The twins asked about the price of the green car with the sunroof.

Personal Pronouns

With the addition of the prepositional-phrase option to noun-phrase rule 9, our grammar can generate a great variety of different noun phrases, including these:

15	a. *George* amazed Evelyn.
	b. *The acrobats* amazed Evelyn.
	c. *The zany, spontaneous exuberance of the chimpanzee in the circus* amazed Evelyn.

Another class of words can also act as noun phrases. In fact, these words can take the place of the noun phrases in 15:

16	a. *He* amazed Evelyn.
	b. *They* amazed Evelyn.
	c. *It* amazed Evelyn.

The words *he, they,* and *it* in 16a–16c are called ***personal pronouns*** (abbreviated ***Pro*_P**). In traditional grammar a pronoun is defined as a word that is used as a substitute for a noun. Actually, a pronoun substitutes for all the words in a noun phrase. In the sentences of 16, the pronouns are equivalent to the entire italicized noun phrases in 15. For example, the *it* in 16c is used instead of (and with the same meaning as) *the zany, spontaneous exuberance of the chimpanzee in the circus* in 15c.

Since a noun phrase can consist simply of a pronoun, our phrase-structure rule needs to be expanded:

17 NP → $\left\{ \begin{array}{c} \text{(Art)} \ \ \text{(Adj)}^+ \ \ \text{N} \ \ \text{(PP)} \\ \text{Pro}_P \end{array} \right\}$

Rule 17 states that a noun phrase can be one of two things: either a phrase consisting of a noun with or without the optional modifiers, or else a simple pronoun. This rule allows the grammar to generate sentences such as the following:

18

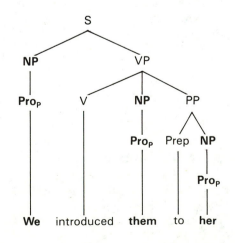

The following is a chart of the English personal pronouns:

19

PERSONAL PRONOUNS		
	SINGULAR	PLURAL
1st person	I / me	we / us
2nd person	you / you	you / you
3rd person	she / her	they / them
	he / him	
	it / it	

Of the three "persons" in the chart, *first person* refers to the speaker; *second person* refers to the hearer, the person spoken to; and *third person* refers to the person or thing spoken about. A *singular* pronoun refers, of course, to a single person or thing, while a *plural* pronoun refers to more than one. Notice that for the second person, *you* is used for both singular and plural. Several centuries ago English had a distinct second-person-singular form *thou/thee*, but that form has become obsolete. In casual conversation, however, it is sometimes useful to make a distinction between singular and plural, and some regional dialects use special plural forms in informal situations. These include *y'all, y'uns, yuz,* and *you guys.* Are any of these informal plurals used in your region of the country?

The difference between the *I* and *me* (and between members of each of the other pairs divided by a slash in the chart) is that the former is in the *nominative* (or *subjective*) *case,* while the latter is in the *objective case.* The nominative form is used in a *subject* noun phrase (the noun phrase that precedes the verb, such as *we* in tree 18), while the objective form is used in a *direct object* (the noun phrase that follows a transitive verb, such as *them* in 18) or in an *object of a preposition* (the noun phrase that follows a preposition, such as *her* in 18). These cases are labeled in tree 20 on page 48:

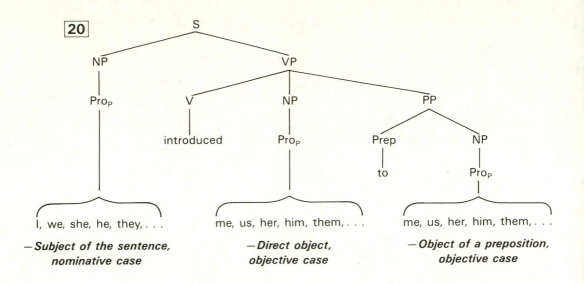

20

—*Subject of the sentence, nominative case* (I, we, she, he, they, . . .)

—*Direct object, objective case* (me, us, her, him, them, . . .)

—*Object of a preposition, objective case* (me, us, her, him, them, . . .)

Whether or not you are familiar with the names of these cases, you certainly know about them subconsciously, and you use the right forms in the right situations. No speaker of English is likely to mistake them as in 21:

21   *Us introduced they to she.

Although we will not try to formulate them, we will assume that our grammar has rules that assign the proper number, person, and case to personal pronouns.

A Further Word on Inflections

Since different forms of personal pronouns are used for singular and plural number and for nominative and objective cases, we can say that the pronouns are *inflected* for number and case. *Inflections* are the different forms or endings a word takes to communicate different grammatical information. In addition to pronouns, other inflected parts of speech include nouns (which usually take *-s* for the plural, for example), verbs (which often take *-ed* for the past tense), and adjectives (which often take *-er* and *-est* for the comparative and superlative forms).

Compared to many other languages (such as German, Greek, or Russian), English is not highly inflected. Unlike pronouns, for example, nouns and articles in English do not take different inflections for the nominative and objective cases. Consider the noun phrases in sentence 22:

22 The boy teased the girl.

In many other languages different forms of the nouns (*boy* and *girl*) or of the article (*the*) would be used to show that *the boy* is in the nominative case and *the girl* in the objective case. In English, however, neither of these noun phrases is inflected to show case information. Nevertheless, we have no doubt that it is the boy who is doing the teasing and the girl who is being teased. We are given this information by the sentence's word order. A noun phrase that comes before the verb is generally the subject in an English sentence. A noun phrase that comes afterward is generally the direct object. A language like English that relies largely on word order rather than inflections to convey case information is called a ***word-order language***. A language that relies largely on inflections rather than word order is called an ***inflected language***.

Languages are constantly changing, and English has changed greatly in the past thousand years. The English of a thousand years ago (called Old English or Anglo-Saxon) was a highly inflected language, and it placed less importance than does modern English on word order. In more recent centuries, however, word order has become increasingly important, and we have gradually lost most of the inflections which no longer serve a useful purpose. The nonessential distinction between *who* and *whom* is one that is being lost within our own century. Of all the parts of speech, the personal pronouns retain the most inflected forms. It is conceivable that a century or two from now, either the nominative or the objective pronouns will have died out, and our descendants may speak sentences such as *Me introduced them to her*.

Exercises

PS RULES

S → NP VP

NP → $\left\{ \begin{array}{c} \text{(Art)} \quad \text{(Adj)}^+ \quad \text{N} \quad \text{(PP)} \\ \text{Pro}_P \end{array} \right\}$

VP → V (NP) (PP)

PP → Prep NP

---

1. Using the above phrase-structure rules and the appropriate lexical items, draw trees for the following sentences:

   a. We warned her.
   b. A present for them arrived in the mail.

    c. She maintained a fast pace until the middle of the last lap.

    d. The collision broke it into pieces.

2. Use the above rules and words of your own choosing to generate four additional sentences. The sentences that you invent should include some pronouns and prepositional phrases.

Varieties of English

When scholars engage in any quest for knowledge, their inquiry is inevitably based on certain assumptions, and it is important for them to be aware of what those assumptions are and, if necessary, to question them. From time to time in our quest to discover the structure of the English language, we have paused to examine our assumptions. The most basic assumption of all—one that we have left unexamined until now—has been that there really is such a thing as *"the* English language." In fact, that is hardly the case. The English spoken by a British aristocrat differs markedly from that spoken by a teenager in a California suburb or that spoken by an Australian sheep rancher.

Even the very same person will use several different "Englishes." For example, there are noticeable differences between the language used by a government leader when delivering a prepared speech to a large audience and when answering questions at a press conference. And that same person may sound quite different still when talking informally with family members. You too sound different—you use a different variety of the language—when you talk comfortably with friends and when you speak on the telephone to an elderly great aunt. And the varieties of language you use in speaking are different from those you use in writing. The latter tend to employ longer sentences, a wider vocabulary, and a greater variety of syntactic constructions. (If, instead of writing, I were talking individually to you, I probably would not have spoken a sentence as long as the previous one nor have used such a "literary" word as "employ.")

Since English is so varied, what is the grammarian to do? How can we describe the structure of English when no single entity called "English" exists?

The answer is that our task is to describe an *idealized language*, if not in all respects an actual one. It is English as *generally* used by educated native speakers. It is, in short, a consensus of what most people agree is the English language. Each of us is different, of course, and there are unique and distinctive features to our individual speech and writing, but the general features and rules that we are attempting to describe are those about which there is general agreement.

Another characteristic of our grammar study is that it is *descriptive*, not *prescriptive*. Although it is of necessity based on an idealized language, our inquiry must be grounded securely in actual usage. Our goal is not to *prescribe* what English would be like if everyone spoke the way we decided they should speak. Instead it is to discover and *describe* the English that the majority of educated speakers actually produce. For example, if most literate users of the language routinely begin sentences with conjunctions or end them with prepositions, we have no choice but to accept those practices as "good English."

Written English, I have said, differs from *spoken English* in several ways. The sentences that we have been analyzing in this book would, for the most part, be considered grammatical both in speech and in writing. But since there is much less variation in written than in spoken English (people from different regions, for example, who sound very different in speech produce a very similar style of language when they write), the idealized language that we examine is much like written language. We will have occasion, however, to look at some distinctly oral constructions as well.

There are many other varieties of English that we could mention before we return to our idealized variety. Different groups of people speak different varieties, or *dialects*, of English. These include *regional dialects* (Southern American English, for example, differs from Northeastern American English), *class dialects* (a working-class Londoner speaks differently from an aristocratic Londoner), and *ethnic dialects* (the speech of many black Chicagoans is different in certain ways from that spoken by many Polish-descent Chicagoans). Dialects are characterized by differences in accents, lexicons, and even phrase-structure rules, and each dialect could be analyzed and described in the same way in which we are here describing our idealized "standard" English. Indeed, it is important to see that what distinguishes one dialect from another is not an *absence* of rules or a *violation* of rules but simply a *different set* of rules.

In addition, all sophisticated speakers and writers of English employ a range of *formal* and *informal* varieties of the language. For example, when you invite someone to join you for a meal, your language can range from the extreme formality of an engraved invitation (". . .requests the pleasure of your company at. . .") to an extremely casual and informal spoken invitation ("'J'eat yet?'").

There are also specialized aspects of language shared by interest groups. These include *slang*, the informal fad language used by teenagers, musicians, or similar in-groups. Slang words constantly enter the language and just as quickly disappear. What was "cool" in the 1950s, "groovy" in the 1960s, and "far-out" in the 1970s might now be "fresh" or "city"—at least for the moment among high school students in the town where I live. Groups that share a special interest may also have their own private lexicon, or *jargon*. Brain surgeons have their own jargon, and so do flight attendants, skiers, and ham-radio enthusiasts. Terms of linguistics jargon that are now familiar to you (but not to the general public) include *phrase-structure rules* and *trees*.

As we continue our exploration of the structure of an idealized version of the English language, you may also wish to think about the rules behind other varieties with which you are familiar.

5 Coordinate Phrases and Complement Clauses

Coordination

Coordinate Noun Phrases

Our rules seem to be getting more and more complex. To the simple noun-phrase rule that we started with in Chapter 2, we have added provisions for optional adjectives, prepositional phrases, and pronouns:

1
$$NP \rightarrow \begin{Bmatrix} (Art) \quad (Adj)^+ \quad N \quad (PP) \\ Pro_P \end{Bmatrix}$$

And we aren't finished yet! At times a noun phrase can have multiple membership:

2
a. *The man and the woman* greeted Donald.
b. The workers demanded *higher pay and better benefits*.
c. They struggled without *food or a reliable source of water*.

Sentence 2a has only one verb phrase (*greeted Donald*), but two noun phrases seem to constitute its subject (*the man* and *the woman*, joined by the word *and*). In sentence 2b, two noun phrases joined by *and* constitute the sentence's direct object. And in 2c, two noun phrases joined by *or* act as the object of the preposition *without*. The words *and* and *or*, which connect the noun phrases, are called ***coordinating conjunctions*** (abbreviated ***Cj_C***).

To account for sentences 2a–2c, we will write a rule that says the slot usually filled by a single noun phrase can also be filled by two noun phrases joined by a conjunction:

3 $NP \rightarrow NP \quad Cj_C \quad NP$

The two rules 1 and 3 allow us to generate sentences like these:

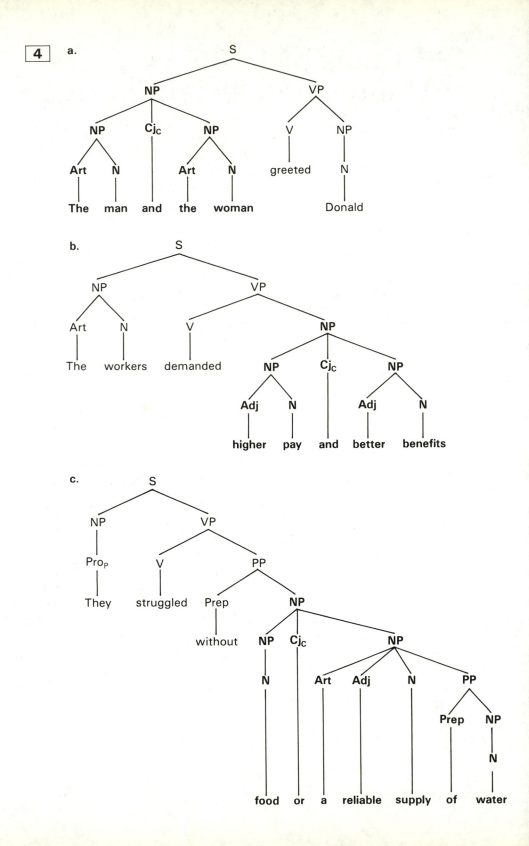

Look carefully at the coordinate noun phrases in 4a–4c. Notice that in each of these phrases the noun phrase "splits" into two noun phrases, each of which behaves like an ordinary noun phrase. Practice generating coordinate noun phrases in the following exercise:

Exercises

Use this grammar to draw trees for the sentences that follow:

$$
\begin{aligned}
&\text{PS RULES}\\
&\text{S} \rightarrow \text{NP} \quad \text{VP}\\
&\text{NP} \rightarrow \left\{\begin{array}{c} \text{NP} \quad \text{Cj}_C \quad \text{NP} \\ \text{(Art)} \quad \text{(Adj)}^+ \quad \text{N} \quad \text{(PP)} \\ \text{Pro}_P \end{array}\right\}\\
&\text{VP} \rightarrow \text{V} \quad \text{(NP)} \quad \text{(PP)}\\
&\text{PP} \rightarrow \text{Prep} \quad \text{NP}
\end{aligned}
$$

1. The rain and the insects spoiled the party.
2. Frank chose Myron or Stella.
3. Leonora worked with a hammer and a saw.
4. The explorer and the wolves lived in peace and harmony.
5. The detective and I solved the mystery through simple logic and a month of tedious labor.

Another Case of Ambiguity

The following sentence is ambiguous. Can you see its two different interpretations?

5 | Pat and Phil or Katie won the award.

The different readings may become more evident when brackets are put around different groupings of noun phrases:

6 | a. [Pat and Phil] or [Katie] won the award.
b. [Pat] and [Phil or Katie] won the award.

Sentences 6a and 6b have the same meaning, respectively, as the following two sentences:

 7
a. Either Pat and Phil won the award, or else Katie won it.
b. Pat won the award along with either Phil or Katie.

By applying rule 3 twice (but in different ways) we can generate sentences that correspond with the two readings of 5:

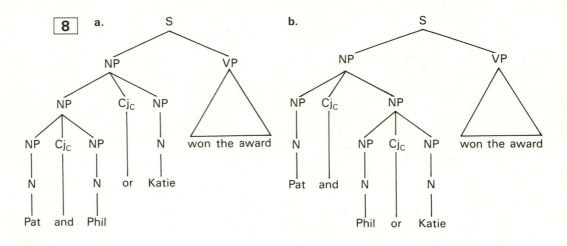

8 a.

b.

These two trees introduce a new shorthand device, a triangle used to represent missing steps. I did not fully analyze the verb phrase in either of these trees, since the analysis is not relevant to our discussion. When we draw a triangle as in 8a, it means that the verb phrase has internal constituents which we could analyze if we wanted to, but to avoid complicating the tree, we choose not to.

Exercises

1. Which tree, 8a or 8b, represents the sentence with the same meaning as 7a?

2. The following sentence is ambiguous:

   The banquet honored Smith or Jones and Brown.

   a. Draw the tree for that sentence when it means that either Smith was honored by himself, or else Jones and Brown were honored together.
   b. Draw the tree for the sentence when it means that either Smith or Jones was honored, and that Brown was also honored.

Other Conjoined Phrases

Noun phrases are not the only phrases that can be joined by conjunctions. Both verb phrases and prepositional phrases can also occur in coordinate pairs:

9
  a. James *dated Susan but married Phyllis*.   *—VP Cj$_C$ VP*

  b. Stephanie stepped *off the pier and into the lake*.   *—PP Cj$_C$ PP*

The grammar is getting complicated as it would seem to need at least three different rules to account for coordination:

10
  a. NP → NP Cj$_C$ NP

  b. VP → VP Cj$_C$ VP

  c. PP → PP Cj$_C$ PP

But these separate rules miss a generalization. *All* phrases can be conjoined. We can capture this general observation about conjunctions in a single phrase-structure rule that uses the term **XP** to stand for any type of phrase:

11
  XP → XP Cj$_C$ XP

Rule 11 replaces the three rules 10a–10c. It states that any phrase can consist of two of itself, joined by a coordinating conjunction. With this simplification, our grammar now looks like the following (included in the lexicon are the five coordinating conjunctions in English):

12

PS RULES	LEXICON
S → NP VP	. . .
NP → $\left\{ \begin{array}{c} \text{(Art) (Adj)}^+ \text{ N (PP)} \\ \text{Pro}_P \end{array} \right\}$	
VP → V (NP) (PP)	
PP → Prep NP	
XP → XP Cj$_C$ XP	

Our grammar can now generate sentences 9a and 9b. Trees for them look like the following:

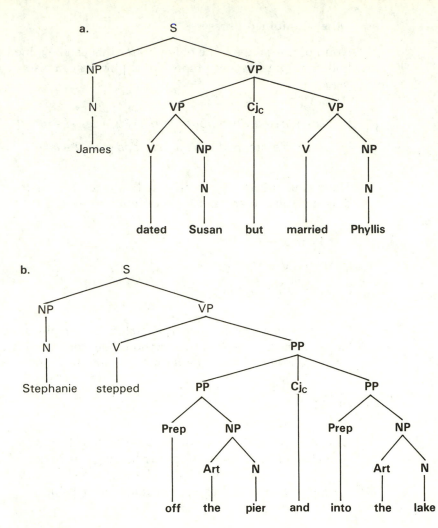

Exercises

1. Circle the conjunctions in each of the following sentences. Then underline the phrases on both sides of each conjunction and label each of them
   as NP, VP, or PP. Finally, use grammar 12 to draw the tree for each
   sentence.

   a. Kit admired Lucy and Alex.
   b. The boxes of foodstuffs and of supplies filled the warehouse.
   c. A half-empty glass of Scotch and soda lay beside the victim of the
      crime.
   d. Norman did the work yet failed the oral exam.

e. The child and an elderly woman entered the station and bought tickets.

Check your trees to be certain you have followed the phrase-structure rules carefully. Note that whenever you have a conjunction, it will be surrounded by a trio of identical phrase labels, like these:

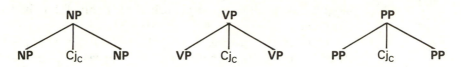

Make sure that all of the coordinate phrases in your trees have this structure.

2. In addition to the coordinate phrases we have examined so far, there are some coordinate phrases that have more than two members. Sometimes they are all joined by conjunctions (*Bob and Ted and Carol and Alice*), and sometimes all conjunctions but the last are omitted (*Barb, Ned, Carl,* and *Alison*). I will not list these rules here, but you might find it interesting to hypothesize about what those rules might look like.

Coordinate Sentences

Like phrases, entire sentences can also be joined by a conjunction:

14 Albert cooked the dinner, and Dominique brought the dessert.

A complete sentence occurs on either side of the conjunction. We can add a new rule, 15, to our grammar and use it to generate trees such as 16.

15 S → S Cj$_C$ S

16

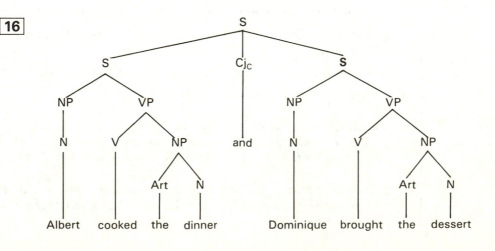

Rule 15 tells us that a larger sentence can be constructed out of two smaller sentences by joining them with a conjunction. Note that each of the lower S-groupings in 16 could stand by itself as an independent sentence. A sentence that contains only a single S-grouping (such as *Albert cooked the dinner*) is called a **simple sentence**. A sentence such as 14 that has two S-groupings joined by a coordinating conjunction is called a **compound sentence**.

Although we proposed rule 15 to account for compound sentences, its addition to our grammar is not really necessary, since sentence coordination can be covered by our general coordinating rule 11, which allows the conjoining of any two phrases. We defined a phrase as any group of words that acts as a constituent, so an S is also a type of phrase, the same as an NP, a VP, or a PP.

Although S-groupings are technically phrases, in common speech the term *phrase* usually refers to a grouping smaller than a sentence, such as a noun phrase or verb phrase. A sentence grouping (on a tree, the words that branch out beneath an S) is usually called a **clause**. Sentence 16 consists of two clauses joined by the coordinating conjunction *and*. Although this distinction is usually made between phrases and clauses, it should be remembered that a clause is a particular type of phrase, and any rule, such as 11, that applies to phrases can also apply to clauses.

Exercises

Draw trees to show how grammar 12 can generate the following sentences with coordinate clauses and phrases. Because some of them are long, your trees may fit better on the page if you turn your paper sideways. Always leave plenty of room for your trees. If you do not, the trees will be cramped and will lose their effectiveness as clear diagrams of the sentences' structures.

1. A nail caused the puncture, and Shirley changed the tire.
2. Victor and Constance dreamed glorious dreams, yet they lived mundane lives.
3. Caesar invaded Britain, but Britain withstood Napoleon and Hitler.
4. Julio rescued the crew and won a promotion.

You should have discovered that one of the above sentences has coordinate phrases but not coordinate clauses. Now that you have gotten this far, you may be ready for a final challenge, a sentence that has everything:

5. The holy man and I climbed the steps and entered the lost temple, but the priestesses captured us and threatened us with torture or with a slow death by starvation.

If you overcame that last challenge, you are certainly on top of the subject, and you have demonstrated considerable aptness as a grammarian.

A note on usage: In writing, a comma is usually placed before a conjunction when it joins two clauses (for example, in sentences 1 through 3 above), but not when it joins two simple phrases (as in sentence 4 above).

Complement Clauses

Sentential-Complement Clauses

At the beginning of this chapter, we observed that noun phrases can take various forms. For example, the direct-object slot in the following tree can be filled with many different kinds of constituents, including one we have not previously seen:

17

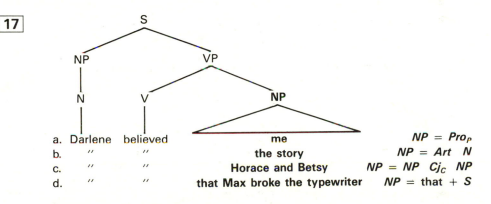

a.	Darlene	believed	me	$NP = Pro_P$
b.	"	"	the story	$NP = Art\ N$
c.	"	"	Horace and Betsy	$NP = NP\ Cj_C\ NP$
d.	"	"	that Max broke the typewriter	$NP = $ that $+ S$

In sentence 17d, the object noun phrase, the thing that Darlene believed, is an entire sentence. Such sentences are called *complement clauses* (more specifically, *sentential complements*), because they are clauses that complement (or complete) the main clause. They are also called *nominal clauses* because they function as noun phrases. Sentential-complement clauses can occur as subjects as well as objects of sentences:

18

a. *That Tom remembered the appointment* amazed the doctor.

                                       —*Clause as subject*

b. The doctor warned *that nicotine causes cancer.*

                                       —*Clause as object*

The word *that*, which introduces the complement clauses in the two sentences, is called a *complementizer* or a *complementizing conjunction* (abbreviated **Cj_{Cl}**). It has no meaning by itself, but rather serves a grammatical purpose by alerting the listener or reader that a complement clause (and not an independent sentence) is about to follow. Notice how confusing sentence 18a would be if the "meaningless" complementizer *that* were omitted. Parts of speech such as complementizers which have no independent meaning but which instead express a relationship between other words in a sentence are called ***grammatical words***. In addition to complementizers, articles, prepositions, and coordinating conjunctions are usually classified as grammatical words. Words that do have independent meaning, such as nouns, pronouns, verbs, and adjectives, are called ***lexical words***.

We will represent complement clauses by the abbreviation ***CompP***. (The P in the abbreviation stands for *phrase*; we could use the abbreviation CompC, but we will find CompP more convenient. In later chapters, we will encounter complements which are phrases rather than complete clauses. CompP is a useful term to describe *all* complements.) The following addition to our NP rule expresses our discovery that a noun phrase can be an entire complement clause:

19   NP → CompP

Sentences 18a and 18b will have this structure:

20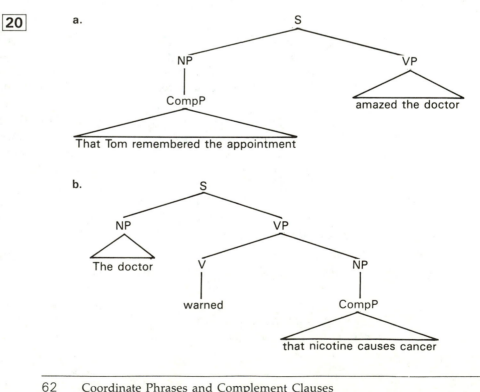
a.

b.

Notice that in 20a, something amazed the doctor. That something could have been a simple noun phrase (such as *the trick*), but instead it is a complete sentence that amazed the doctor, namely *that Tom remembered the appointment*. We can observe, then, that each of the two complement clauses consists of the complementizer *that* and a complete sentence. We can state this observation in the following rule:

21 CompP → Cj$_{Cl}$ S

With rules 19 and 21 we can now draw the complete trees for 18a and 18b.

22 a.

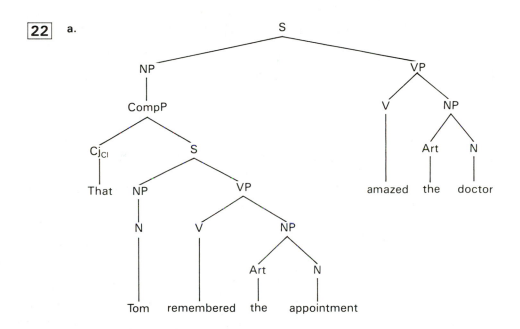

b.

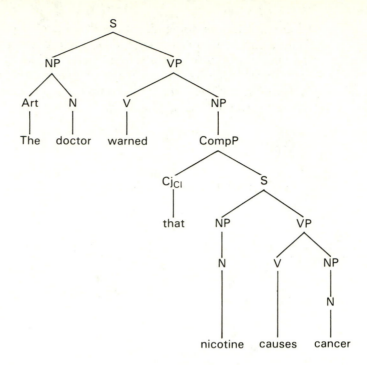

Each of the two lower S clauses in 22a and 22b is a constituent of a noun phrase in the higher S. When one S is a constituent of another, it is said to be *embedded* in that S; it is also called an *embedded clause*. The clause *nicotine causes cancer* is embedded in sentence 20b.

When rule 19a is incorporated into the grammar, the comprehensive NP rule looks like this:

$$\boxed{23} \qquad NP \rightarrow \left\{ \begin{array}{c} Pro_P \\ (Art) \quad (Adj)^+ \quad N \quad (PP) \\ CompP \end{array} \right\}$$

It should be clear that when a rule such as 23 provides options, any one of the options may be chosen whenever a noun phrase occurs. There is no significance to the order in which I listed the three options in 23. For example, the rule would have had exactly the same meaning if I had placed the pronoun option in the middle or on the bottom instead of on top.

Exercises

1. Underline the embedded complement clauses in the following sentences, and note whether each complement clause acts as the subject or direct

object of the sentence. Finally, draw trees to show how a grammar that incorporates rule 23 can generate the sentences:

   a. Roscoe knew that roses have thorns.
   b. That a computer had bugs caused anxiety for the squeamish programmer.
   c. Willie doubts that babies understand geometry.
   d. That Margot testified about the burglary resulted in the conviction of the notorious slasher.

Sometimes a sentence can have more than one complement clause:

   e. That the sun shone meant that the groundhog saw a shadow.

And sometimes one complement clause can be embedded in another:

   f. Pedro thought that Pierre believed that Olga loves Hans.

2. All the complement clauses so far have been either subjects or direct objects. What is the role of the complement clause in the following sentence? How would you diagram it?

   He believed nothing except that television rots the brain.

3. Invent two additional sentences with complement clauses, and diagram them.

Complement Clauses without "That"

Complement clauses present some additional options that we have not yet considered. Sometimes, when the complementizer *that* is not needed to avoid confusion, it can be omitted. Compare these two sentences:

24   a. We knew that Murray preferred tea to coffee.
     b. We knew Murray preferred tea to coffee.

The complementizer can usually be omitted when the complement clause acts as the direct object of the main sentence. It is needed, however, when the complement clause is the subject of the sentence:

25   a. That Perry ran for public office amazes me.
     b. *Perry ran for public office amazes me.

The purpose of the complementizer *that* is to alert the hearer that a complement clause is about to follow. It is not needed in 24b for that purpose, but if it is omitted in 25b, the hearer has no way of knowing that *Perry ran for public office* is an embedded clause and not the main clause of the sentence.

Rule 21 needs to be revised to reflect the fact that the complementizer can sometimes be omitted:

26   CompP → (Cj$_{Cl}$)   S

It is important to note, however, that the complementizer is required when the complement clause is the subject of the sentence.

Nominal-Complement Clauses

In the previous examples, complement clauses acted as noun phrases. In the following sentences, complement clauses follow (and complement) other noun phrases:

27   a. The theory *that Martians inhabit Vermont* amazed Clarence.

b. He conceived the idea *that insomnia prolongs life*.

c. We laughed at the ridiculous notion *that Cynthia resembles Linn*.

The italicized complement clauses in 27 are called **nominal-complement clauses** because they complement or complete the meaning of the nouns that they follow. In 27a, for example, the complement clause *that Martians inhabit Vermont* "complements" the noun phrase *the theory*; that is, it completes its meaning by explaining what the theory is. We can introduce still one more option in our NP rule:

28   NP → (Art) (Adj)$^+$ N (PP) **(CompP)**

In addition to its other constituents, a noun phrase can include a nominal-complement clause. This rule allows us to generate the sentences of 27. Here are trees for 27a and 27c:

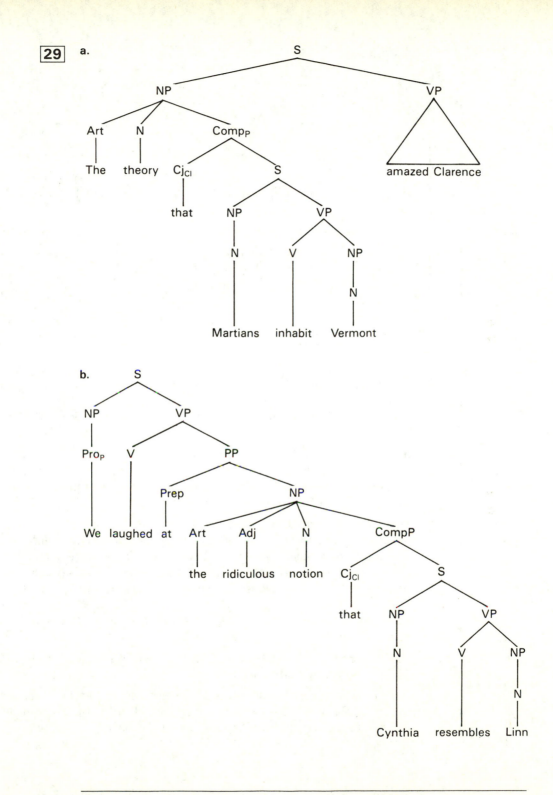

Exercises

1. Our grammar now includes the following phrase-structure rules:

```
                            PS RULES
            S  →  NP   VP

                                      Pro_P
            NP →   { (Art)  (Adj)+   N   (PP)   (CompP) }
                                      CompP

       CompP →  (Cj_Cl)   S

                      ( V   (NP)  PP )
            VP →   {    V_L { NP  }    }
                      (        { Adj } )

            PP →  Prep   NP
            XP →  XP   Cj_C   XP
```

Draw trees to show how these rules can generate the sentences below. If you have difficulty, be sure you are applying rule 28 at the appropriate noun-phrase label. Compare each NP in your trees with those in **29a** and **29b**.

a. The news that the forecasters predicted rain cheered the farmers.
b. Moscow issued a statement that the premier signed the treaty.
c. The defendant denied the allegation that he committed perjury.
d. We convinced Geoffrey of the necessity that he make a will.

Notice the construction he make *instead of* he makes *in exercise 1d. This is one of the few vestiges in modern English verbs of the* **subjunctive mood**. *Another remains in the familiar expression* if I were you, *where* were *is used instead of* was. *These subjunctive forms are used to describe hypothetical situations, imaginary events that have not actually happened. Except for third-person-singular forms (where the -s inflection is left off the verb), subjunctive forms are identical with forms in non-subjunctive statements (called the* **indicative mood**), *such as the subjunctive verb* live *in exercise 1e:*

e. The strong wish of the American people that the major powers live in peace swayed the election.

Be certain that the complement clause in exercise 1e is attached to (complements) the appropriate NP. The sense of the sentence is not "the people *that the major powers live in peace" but "the* wish . . . *that the major powers live in peace." The structure of your tree should reflect this.*

The following sentences contain both sentential complements and nominal complements:

  f. The proposal by the commission that students wear suits and dresses to class shows that they desire a return to the past.

  g. That Paula and Marc married confirmed the theory that opposites attract.

2. We have seen nouns such as *theory, belief,* and *notion* taking nominal complements. List as many nouns as you can that can be followed by complement clauses. What do these nouns have in common?

Adjectival-Complement Clauses

Just as certain nouns can be complemented by clauses that complete their meaning, so can certain adjectives be complemented by clauses as well:

30
  a. Randolph was angry *that the neighbors threw a wild party*.
  b. Lana is confident *that she knows the correct answers*.

An *adjectival-complement clause* complements an adjective that follows a linking verb. Together, the adjective and the complement clause constitute a phrase, which we will call an *adjectival phrase* or **AdjP**. Our phrase-structure rules can be adjusted as follows:

31

$$VP \rightarrow V_L \left\{ \begin{array}{c} NP \\ AdjP \end{array} \right\}$$

$$AdjP \rightarrow Adj \ (CompP)$$

With these rules we can draw the tree for 30a:

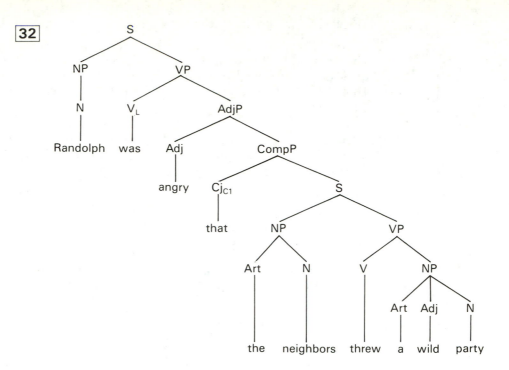

Exercises

1. Draw trees for these sentences with adjectival-complement clauses:
   a. The students were certain that they understood calculus.
   b. The Indians are furious that the cowboys broke the treaty.
   c. Vincent seemed happy that the vacation started.

2. The CompP that follows an adjective can be a complement clause, as in the sentences in exercise 1. But prepositional phrases can also complement adjectives, as in these examples:
   a. The students were certain of their knowledge.
   b. The Indians were angry at the cowboys.
   c. Vincent seemed happy with his schedule.

   How might you adjust our grammar to account for these sentences?

6 Determiners, Adverbs, and Other Modifiers

After witnessing our grammar's NP rule grow ever more complicated, you may wonder if at last we have got it the way we want it—at the point where it can generate all the possible noun phrases in English. It cannot, at least not yet, but having come this far, you are well prepared to take any additional modifications in stride. Look at the positive side: With each change we have made, our grammar has become more and more powerful, able to produce ever more varied types of English sentences.

Our noun-phrase rule to date is as follows:

1

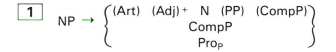

$$NP \rightarrow \left\{ \begin{array}{l} (Art)\ (Adj)^{+}\ N\ (PP)\ (CompP) \\ CompP \\ Pro_P \end{array} \right\}$$

Determiners

We will take another look at the top line of rule 1, which generates noun phrases such as this one:

2

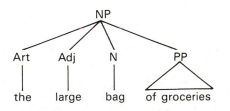

In particular, let us consider the slot occupied by the category Art in that phrase. In addition to the articles (*a*, *an*, and *the*), other words could also fill that slot in a grammatical phrase:

3

This
Each } large bag of groceries
John's
My

Each of these four words can occur instead of *the* in the sample noun phrase. A few more tests can help us decide if these words can be true replacements for the Art category. First, none of them can occur along with *the*:

4

*The this
*This the
*The each } large bag of groceries
*John's the
*The my

Second, just as two articles cannot occur in a phrase (**the a bag*), the four words also cannot occur with each other:

5

*This each
*John's this } large bag of groceries
*Each my

Finally, like the article, each of the four substitutes must precede the adjective; none can follow it:

6

*Large this
*Large each } bag of groceries
*Large John's
*Large my

The apparent exception, *Large John's*, has a different meaning. It is ungrammatical if it is to retain the meaning that the bag is large.

From these tests, we conclude that the four words, *this, each, John's,* and *my,* do fill the same slot in the noun phrase as the article. A larger grammatical category is needed, one that will include articles as well as these four as-yet unlabeled words. We will call all such words ***determiners*** (abbreviated ***Det***). The first line of rule 1 now becomes:

7 NP → **(Det)** (Adj)+ N (PP) (CompP)

Determiners can be a variety of things, including articles as well as our four substitute words. Once we find categories for them, we can insert their names in place of the dotted lines in this rule:

8   Det → $\left\{ \begin{array}{c} \text{Art} \\ \ldots \\ \ldots \end{array} \right\}$

Demonstratives and Quantifiers

The words *this, that, these,* and *those* are called ***demonstrative modifiers*** (abbreviated ***Dem***), because they *demonstrate* (point out definitely) which particular bag of groceries is being discussed. The word *each* is called a ***quantifier*** or ***Quant*** (also called an ***indefinite modifier***). Other quantifiers include *any, all, enough, every, few, many, more, much, most, several, no,* and *some*. They are called quantifiers because they quantify (provide quantity information about) the nouns that follow them.

So far we have named three options to fill the missing categories in rule 8:

9   Det → $\left\{ \begin{array}{c} \text{Art} \\ \text{Dem} \\ \text{Quant} \\ \ldots \end{array} \right\}$

Rules 7 and 9 allow us to generate trees such as the following:

10

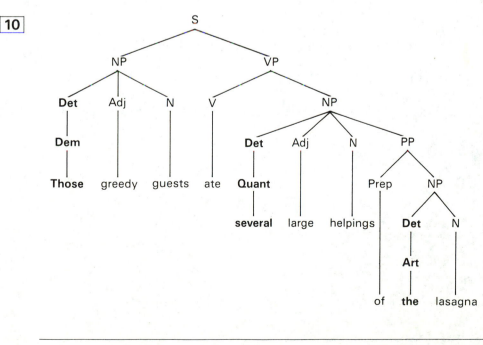

Exercises

Draw trees to show how a grammar with rules 7 and 9 can generate the following sentences:

1. That play had many funny scenes.

   Notice that the demonstrative that *in exercise 1 is a different word from the complementizer* that *(such as the second word in this sentence).*

2. They preferred all rural locations to this city.

3. The hikers packed enough supplies for any emergency.

Possessive Nouns and Pronouns

The third new determiner that we saw in 3, *John's*, is a ***possessive noun***, indicating ownership. In fact a whole range of possessive noun phrases can fill the same slot as *John's*:

11

John's
The boy's
An entire family's
Both twins'
} large bag of groceries

In written English, possession for nouns is indicated by adding *'s* (or an apostrophe alone for plural words such as *twins* that already end in *s*). We can indicate this option for determiners with a rule (12). ***Poss*** represents the appropriate possessive ending for the noun.

12 Det → NP Poss

Rule 12 allows us to generate noun phrases such as those in tree 13.

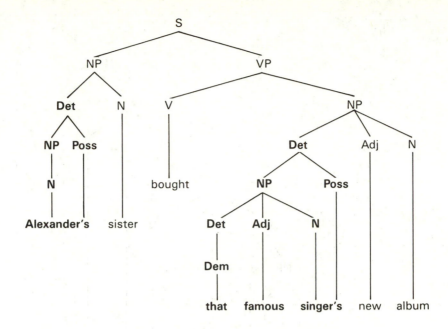

Study this tree, and particularly its subject and object noun phrases, very carefully. First notice how rules 7 and 12 generated the phrase *Alexander's sister*. Then examine the more complicated noun phrase, *that famous singer's new album*. Begin by analyzing it from top to bottom, starting with the label NP, and seeing how the rules generated it. Next, analyze it from bottom to top. Note that *that famous singer* is a grouping or constituent, and when the possessive ending is added, *that famous singer's* is also a grouping which, as a unit, modifies *new album*. Notice that the entire noun phrase contains two adjectives, *famous* and *new*. The tree shows clearly that *famous* modifies *singer* and that *new* modifies *album*. Certainly it is the singer, not the album, who is famous, and the album, not the singer, that is new.

Because rules 7 and 12 allow for recursion (with noun phrases occurring within other noun phrases), phrases with multiple possessives such as 14 are possible.

14

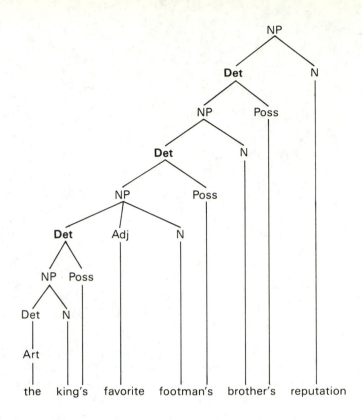

In addition to nouns, pronouns can also be possessive. The ***possessive pronouns*** (abbreviated **Pro$_S$**) are *my, our, your, her, his, its,* and *their*. Here is our final option for the determiner category, along with a sample phrase which the rule can generate:

15   Det → Pro$_S$

16

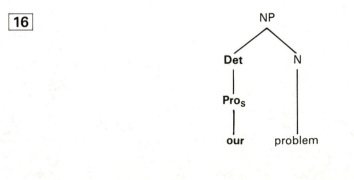

Since we have made many adjustments to our grammar, it is time we reviewed its current state:

17

PS RULES	LEXICON

$S \rightarrow NP \ VP$

$NP \rightarrow \begin{cases} (Det) \ (Adj)^+ \ N \ (PP) \ (CompP) \\ CompP \\ Pro_P \end{cases}$

$CompP \rightarrow (Cj_{Cl}) \ S$

$Det \rightarrow \begin{cases} Art \\ Dem \\ Quant \\ NP \ Poss \\ Pro_S \end{cases}$

$VP \rightarrow \begin{cases} V \ (NP) \ (PP) \\ V_L \begin{cases} NP \\ AdjP \end{cases} \end{cases}$

$AdjP \rightarrow Adj \ (CompP)$

$PP \rightarrow Prep \ NP$

$XP \rightarrow XP \ Cj_C \ XP$

LEXICON

Art: the, a, an
Dem: this, that, these, those
Quant: any, all, each, enough, every, few, many, more, much, most, several, some
Pro_S my, our, your, her, his, its, their
Poss: 's, '
. . .

Exercises

1. Use grammar 17 to generate trees for the following sentences:
   a. Your happiness is my fondest wish.
   b. They speak the Queen's English in Tasmania.
   c. The elderly butler's favorite book of limericks disappeared.
   d. My opinion of Sam's cousin was unfavorable.
   e. Those scoundrels impressed few people with their honesty.

2. Draw trees for both of these two noun phrases (start with the NP symbol):
   a. the whole class's favorite novel's author's latest book
   b. the latest book by the author of the favorite novel of the entire class

   Note that your tree for a in exercise 2 branches down and to the left, while your tree for b branches down and to the right. Can you speculate about why people generally find sentences with right-branching trees easier to understand?

3. The quantifiers *much* and *many* have similar meanings, but they are used to modify different nouns. Which nouns from the following list would be preceded by *much* and which by *many*?

water	gallons	sheep
sand	children	love
people	attempts	snow
snowstorms	embarrassment	

When you speak, how do you know whether to use *much* or *many*? Can you think of a principle that would determine whether a noun would take one or the other of the two quantifiers? Would the same principle also apply to *little* and *few*?

4. As lengthy as it seems, our list of determiners may not yet be complete. Decide whether the **cardinal numbers** (*one, two, three,* and so on) and the **ordinal numbers** (*first, second, third,* and so on) should be regarded as determiners or adjectives.

5. Our classification of determiners may still not be as neat as we would like. Here is a more difficult problem: How should we account in our grammar for such expressions as *a few pencils, the first six pens, many a fine eraser,* and *such an unusual crayon*? Do they indeed disprove the claim that a noun phrase can have no more than one determiner?

Adverbs

Adverbials that Modify Verbs

One major part of speech that we have not yet explored is the **adverb** or **Adv**. Adverbs can modify verbs, as the italicized adverb does in this sentence:

18 Winifred gazed at the sky *intently*.

Intently tells how Winifred did the gazing, and so it modifies the verb. We can add an adverb option to our VP rule:

19 VP → V (NP) (PP) **(Adv)**

Our tree for 18 looks like this:

20

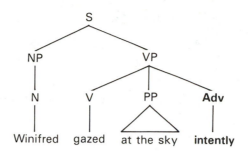

Most adverbs are easy to spot because they are formed by adding the inflection *-ly* to an adjective: *rapidly, angrily, happily*. Adverbs that do not end in *-ly* include *well, much, little, once, twice,* as well as many place adverbs such as *here, there, eastward,* and *skyward,* and also many time adverbs such as *soon, often, yesterday, now,* and *then.*

While it generated sentence 20, rule 19 is still not satisfactory. It can generate an adverb following a prepositional phrase, but some grammatical sentences have the reverse order:

21   Winifred gazed intently at the sky.

Perhaps we need a second verb-phrase rule to allow for adverbs preceding prepositional phrases. But the following sentences show that there are still other possibilities as well:

22

Winifred gazed
- intently at the sky yesterday.   *—Adv PP Adv*
- at the sky intently with binoculars.   *—PP Adv PP*
- intently yesterday at the sky with binoculars.
           —Adv Adv PP PP

Prepositional phrases and adverbs seem to occur interchangeably in a variety of combinations. We could write a separate rule for each of them, but clearly there are many other possibilities as well—in fact, a limitless number of them—and we cannot write rules for all of them.

Despite these problems, a solution is in sight. Since adverbs and prepositional phrases are interchangeable, we can hypothesize that they belong to the same kind of category. Further evidence is the fact that some adverbs and prepositional phrases are equivalent in meaning, such as *enthusiastically* and *with enthusiasm*. We will give the category that includes them both the name *adverbial phrase* or **AdvP**. Any number of adverbial phrases can occur within a verb phrase. Our revised rules look like this:

23

$$VP \rightarrow V \ (NP) \ \mathbf{(AdvP)+}$$

$$AdvP \rightarrow \begin{Bmatrix} Adv \\ PP \end{Bmatrix}$$

The rules of **23** can generate verb phrases with multiple adverbs and prepositional phrases such as this one with four adverbial phrases:

24

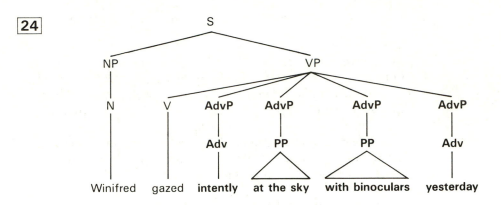

Exercises

Draw trees for the following sentences to show how the rules of **23** can generate verb phrases with adverbial phrases:

1. She gets headaches lately.
2. The dancers glided effortlessly across the patio.
3. Alexis helped Carl gladly with his project recently.
4. That he glared fiercely at me discomforted me greatly.

Like all other phrases, adverbial phrases can be conjoined by the XP rule:

5. The music stopped abruptly and without any warning.

Remember the difference between prepositional phrases that modify nouns and those that modify verbs:

6. Luke sat in the front of the car on the trip to Mexico.

The following sentence is ambiguous because it is unclear whether the adverb *yesterday* is a constituent of the VP that includes *learned* or the VP that includes *won*:

7. We learned that he won the medal yesterday.

   a. Draw a tree for the sentence when it means that yesterday was when he won it.
   b. Draw a tree for the sentence when it means that yesterday was when we learned it.

   Note: An adverb can follow the object noun phrase within a verb phrase, even when that noun phrase is an entire embedded clause.

And finally:

8. George sat impassively for five minutes alone on the couch without any sign of life.

Adverbials that Follow Linking Verbs

Earlier, we saw that a linking verb can be followed by a noun phrase (for example, *The plane is a jet*) or an adjectival phrase (*The plane is new*). An adverbial phrase can also follow a linking verb:

25
    a. The plane is *here*.

    b. The plane is *on the runway*.

    c. The departure is *tomorrow*.

Our phrase-structure rule for linking verbs can be revised to include adverbials:

26
$$VP \rightarrow V_L \left\{ \begin{array}{c} NP \\ AdjP \\ \mathbf{AdvP} \end{array} \right\}$$

There is a restriction, however, on the occurrence of adverbials in this position. Not all adverbial phrases can follow linking verbs, but only adverbials of place (such as *here* and *on the runway*) or of time (such as *tomorrow*). Other adverbials cannot occur in this position (**The plane is quickly*).

Sentence 25a can be diagrammed as shown in 27.

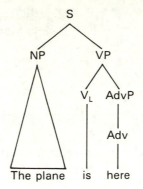

27

The plane is here

Exercises

Draw trees to show the derivations of the following sentences:

1. The coach says that the future is now.
2. The boys were at the concert.
3. Pandemonium is everywhere.

Degree Modifiers

Adjectives and adverbs are both modifiers. Adjectives modify nouns, while adverbs modify verbs. But both adjectives (28) and adverbs (29) can themselves be modified:

28
very quick
most polite
quite happy
extremely tall
slightly sick

29
very quickly
most politely
quite happily
too soon
almost always

These modifiers of modifiers (*very, too, slightly...*) are sometimes classified as adverbs (note that some of them end in *-ly*). We will call them *degree modi-*

fiers (abbreviated **Deg**) because when a word like *very* modifies *quick* or *quickly*, it tells us the *degree* of quickness. In addition to adjectives and adverbs, at least some prepositional phrases can also take degree modifiers: *almost without exception, gravely in error, nearly on time, slightly above the average.*

Let us first add degree modifiers as options to our rule for adverbial phrases:

30 $\quad$ AdvP $\rightarrow$ (Deg) $\begin{Bmatrix} \text{Adv} \\ \text{PP} \end{Bmatrix}$

When a degree modifier precedes an adjective, as in 28, the two words constitute a phrase and so can be called an *adjectival phrase* or AdjP. The grammar needs to be revised accordingly:

31 $\quad$ NP $\rightarrow$ (Det) **(AdjP)**$^+$ N (PP) (CompP)

$\quad\quad$ AdjP $\rightarrow$ (Deg) Adj

An adjectival phrase can take a degree modifier whether it precedes a noun (the very old shoe) or follows a linking verb (The shoe was very old). But notice that an adjectival-complement clause (see pages 69–70) can occur in an adjectival phrase only when the adjectival phrase follows a linking verb (I am happy that you came) but not when it precedes a noun (*the happy-that-you-came person). We might wish to distinguish between adjectival phrases in the two positions—that is, between an AdjP (which precedes a noun) and an AdjP$_L$ (which follows a linking verb). If so, we can write our phrase-structure rules as follows:

$\quad\quad$ AdjP $\rightarrow$ (Deg) $\quad$ Adj

$\quad\quad$ AdjP$_L$ $\rightarrow$ (Deg) $\quad$ Adj $\quad$ (CompP)

In the same manner, we can distinguish between two different adverbial phrases—that is, between an AdvP (which modifies a transitive or an intransitive verb) and an AdvP$_L$ (which follows a linking verb). Unlike an AdvP, an AdvP$_L$ is restricted to adverbials of time and place. The rule for linking verbs would be revised as follows:

$\quad\quad$ VP $\rightarrow$ V$_L$ $\begin{Bmatrix} \text{NP} \\ \text{AdjP}_L \\ \text{AdvP}_L \end{Bmatrix}$

Rules 30 and 31 allow the grammar to generate trees such as this one:

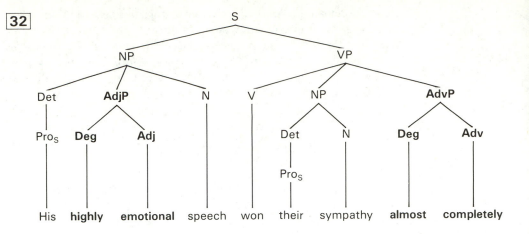

32

Tree diagram for the sentence:

His highly emotional speech won their sympathy almost completely

S
- NP
  - Det → Pro_S → His
  - AdjP
    - Deg → highly
    - Adj → emotional
  - N → speech
- VP
  - V → won
  - NP
    - Det → Pro_S → their
    - N → sympathy
  - AdvP
    - Deg → almost
    - Adv → completely

Exercises

Use rules 30 and 31 to generate trees for these sentences:

1. The fire had terribly sad consequences.
2. The grossly overweight athlete began his diet almost immediately.
3. They schedule the most important classes too infrequently.

   Note that the word most *can be either a degree modifier* (the most unusual person) *or a quantifier* (Most people have jobs).

4. Ruby was absolutely furious that Arthur forgot his manners.
5. He arrived unfashionably early in an extraordinarily garish tuxedo.

Noun Phrases as Modifiers

Nouns can be modified by adjectives, but they can also be modified by other nouns. Look at these examples:

33

| tennis racket | dorm director | surprise party |
| carpet sweeper | stamp collection | sausage pizza |

We can make noun modifiers a second option in adjectival phrases:

34

$$\text{AdjP} \rightarrow \left\{ \begin{array}{l} \text{(Deg) Adj} \\ \text{N} \end{array} \right\}$$

Rule 34 describes an adjectival phrase that precedes a noun. With this rule we can generate noun phrases such as this one:

35

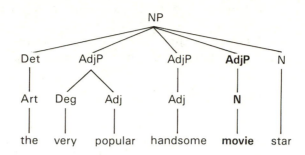

Exercises

1. Use the noun–phrase rule of **31** and the adjectival-phrase rule of **34** to generate these noun phrases:

    a. the Bronze Age
    b. my favorite grammar book
    c. all rock videos
    d. designer jeans with leather cuffs
    e. creamy milk shakes
    f. friendly purple people eater

2. Draw trees for these sentences:

    a. The child prodigy wrote a piano concerto.
    b. An overly enthusiastic sports fan demanded an autograph.
    c. Jake's obnoxiously loud record player caused a riot in Farley Hall.

3. Adjectival phrases, like all other phrases, can be joined with conjunctions by the XP rule. Draw a tree for this sentence:

    The sadder but wiser champion won an exceptionally bloody but meaningless contest.

4. In the noun phrase *the violent thunder storm,* the adjective modifier (*violent*) precedes the noun modifier (*thunder*). Do adjectives always precede nouns when both are modifiers in the same noun phrase? Can you think of any noun phrases with the reverse order?

5. Sometimes the distinction between noun modifiers and adjectives is blurred. For example, in the phrases *silver spoon* and *silver hair,* is it clear what kinds of adjectival phrases the two instances of *silver* are?

6. Sometimes noun modifiers are themselves modified. For example, in *chicken salad sandwich*, the noun *chicken* modifies *salad* rather than *sandwich*. In *old age home*, the adjective *old* modifies *age* and not *home*. Can you revise rule 34 to allow for such phrases?

As the preceding exercise 6 demonstrated, rule 34 needs to be revised to allow for modifiers which are themselves complete noun phrases:

36 $\quad$ AdjP $\rightarrow \left\{ \begin{array}{c} \text{(Deg)} \quad \text{Adj} \\ \textbf{NP} \end{array} \right\}$

With this rule we can generate noun phrases such as *the delicious fresh deviled-egg-and-ham salad sandwiches*. This phrase is ambiguous, with more than one possible interpretation, depending on which modifier is seen as modifying which noun. Here is one interpretation:

37

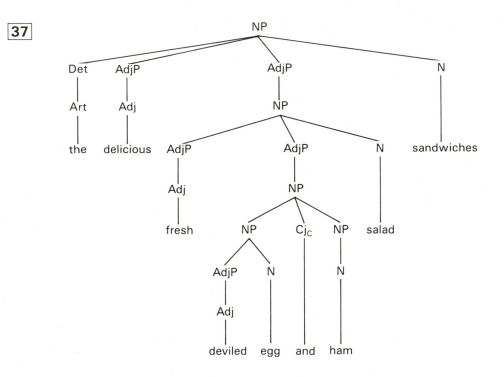

In the interpretation offered by diagram 37, *delicious* modifies *sandwiches* (it is the sandwiches that are said to be delicious); *fresh* modifies *salad* (it is the salad that is said to be fresh); and the conjoined phrase *deviled-egg-and-ham* also modifies *salad* (the salad consists of those ingredients).

Exercises

1. Use rule **36** to diagram these sentences:

   a. They served peanut butter sandwiches in the old age home.
   b. He bought the giant economy size cough medicine bottle

2. Diagram the phrase *the delicious, fresh deviled-egg and ham-salad sandwiches* so that it means that the sandwiches were made from two ingredients: (a) delicious, fresh deviled eggs and (b) ham salad. Note how your tree differs from **37**, which offers a different interpretation of the phrase. What other interpretations of the phrase are also possible?

3. It is possible to describe a person as *a loyal fan of the Red Sox* but not as *∗a loyal the Red Sox fan*. In the latter phrase, the article *the* must be omitted before *Red Sox*: the friend is *a loyal Red Sox fan*. Do you find a general restriction on the use of determiners in noun phrases when they modify other noun phrases?

4. Note that the phrase *wild horse trainer* is ambiguous, since it is not clear what *wild* modifies. Use your revised rule to draw a tree for that noun phrase when it means that the horse is wild, and another tree which indicates that the trainer is wild.

5. In written English, punctuation is sometimes used to eliminate ambiguity among modifiers, as in these examples:

   a. Anna is a hyperactive child psychologist.
   b. Anna is a hyperactive-child psychologist.

   How do the two sentences differ in meaning? Would you insert a hyphen in *wild horse trainer* if you wanted to show that the horse, not the trainer, is wild? State the general principle for using hyphens in such cases to avoid ambiguity.

7 Transformational Rules: Altering Elements in a Sentence

Particles

Sometimes words can do double duty as two different parts of speech. For example, the same words that act as prepositions can also act as an entirely different category, called *particles* (abbreviated ***Prt***). The italicized words in the following sentences are all particles:

1   Bonnie shut *off* the engine.

Eliza looked *up* the address in the directory.

The announcer called *out* the winner's name.

Clyde turned *in* the counterfeit money.

At first it may appear that the italicized words are prepositions. But notice the difference in the way *on* is used in the following two sentences:

2   a. Terry cried on my shoulder.

b. Terry tried on my sweater.

In 2a, *on my shoulder* is a prepositional phrase. We feel intuitively that the preposition *on* is connected with the noun phrase *my shoulder*. As a whole, the prepositional phrase *on my shoulder* tells us where Terry did the crying. It has the feel of a unit in a way that *on my sweater* in 2b certainly does not.

By contrast, if we have a sense about groupings in 2b, we would say that *on* belongs with *tried* rather than *my sweater*. In fact, the verb *tried* and the particle *on* together constitute the action: *trying on* was what Terry did. We can define a particle as a word that has no meaning by itself but that can pair with a verb to describe an action. Sentences 2a and 2b can be diagrammed as follows:

3

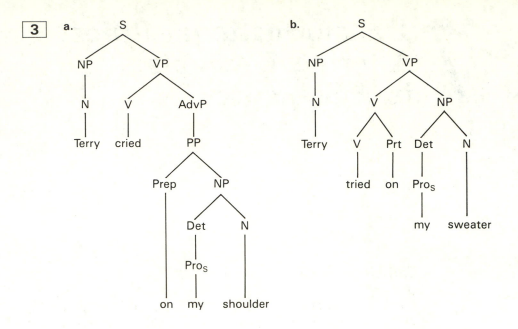

Diagram 3b shows the "verb" or "action" of that sentence to consist of two words, the verb *tried* and the particle *on*. A phrase-structure rule can allow for such verb-particle combinations:

4 (V → V Prt)

Rule 4 states that, as an option, a verb can have two constituents: the verb itself and a particle.

This rule is somewhat different from other phrase-structure rules that we have written in that it is an entirely optional rule. Consider the procedure for applying phrase-structure rules: To generate a sentence, we begin with the S rule and continue to apply rules until we cannot apply any more. Often the grammar allows us a choice between rules. For example, whenever the rules generate the category NP we must then apply one or another of the NP (or XP) rules in order to generate that noun phrase. The tree cannot simply stop at the NP label. On the other hand, it can stop at the V label. Rule 4 is placed in parentheses to show that when we encounter the category V, we have the option either of applying rule 4 or of applying no further phrase-structure rules before inserting a verb from the lexicon.

Exercises

1. For each of these pairs of sentences, decide which sentence has a verb-particle combination and which has a prepositional phrase:

a. He walked up the street.
   He looked up the phone number.
b. She thought over the offer.
   She jumped over the fence.
c. We took out the garbage.
   We stared out the window.
d. They strolled in the garden.
   They took in the orphan.
e. You drove off the road.
   You turned off the radio.

2. Draw trees for these sentences with particles:

   a. Belinda called up her friend.
   b. Julian knocked over the statue.
   c. Knute's army drove out the barbarian invaders.
   d. Sigmund figured out the solution without any help from me.

3. Draw trees for the sentences in exercises 1a and 1b.

Moving the Particles

In writing rule 4, we placed the particle right after the verb, since that is
where it occurred in all our sample sentences. It makes sense that verbs and
particles would occur next to each other since we observed that together they
state the sentence's action. For example, if Joe has put out a fire, we would
describe his action not as *putting* but as *putting out*.

   Nevertheless, we also find particles occurring after the direct-object noun
phrase. Compare the sentences of 1 with those of 5:

5 Bonnie shut the engine off.

   Eliza looked the address up in the directory.

   The announcer called the winner's name out.

   Clyde turned the counterfeit money in.

The sentences of 5 are identical in meaning with those of 1. The only syntactic difference is that in 1, the particle precedes the direct-object noun
phrase, while in 5 the particle follows it.

   A problem that faces us is how we should account for the sentences of
1 and 5. We could add to our phrase-structure rules to allow particles to
occur directly in verb phrases, following the direct object.

6 VP → V (NP) (Prt) (AdvP)+

The following two sentences would then be derived in very different ways:

7

a. Biff put on a suit.

b. Biff put a suit on.

Whereas the particle in 7a would be generated by rule 4, the particle in 7b would be generated directly by rule 6.

But besides complicating the grammar, the existence of two very different ways of generating particles is unsatisfactory because it implies that pairs of sentences such as 7a and 7b are entirely different and independent of each other, since they are created in independent ways. Most people, however, have the intuitive feeling that a sentence such as 7b is really a stylistic variant of 7a—that they are in a sense the same sentence, with the words arranged in different orders. We would want our grammar to capture this feeling.

To solve our problem we will introduce a new kind of rule, called a *transformational rule*, which can allow the grammar to rearrange or transform sentences already generated by the phrase-structure rules. Instead of the two ways of generating particles—by rules 4 and 6—we will adopt only 4 and then add a transformational rule:

8

Particle-Movement Transformation (T-Prt): When a sentence with a verb-particle combination has been generated by the phrase-structure rules, the particle may then be moved to a position following the first noun phrase within the verb phrase.

Transformational rule 8, called *particle movement* (abbreviated *T-Prt*) states that after the phrase-structure rules have generated a sentence with a particle before a noun phrase, the particle can then be moved after the noun phrase to create a variant sentence.

A transformational rule such as 8 operates only after a sentence has been generated by the phrase-structure rules. For example, let us show how sentences 7a and 7b can now be formed, depending on whether transformational rule 8 is applied. A grammar with phrase-structure rule 4 can produce the tree in 9.

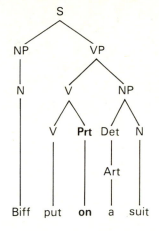

If the transformational rule T-Prt is not applied, no changes are made and the grammar has generated a sentence, *Biff put on a suit*. If, on the other hand, T-Prt is applied, tree **9** can be altered to produce *Biff put a suit on*. One way to represent this change in a diagram might be to circle the element to be moved and use an arrow to show its new location:

10

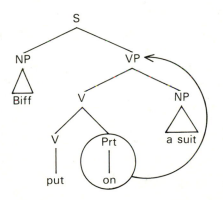

But a clearer way is to draw two trees, the first showing the original form of the sentence as generated by the phrase-structure rules and the second showing the sentence's final form as altered by the transformational rule. An arrow with a double line (⟹) is drawn between them and labeled with the name of the transformational rule that has caused the change:

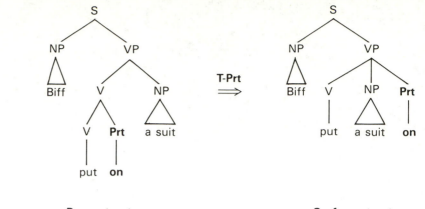

−*Deep structure*   −*Surface structure*

We can call the first tree, which is produced by the phrase-structure rules, the **underlying form** or **deep structure** of the sentence. The second tree, representing what is actually spoken or written, can be called the **surface structure** of the sentence. It shows the changes in the sentence after the transformational rule has been applied. The two trees of diagram 11 show the particle *on* being removed from its original position as a partner of *put* and moved to a position at the end of the verb phrase.

*I have slightly simplified the drawing of the surface-structure tree. The verb in the deep-structure tree of **11** looks like* i *below. After the particle has been removed the remaining structure should then look like* ii. *But since the second V label now serves no purpose, it is permissible to delete it; that is, we can represent the resulting structure as in* iii. *This is how I represented the verb in the surface structure of **11**.*

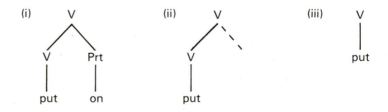

A set of one or more trees that shows how a sentence has been produced by the operation of the phrase-structure and transformational rules is called the **derivation** of that sentence. Diagram 9, which consists of one tree, is the derivation of *Biff put on a suit*, and diagram 11, which consists of two trees, is the derivation of *Biff put a suit on*. Note that in **9**—where the transformational rule has not been applied—the deep structure is also the surface structure. In 11, however, the deep and surface structures are different.

Note also that both 9 and 11 have the same deep structure. It is only their surfaces that differ. This captures our intuitive feeling that sentences 7a and 7b are not independent of each other either in meaning or in origin, but that they are really two different variations of the same basic sentence.

Exercises

1. Unlike a preposition, a particle can occur on either side of a noun phrase. A good test of whether a word such as *on* or *down* is acting as a particle or as a preposition in a particular sentence is to see whether T-Prt can apply: Can the word in question be moved behind the direct object? For example, we can try this test on sentences 2a and 2b. Sentence 2b with a particle passes the test:

$$\text{Terry tried on my sweater} \overset{\text{T-Prt}}{\Longrightarrow} \text{Terry tried my sweater on}$$

However, sentence 2a with a preposition does not:

$$\text{Terry cried on my shoulder} \overset{\text{T-Prt}}{\nRightarrow} *\text{Terry cried my shoulder on.}$$

Since T-Prt cannot apply in the second case, *on* is a preposition and *on my shoulder* is a prepositional phrase. In the first case, however, T-Prt can apply, so *on* in that sentence is a particle. Apply this same test to the sentences in the exercises on pages 90–91. In particular, see if it works with the sentences of the first exercise to distinguish those with particles from those with prepositions.

2. The following grammar contains both phrase-structure and transformational rules:

PS RULES	LEXICON	
S → NP VP	Det:	a, the, their, some
NP → { Prop / (Det) (AdjP)⁺ N (PP) }	Adj:	splendid
	Prop:	he
AdjP → (Deg) Adj	N:	Mavis, dessert, Mason,
VP → V (NP) (AdvP)⁺		groceries, car, project, kids,
(V → V Prt)		friends, tornado, buildings,
AdvP → (Deg) { (Adv) / PP }		wind, paper, alley
	V:	whipped, brought, put,
PP → Prep NP		rounded, blew
	Prt:	up, in, off, down
	Adv:	repeatedly
	Prep:	down
T-RULES		
T-Prt		

Note that this is a simplified grammar; for the sake of clarity I have omitted rules that do not apply to the current discussion. I will continue to do the same in future chapters. To simplify things further, from now on I will also list articles, possessive pronouns, demonstrative modifiers, and quantifiers together in the lexicon simply as determiners.

Using this simplified grammar, draw trees to show the derivations of the following sentences:

a. Mavis whipped up a splendid dessert.   *–Requires one tree*
b. Mason brought the groceries in.   *–Requires two trees*
c. He put the project off repeatedly.
d. The kids rounded up their friends.
e. The tornado blew some buildings down.
f. The wind blew the paper down the alley.

Notice that you are being given surface structures (final versions) and asked to show where they came from. For each sentence, determine if it contains a particle and, if so, whether the particle occurs before or after the direct-object noun phrase. If it occurs before, then the particle-movement transformation has not applied, and only one tree will need to be drawn. If it occurs afterward, however, T-Prt has applied, and the derivation will contain two trees. Draw the first (the deep-structure tree) from the phrase-structure rules. If needed, draw the second (surface-structure tree) by changing the first as directed by the transformational rule.

3. Derivation 11 makes the claim that *Biff put on a suit* is a more basic form than *Biff put a suit on*. Does this hypothesis correspond with your intuitions about these two sentences?

4. Words such as *by*, in addition to acting as both prepositions and particles, can act also as more direct components of verbs. For example, in the sentence, *McDuck came by his wealth honestly,* the "action" is stated by the phrase *came by. By* is not a preposition, since *by his wealth* is not a phrase in this sentence, nor is *by* a particle, since we cannot move it (*McDuck came his wealth by honestly*). Instead *came* and *by* together are said to constitute a single **phrasal verb**. *Came* and *by* are written as separate words but act as if they were a single verb (and so are treated as a single word in the grammar). Other phrasal verbs include *look forward* (*Oscar looks forward to lunchtime*), *take off* (*The plane took off for Aruba*), and *pass out* (*Chita passed out at the sight of blood*). In the following sentence, decide if *on* is a preposition, a particle, or part of a phrasal verb:

The salesman calls on a dozen accounts each day.

What criteria did you use to make your decision?

Our Goals—A Review and Update

In the first chapter I claimed that our goal in this book is to discover a grammar for English with two important qualities: First, it should be capable of generating the grammatical sentences of English. Second, and far more ambitiously, it should also be a model of our mental grammars, reflecting in some way the process our minds go through as we create sentences.

We have been successful so far in our first goal. Every time we have introduced new data in the form of additional sentences, we have been able to augment or modify our grammar to accommodate it. We have made our rules as simple as we could, while still being capable of producing grammatical sentences.

Success in our second goal is far less certain. We have no means of verifying it, since we cannot directly observe the working of our minds in order to make the comparison. The best we can do is hope that if we have created a grammatical model that generates good sentences in the most efficient way possible and that captures most accurately our intuitive feelings about our language, then such a grammar comes closest to doing what our mental grammars do.

Linguists continue to debate the nature of the ideal grammar. Whether ours attains both of our goals is open to question, and we should keep an open mind as we continue to develop our model. Remember that we are constructing hypotheses about language and then testing them. We must always be willing to change or reject a hypothesis if it does not work or if a better explanation presents itself. The quest for understanding about our language continues, and we must remain active and honest participants in the quest.

For now, let us continue to hypothesize that in some way our grammar reflects what the mind does when it generates language. One consequence that follows from this hypothesis is the claim that, in producing sentences, our minds observe the equivalent of phrase-structure and transformational rules. This will not seem far-fetched if we consider what the "rules" really mean. We should not think of our minds as blindly and mechanically directed by a set of mathematical formulas. Rather, we should think of the rules as descriptions of what our subconscious minds must do in order to produce sentences.

For example, the first phrase-structure rule (S $\rightarrow$ NP VP) reflects our subconscious knowledge that when we begin a sentence with a noun phrase, we must keep track, no matter how complex that noun phrase may be, of the fact that a verb phrase must follow. Surely that is what happens whenever we speak. Similarly, the NP and VP rules are statements of what options we have for those categories. The test of whether these and the other phrase-structure rules are accurate is whether we produce the sentences they describe, and indeed we do just what the rules say.

Transformational rules raise other questions, such as Exercise 3 on page 96. You may ask whether derivation 11 is an accurate account of how your mind produces the sentence *Biff put a suit on*. Again it is important to consider what the model is *not* saying. It does not mean that first you think the completed sentence *Biff put on a suit* and then you create another one with the words switched around. What it is saying is that the mind generates a basic structure that it can then easily—and almost instantaneously—alter in a certain way if it decides to. In order to show the details of this change clearly on paper we draw an entirely new tree, but that should not deceive us into thinking the change is more complicated than it is. Remember that the rules that we state and the trees that we draw are meant only as visual aids to our understanding. It is important that you consider carefully what it is they are intended to show and that you use them to help you better understand your own mind and what it does when you use language.

Optional and Obligatory Rules

A grammar with both phrase-structure and transformational rules is called a *generative-transformational grammar*. So far we have introduced one transformational rule, called the particle-movement transformation or T-Prt. It is an *optional rule* because whenever a particle occurs we have the choice whether to apply it. A grammatical sentence results whether T-Prt is or is not applied.

But to be more accurate, I should say that it is not always optional. T-Prt *must* be applied if the direct-object noun phrase is a pronoun. Compare 12a, whose direct object is a noun, with 12b, whose direct object is a pronoun:

12

a. Ed took up golf $\overset{\text{T-Prt}}{\Longrightarrow}$ Ed took golf up   —*T-Prt is optional*

b. Ed took up it $\overset{\text{T-Prt}}{\Longrightarrow}$ Ed took it up   —*T-Prt is obligatory*

Since the deep structure of 12b would not be a grammatical surface structure, we say that T-Prt is otherwise optional but *obligatory* when the direct object is a pronoun.

Exercises

Show the derivations of these surface structures:

1. Her skillful performance showed us up.

2. You held it up over your head.

3. The reporter put down her words on paper.

4. The judges looked them over carefully.

It may seem uncomfortable to generate a deep-structure tree that would not itself be an acceptable spoken sentence such as Her skillful performance showed up us, *but remember that the deep structure represents the underlying* idea *of the sentence, not the words actually spoken or written. Only the final version (the surface structure) represents what we actually speak or write.*

8 Three More Transformational Rules

Moving Adverbial Phrases

Whether they occur before or after the direct object in the surface structure, particles are always located next to the verb in the deep structure, generated by these rules:

1 VP → V (NP) (AdvP)+

(V → V Prt)

Particles are not the only elements in verb phrases that can be moved. Adverbial phrases can also occur in various places in surface sentences:

2
a. He opened the present *eagerly*.
b. He *eagerly* opened the present.
c. *Eagerly* he opened the present.

If we were to regard these as three unrelated sentences, the phrase-structure rules would need to account separately for all three occurrences of the adverbial phrase. First, the VP rule would need to allow adverbial phrases to occur both at the beginning and at the end of the verb phrase:

3 VP → (AdvP)+ V (NP) (AdvP)+

And in order to account for 2c, the S rule would have to allow for an adverbial phrase beginning the sentence:

4 S → (AdvP)+ NP VP

If we were to adopt this analysis, we would indeed begin to clutter our grammar, and in a way that would make little sense. These complicated rules fail to capture a generalization we intuitively feel—that the adverb *eagerly* means the same thing in all three sentences (2a–2c), and in all three it modifies the verb *opened*, telling how he opened the present. When we speak or write, we can put the adverb in different positions for reasons of style or emphasis, but we expect our grammar to show the fundamental similarity of all three sentences. Our solution is to derive all three surface structures from the same underlying or deep structure. A transformational rule can account for the surface variations.

We will retain the phrase-structure rules of 1 as the sole means of generating adverbial phrases in the deep structure. On the surface the adverbial phrases can be moved to other positions by this optional transformational rule:

5 **Adverbial-Phrase-Movement Transformation (T-AdvP):** An adverbial phrase may be moved to a position either at the beginning of the S or at the beginning of the VP.

If we want to show how the grammar generates 2b, we first draw the deep-structure tree and then use T-AdvP to move the adverb to the front of the verb phrase. Here is the derivation of 2b:

6

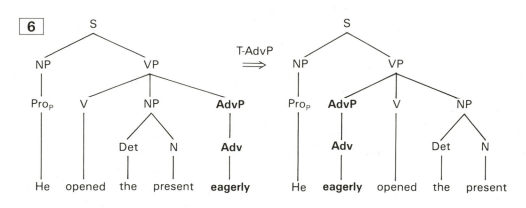

And here is the derivation of 2c:

7

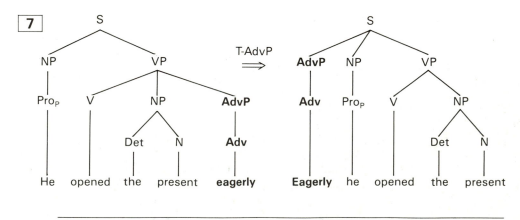

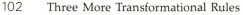

In 6, *eagerly* is moved to the beginning of the verb phrase, while in 7 it is moved to the beginning of the sentence. The same deep structure underlies both these sentences as well as sentence 2a, in which the transformational rule does not apply.

In addition to adverbs, prepositional phrases can also be moved by T-AdvP. If we were to derive *With a shout, the police quickly entered the building,* we would need to apply T-AdvP twice, once to move the adverb *quickly* and again to move the prepositional phrase *with a shout.* Here is the derivation:

8

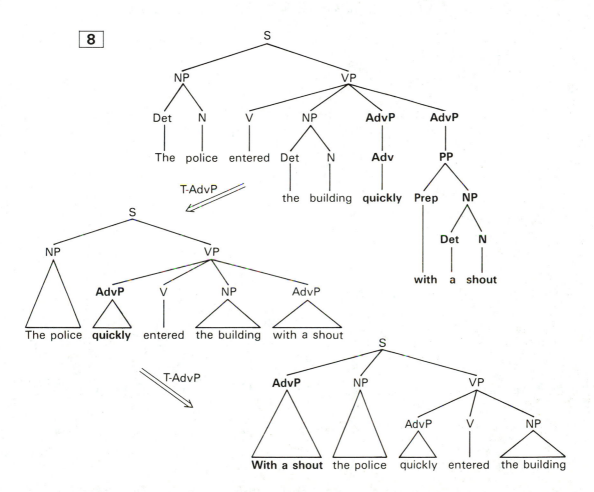

When applied the first time, T-AdvP moved *quickly* to the front of the verb phrase. When applied the second time, it moved *with a shout* to the beginning of the sentence. There is no significance to the order in which the movement of the two adverbial phrases is shown; the effect would have been the same if the movement of *with a shout* were shown first. Note that each tree in a derivation is identical to the previous one except for the change caused by the transformational rule.

Note that T-AdvP applies only to "standard" adverbials, not to "linking" adverbials (AdvP$_L$—see note on page 83). For example, in the sentence The comb is on the dresser, *the prepositional phrase* on the dresser *cannot be moved.*

Our grammar now contains two tranformational rules, T-Prt and T-AdvP. Sometimes the derivation of a surface sentence requires the operation of both rules. Here is the derivation of *The pitcher easily struck Casey out*:

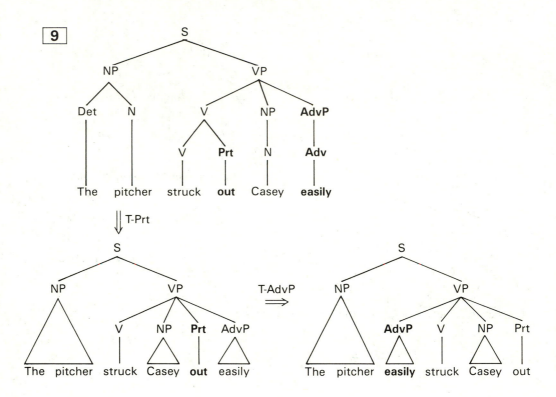

Exercises

Show the derivation of sentences 1 through 6 below. Follow the same procedure I used in derivations 8 and 9. Draw a complete tree for the deep structure—one that shows all the constituents. To save steps in drawing the transformed trees you may use triangles for the constituents whose membership has not been altered.

1. Jocelyn arrived punctually for class at noon yesterday.
   —No transformations required
2. Barnabas usually knew the correct answer.
3. Smugly, the detective revealed the solution.
4. The man with the wooden leg without assistance climbed the ladder.
5. Over the field they doggedly pursued their quarry.
6. Foolishly Brenda passed every opportunity up.

Indirect Objects

The noun phrase that follows a transitive verb is called a **direct object**. In addition to a direct object, a second noun phrase sometimes follows a verb, as in the sentences of 10. The italicized noun phrases that occur between the verbs and the direct objects in these sentences are called **indirect objects**:

10
a. Carmen gave *José* a cigarette.
b. George did *his mother* a favor.
c. We told *him* a secret.
d. The experience taught *Mona* a valuable lesson.
e. I asked *the wise swami* a question.

In 10a, *a cigarette* is the direct object, and *José* is the indirect object. An **indirect object** names the person or thing to whom or for whom the action is performed. We could diagram 10a as follows:

11

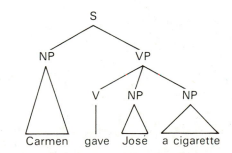

For each sentence with an indirect object, there corresponds an equivalent sentence with a prepositional phrase. These prepositional phrases begin with the prepositions *to*, *for*, or *of*:

12
a. Carmen gave a cigarette *to José*.

b. George did a favor *for his mother*.

c. We told a secret *to him*.

d. The experience taught a valuable lesson *to Mona*.

e. I asked a question *of the wise swami*.

The question that faces us is how our grammar should account for indirect objects. We could alter our VP rule to allow verbs to be followed by two noun phrases, but that would have two disadvantages. First, it would make the VP rule more complicated and, second, it would not account for the similarity between the sentences of 10 and 12. Another solution—the one we will adopt—is to keep our current VP rule, which can generate the sentences of 12, and to claim that the sentences of 10 are created from them by a transformational rule:

13 **Indirect-Object Transformation (T-IO):** An indirect object can be created from a prepositional phrase which states to whom, for whom, or of whom an action is performed. The preposition *to, for,* or *of* is deleted, and the following noun phrase is moved to a position immediately following the verb.

Sentences 12a and 10a have identical deep structures in this analysis; 12a is created by applying the transformational rule. Here is its derivation:

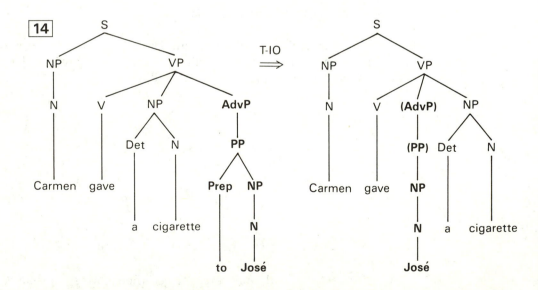

14

The direct-object noun phrase and the adverbial phrase have switched positions, and the preposition *to* has been deleted in the surface tree. Since the indirect object is no longer a prepositional phrase, the category labels AdvP and PP can be deleted from the tree or else placed in parentheses to show they no longer apply.

This analysis applies to indirect objects even when the direct object is a complement clause. Here is the derivation of *Arthur showed Laura that lizards eat crickets*:

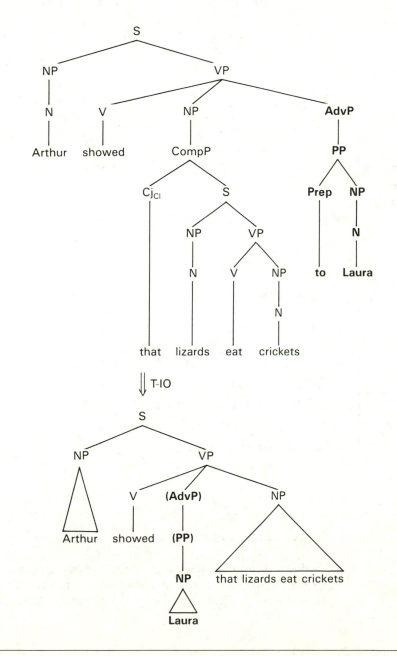

Our grammar now contains three transformational rules. (For the sake of simplicity, I have omitted some phrase-structure rules from the following grammar. I have also continued to list all determiners together in the lexicon.)

PS RULES	LEXICON

PS RULES

S → NP VP

NP → { Prop / (Det) (AdjP)⁺ N (PP) }

AdjP → (Deg) Adj

VP → V (NP) (AdvP)⁺

(V → V Prt)

AdvP → (Deg) { PP / Adv }

PP → Prep NP

T-RULES

T-Prt

T-AdvP

T-IO

LEXICON

Det: a, the, my, his

Adj: firm, injured, big, fancy

N: Earl, handshake, Isaac, team, player, card, brother-in-law, discount, Arlene, Lionel, age, chef, dessert

Prop: me, her

V: gave, sent, got, asked, whipped

Prt: up

Prep: to, for, of

Adv: rudely

Exercises

Use this grammar to show the derivations of these surface sentences:

1. Earl gave a firm handshake to Isaac.
2. The team sent the injured player a card.
3. My brother-in-law got me a big discount.
4. Arlene rudely asked Lionel his age.
5. The chef whipped a fancy dessert up for her.
6. The chef whipped her up a fancy dessert.

Imperative Sentences

Traditional grammar classifies verbs as having three *moods*. The verbs in all the sample sentences that we have examined so far have been in the *indicative mood*. Indicative verbs occur either in *declarative sentences*, which make statements (for example, *He is a boy scout*) or **interrogative sentences,** which ask questions (*Is she a girl scout?*). We have already mentioned the **subjunctive mood,** which concerns hypothetical, not actual, situations (*If I were a cub scout. . .*). Except for a few expressions, distinct subjunctive forms of verbs have disappeared from modern English. The third mood, and the one we will now consider, is the **imperative mood.** Imperative sentences are commands (*Be a good scout!*).

In commands like *Be a good scout!* or *Open the door!* no subject noun phrase is stated, but it is understood to be the hearer (or *you*) who is being directed to be a good scout or to open the door. In grammatical terms, we can say that the concept *HEARER* (which could also be represented by *YOU*) is the subject of the deep structure of each sentence, but it is deleted from the surface structure by a transformational rule:

16 **Imperative Transformation (T-Imp):** Delete the subject *HEARER* to form a command.

Here is the derivation of the command, *Open the door!*

17

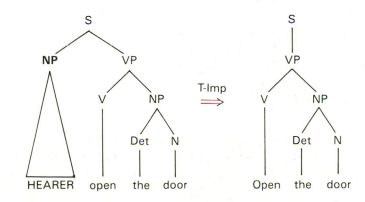

The subject noun phrase is simply removed from the surface-structure tree.

Triangles are used in trees as a convenient device to represent missing steps. In 17, the noun phrase HEARER represents a concept, not an actual word, and so the noun phrase does not need to be analyzed more specifically as a noun or a pronoun or some other part of speech.

Remember that the deep structure represents the concept of the sentence, not the words as they are actually spoken. For convenience, we usually use the spoken words to represent deep-structure concepts, but when we wish to make it clear that a pure concept—not an actual word—is being represented, we can use capital letters for the representation. Thus, the deep-structure subject of 17, the person being addressed, can be represented by *HEARER* (or *YOU* or *READER* or any equivalent symbol).

We can consider the deep-structure/surface-structure distinction as the difference between the idea that we think (deep structure) and the words we actually say (surface structure). In speaking, we proceed from the idea to the words. Conversely, if we were to create a model of how we comprehend the sentences that others speak, we could show the same process in reverse. That is, we could draw the same trees with the transformational arrow pointing in the opposite direction. When we hear the surface structure, the transformational rule allows us to comprehend the idea of the deep structure.

Exercises

1. Our grammar now has four transformational rules: T-Prt, T-AdvP, T-IO, and T-Imp. Draw trees to show the derivations of these sentences. (Note that in sentences *c*, *d*, and *e*, more than one transformational rule applies.)

    a. Eat your oatmeal.
    b. Stop!
    c. Take the garbage out.
    d. Give Larry a medal.
    e. Never raise your voice.

    And for good measure:

    f. Kindly offer Steve and Marlys the recipe for the chowder.

2. Invent three additional sentences that are produced by one or more of these four transformational rules, and show their derivations.

9 Pronouns: Another Analysis

A Personal-Pronoun Transformation

In Chapter 4, a pronoun was defined as a word used in place of a noun phrase. We have used the second option in the following phrase-structure rule to generate personal pronouns such as *I*, *you*, and *they*:

1 $\quad \text{NP} \rightarrow \begin{Bmatrix} \text{(Det)} \quad \text{(AdjP)}^+ \quad \text{N} \quad \text{(PP)} \quad \text{(CompP)} \\ \text{Pro}_\text{P} \end{Bmatrix}$

This rule allowed the grammar to produce sentences such as *She promoted him* and *They amazed us.*

    Another analysis of how pronouns are generated is also possible. To say that pronouns "stand for" noun phrases is another way of saying that they are surface-structure representatives of those noun phrases, derived from them by a transformation. The noun phrases (or, more accurately, the concepts that they represent) are present in the deep structure, but they are replaced by pronouns in the surface structure. For example, in a sentence such as *Elizabeth praised the clerk, and he thanked her,* we understand the second clause to mean that the clerk thanked Elizabeth. What we understand is the deep structure, from which the surface that is actually spoken is derived by this transformation:

2   **Personal-Pronoun Transformation (T-Pro$_\text{P}$):** A noun phrase may be replaced by the appropriate personal pronoun.

Under this analysis, here is the derivation of our sample sentence:

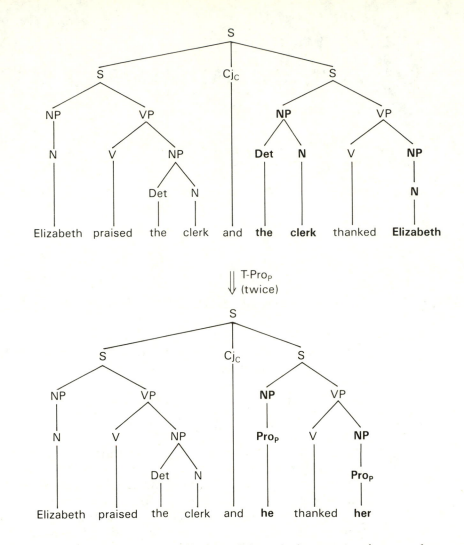

A sentence such as *They liked it* will have little meaning for us unless we know what the pronouns *they* and *it* refer to. For the sentence to make sense, these pronouns must be derived from noun phrases that are known to both the speaker and the listener, as in the analysis in 4.

4

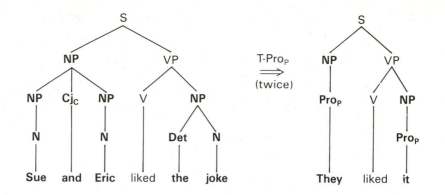

A very important concept to understand—one that bears repeating—is that the deep structure represents the sentence's idea or meaning. The words we write in our diagram across the bottom of the deep-structure tree represent that idea; in the deep-structure stage, the words themselves are not actually spoken or even necessarily formed as words in our minds. For example, if you say *I* in a sentence, that doesn't mean that your mind first thinks your name and then transforms it into the pronoun *I*. It does mean that you think the concept of yourself and transform that concept into the word *I*. If you were to diagram such a sentence, however, in the deep structure you might use your name or some symbol such as *MYSELF* or *SPEAKER* (written in capital letters) to represent the concept of yourself:

5

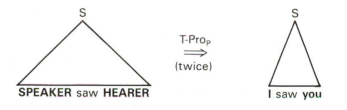

Note that the transformational rule applied twice in derivations 3, 4, and 5. In 4, for example, it applied once to change the noun phrase *Sue and Eric* to the personal pronoun *they,* and again to change *the joke* to *it*. We could draw three trees in each derivation to show the rule applying twice, but it is permissible, as here, to simplify a diagram when doing so would cause no confusion, thus representing both changes on the same transformed tree.

Exercises

Use T-Pro$_P$ to derive the pronouns in the following sentences:

1. Clementine brags that she speaks Hungarian.

2. Dorothy dated Carl and Sean, but she disliked them.

3. That she won the prize astonished Henrietta.

4. Linda and I petted the cat, but it scratched us.

For the following sentences, supply your own meaning for the pronouns; that is, invent appropriate deep structures. Draw the derivations.

5. It followed her to school.

6. They fascinate him.

Reflexive Pronouns

Sometimes instead of a personal pronoun such as *him* or *them,* we use a ***reflexive pronoun*** (abbreviated **Pro$_X$**) such as *himself* or *themselves* to stand for a noun phrase:

6 a. Peter congratulated himself.

   b. The O'Hoolihan twins invited themselves to our party.

When we read a sentence like 6a, we understand the reflexive pronoun *himself* to refer (or "reflect" back) to *Peter.* We can assume that there is a transformation, which we will label T-Pro$_X$, that transforms the underlying concept *Peter congratulated Peter* into the spoken words *Peter congratulated himself*:

7

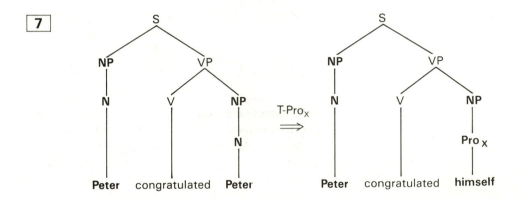

What is the nature of this transformation and when do we apply it instead of T-Pro$_P$? If we had applied T-Pro$_P$ instead of T-Pro$_X$ to the deep structure of 7, we would have produced the surface sentence *Peter congratulated him,* which would be ungrammatical if *him* was supposed to refer to *Peter.* Let us examine some additional data before deciding under what circumstances T-Pro$_P$ and T-Pro$_X$ can be applied.

Exercises

1. Which of the following sentences are grammatical? *Himself* is intended to refer to Peter in each sentence.

   a. Peter congratulated himself.
   b. Himself congratulated Peter.
   c. Jane said that Peter congratulated himself.
   d. Peter said that Jane congratulated himself.
   e. Peter said that himself congratulated Jane.

   Can you draw any conclusions from this data about when a deep-structure noun phrase can become a reflexive pronoun? If not, the additional data in exercise 2 may be of help.

2. The following are all deep structures. For each, decide what would be the appropriate surface structure—that is, for each of the italicized noun phrases, decide whether T-Pro$_P$ or T-Pro$_X$ should apply. You can assume that when a name such as *Mary* appears more than once in a sentence, it refers to the same person.

   a. Mary claimed that *Mary* understood trigonometry.
   b. Maxwell looked at *Maxwell* in the mirror.
   c. Clint tried hard, but *Clint* lost the race.
   d. Hugh and Maggie hosted a party in honor of *Hugh and Maggie*.
   e. Maria said that *Maria* injured *Maria*.

   In the following "intermediate" structure, T-IO has already applied to make the second *Fran* the indirect object. What pronoun transformations would now apply?

   f. Fran promised *Fran* that *Fran* would study harder.

   Can you now state a rule for when a noun phrase can become a personal pronoun and when it can become a reflexive pronoun?

The answer to the last question is that a reflexive pronoun is used only when two identical noun phrases occur within the same clause:

8 [$_S$ *Peter* congratulated *Peter*]

$\Downarrow$ T-Pro$_X$

Peter congratulated *himself*.

But a personal pronoun must be used when two identical noun phrases occur in different clauses:

---

9 $[_S$ *Peter* said that $[_S$ Jane congratulated *Peter*$]$ $]$

$$\Downarrow T\text{-}Pro_P$$

Peter said that Jane congratulated *him*.

The second *Peter* cannot become *himself* since it is not in the same S clause as the first *Peter*.

We can now state our reflexive transformation:

10 **Reflexive Transformation (T-Pro$_X$):** When a noun-phrase occurs twice in the same clause, the second is changed to the appropriate reflexive pronoun.

T-Pro$_X$ is an obligatory transformation.

Exercises

1. Show the derivations of these surface sentences:

   a. The astronaut blamed herself for the mishap.
   b. Katrinka and Scott vindicated themselves.

   For the following sentence, use *SPEAKER* to represent the deep-structure concept of *I*. The derivation will require the application of both T-Pro$_X$ and T-Pro$_P$.

   c. Carla and I treated ourselves to a fancy Chinese dinner.

2. Draw trees for the derivations of sentences produced from deep structures in exercises 2a through 2e on page 115.

Conditions for Applying the Personal-Pronoun Transformation

Like T-Pro$_X$, T-Pro$_P$ can only be applied under certain circumstances. We have already seen that if two identical noun-phrases occur in a deep structure, they must appear in different clauses for one of them to become a personal pronoun. For example, T-Pro$_P$ can apply to the following deep structure because the two *Jennifer*s occur in different clauses:

11 $[_S$ That $[_S$ *Jennifer* won the election$]$ surprised *Jennifer*$]$

In fact, because it can apply to either *Jennifer*, T-Pro$_P$ can generate two different grammatical surface sentences:

12

a. That she won the election surprised Jennifer.

b. That Jennifer won the election surprised her.

Note that both 12a *and* 12b *are ambiguous. Here we are considering only the reading in which* she *and* her *refer to Jennifer.*

In deep structure 11, the *Jennifer* in the embedded S clause came before the *Jennifer* in the upper S clause. Note the difference when the order is reversed, as in this deep structure:

13

[$_S$ *Jennifer* announced that [$_S$ *Jennifer* won the election]]

In this instance only the second occurrence of *Jennifer* can become a pronoun:

14

a. Jennifer announced that she won the election.

b. *She announced that Jennifer won the election.

Sentence 14b is ungrammatical in this case since it does not mean the same thing as 13; we would not understand *she* in 14b to refer to Jennifer.

From our data in 11 through 14 we can conclude that T-Pro$_P$ can only occur under two circumstances:

15

CONDITIONS FOR APPLYING T-PRO$_P$
When a deep structure contains two identical noun-phrases, T-Pro$_P$ can apply only if:
a. the noun-phrases occur in two different clauses, and
b. the noun-phrase to be replaced by a personal pronoun is either the second of the two or else occurs in a lower (embedded) clause.

The first instance of *Jennifer* in 13 could not become a personal pronoun because it is the first of the two occurrences and it occurs in a higher S clause than the second *Jennifer*.

These provisions may seem complicated at first, but if you test them you will see that they perfectly describe the conditions under which you produce personal pronouns. Review this section carefully to make certain these conditions are clear to you.

Exercises

1. Draw trees to show the derivations of sentences 12a, 12b, and 14a. Examine the deep-structure tree for 14a and be certain you understand why, according to 15, it cannot be transformed into 14b.

2. Draw the tree for this deep structure:

   Luke likes most fruits, but Luke dislikes rhubarb.

   Can either instance of *Luke* be replaced by a personal pronoun? Explain why and draw the derivation(s) for the grammatical surface structure(s).

Must Transformations Apply in a Particular Order?

Our grammar now contains six transformational rules:

16 **T Rules**

1. T-Pro$_X$
2. T-AdvP
3. T-IO
4. T-Pro$_P$
5. T-Prt
6. T-Imp

Some sentences are generated by the application of several different transformational rules. One question that linguists debate is whether transformations must apply in a particular order. Let us consider the arguments that at least some rules must apply before certain other rules. Consider the derivation of the command *Excuse yourself*. We will use *HEARER* in the deep structure to represent the concept of the person being addressed.

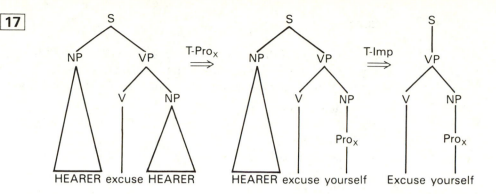

According to the argument for rule ordering, it is important in 17 that the two transformations are performed in this order. We would not achieve the correct surface structure if the order were reversed. That is, if T-Imp were applied first (*HEARER excuse HEARER* ⟹ *Excuse HEARER*), we would not then be able to apply T-Pro$_X$ because the tree would no longer have two identical noun-phrases. But the correct surface is achieved if transformational rules are applied in the order in which they are listed in 16.

There is also an argument for ordering T-Pro$_X$ before T-Pro$_P$, as we did in 16. For example, in drawing the derivation of sentence 1c in the exercise on page 116, it is important to apply transformations in this order:

18   Carla and *SPEAKER* treated *Carla and SPEAKER* . . .

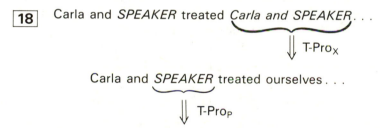

If, on the other hand, T-Pro$_P$ applied first, the two noun-phrases would no longer be identical and T-Pro$_X$ would not then be able to apply.

Other rules may also need to be ordered in a certain way. In Chapter 7 we discovered that, in order to prevent such ungrammatical sentences as *Nan threw out it*, T-Prt is obligatory when the direct object is a pronoun. Consequently, T-Pro$_X$ and T-Pro$_P$ need to have already occurred before T-Prt can take place.

As we consider other transformational rules, we wll continue to consider the order in which they might apply.

Exercises

1. Below are given four deep structures. As was done in **18**, show how the given transformational rules, when applied in order, change those structures. What surface sentences result from these derivations?

    a. Phyllis cheered up Phyllis   [T-Pro$_X$, T-Prt]

    b. *HEARERS* give a reward to   [T-Pro$_X$, T-IO, T-Imp]
       HEARERS

    c. Marvin told [that Marvin   [T-AdvP, T-IO, T-Pro$_P$ (twice)]
       played handball often] to
       SPEAKER

    d. *SPEAKER* told [that Marvin   [T-IO, T-Pro$_P$ (twice). Is the reverse
       played badly] to Marvin   order possible?]

2. Show the derivations of the surface sentences below. Some of these derivations involve more than one transformation. Decide which transformational rules applied. Your derivation should show them applying in the order in which they are listed in **16**.

    If you have difficulty in determining a sentence's deep structure, you may find it useful to work backwards. On scratch paper, draw the tree for the surface structure that you are given. Consider each transformational rule in **15**, starting with T-Imp and working up the list, and ask yourself whether it has applied. If so, "undo" it to determine what the sentence looked like before the rule's application. When you have undone all the transformational rules that have applied, the result is the deep structure. You are then ready to draw the derivation.

    a. Rob rarely exerted himself.
    b. Brace yourself for a shock.
    c. Quickly shut the machine down.

10 More Embedded Sentences: Adverbial Clauses and Relative Clauses

Adverbial Clauses

Previously we have seen that an adverbial phrase can be either an adverb or a prepositional phrase:

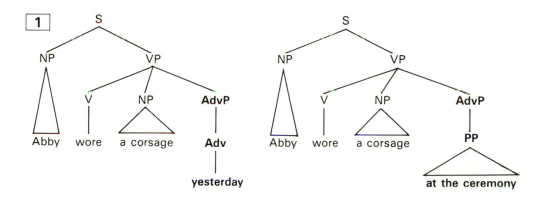

But an adverbial phrase can also be an entire sentence: *Abby wore a corsage when the class graduated*. The embedded sentence, *the class graduated*, is called an **adverbial clause**. It is preceded by *when*, which is a **subordinating conjunction** or **Cj_s**. Here are some other sentences with subordinating conjunctions and adverbial clauses:

2 We bought a new car *because the old Camaro finally broke down*.

They will arrive on time *unless their plane is delayed*.

Jake fell asleep *although he had a good night's sleep*.

Bob worried *almost until the plane taxied to the terminal*.

Our phrase-structure rule for adverbial phrases needs to be expanded to allow for adverbial clauses:

$$\boxed{3} \quad \text{AdvP} \rightarrow \text{(Deg)} \begin{Bmatrix} \text{Adv} \\ \text{PP} \\ \text{Cj}_\text{s} \ \text{S} \end{Bmatrix}$$

If the last option is chosen, the grammar can generate trees such as in 4:

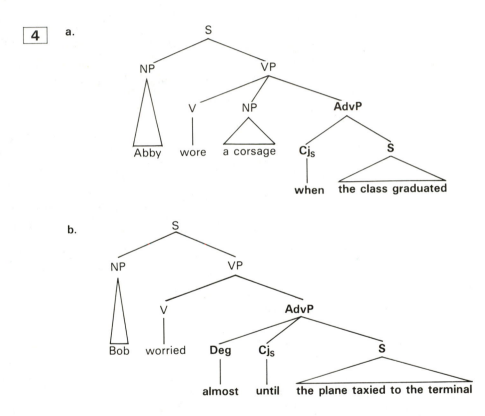

$\boxed{4}$ a.

b.

Unlike coordinating conjunctions such as *and* and *or* that connect two equal or *coordinate* clauses, subordinating conjunctions such as *when* and *until* connect unequal clauses. A subordinating conjunction introduces a clause that is embedded in—or subordinate to—the upper clause. The lower S-clauses in 4 are **subordinate** or **dependent clauses**, while the upper S-clauses are **main** or **independent clauses**. Among the most common subordinating conjunctions are these:

COMMON SUBORDINATING CONJUNCTIONS		
after	if	until
although	lest	when
as	since	whenever
because	though	where
before	till	whereas
for	unless	while

Some other subordinating conjunctions, called *phrasal conjunctions*, consist of more than one word. Although the words that comprise them originally functioned as independent words, they have come to act as if they were single words and can be treated as single words in the grammar. In some cases, such as *inasmuch* and *insofar*, the parts have even come to be joined together in spelling. Here are the most common phrasal subordinating conjunctions:

COMMON PHRASAL SUBORDINATING CONJUNCTIONS		
as if	even if	in order that
as soon as	even though	insofar as
as though	inasmuch as	so that

Exercises

1. Draw trees to show the derivations of the following sentences with adverbial clauses:

   a. The coach has a tantrum if a player commits a foolish error.
   b. Jess hid while Marla searched for him.

   Treat *as if* as if it were a single word:

   c. Milton bought albums as if money grew on trees.
   d. The gardener sees clearly simply because he got new glasses.

   The word *simply* in exercise sentence 1d might be regarded as a degree modifier. Note also that sentence 1d involves the transformation T-Pro$_P$. That and the following sentence have more than one adverbial.

   e. The pipes froze completely in January although Roy insulated the house.

2. Among the multiword subordinating conjunctions listed in **6** are *even if* and *even though*. Do these act as if they were single words or should *even* be treated as a degree modifier like *almost* or *entirely*?

Like other adverbials, adverbial clauses can be moved to other positions in a sentence. In the following derivation, T-AdvP applies twice to produce *While the family slept, the burglar deftly entered the house*:

7

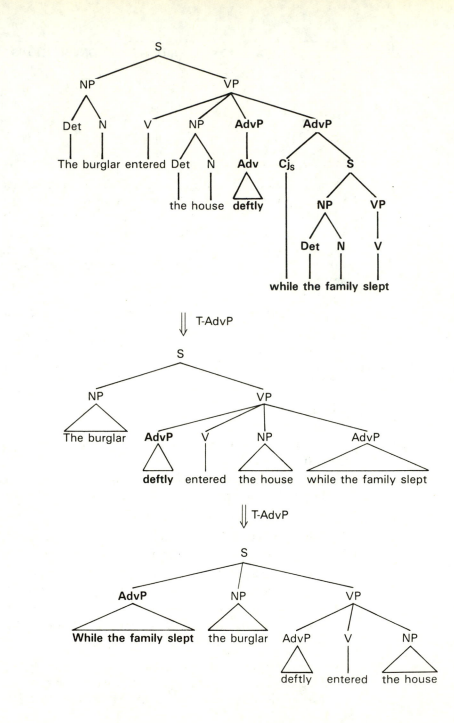

The first transformation placed the adverb *deftly* before the verb, and the second moved the adverbial clause to the front of the sentence.

Exercises

1. Show the derivations of the following surface sentences:
   a. The soprano, because the audience cheered lustily, sang an encore.
   b. Lest the voters forget, the congressman reprinted the entire speech in his newsletter.
   c. Just before the rain came, Emily put away the lawnmower.
   d. Lately, whenever George snores, Martha pokes him.

2. The derivation of exercise sentence 1d requires both T-Pro$_P$ and T-AdvP. Does it matter which of the two transformations is applied first? Consider the sentences below in making your decision. In particular, think about which order is necessary to prevent the ungrammatical sentence *d* from being generated. Remember that T-Pro$_P$ can apply to the first of two identical noun phrases if that noun phrase occurs in an embedded clause but not if the noun phrase occurs in the main clause — see 15 on page 117.
   a. When Jude talks, he mumbles.
   b. When he talks, Jude mumbles.
   c. Jude mumbles when he talks.
   d. *He mumbles when Jude talks.   — *Ungrammatical if* **he** *refers to* **Jude**

Relative Clauses

We have so far encountered several kinds of sentences with multiple clauses. Coordinate sentences have two or more main clauses joined by a coordinating conjunction (for example, *He dances, and she sings*). Other sentences have main and subordinate clauses. Among the subordinate (or embedded) clauses that can occur are complement clauses (*He claims that she sings*) and adverbial clauses (*He laughs when she sings*). Still other embedded clauses are *relative clauses*, which modify nouns. Relative clauses are printed in italics in these sentences:

8

a. The woman *who sings in the choir* is my sister.

b. The shirt *that Amy wore* was pink.

c. Germaine devised a plan *which baffled our opponents*.

d. Don paid the lady *whose car Ed rented*.

e. Marvin reached a decision *which Jo agreed with*

f. Marvin reached a decision *with which Jo agreed*.

Each relative clause modifies—or gives additional information about—the noun it follows. In 8a, for example, *who sings in the choir* tells us which woman is meant.

The relative clauses in 8a–8f begin with the words *who, that, which*, and *whose*, which are called **relative pronouns** (abbreviated **Pro_R**). Like all other pronouns, relative pronouns stand for noun phrases and are derived from those noun phrases by a transformation. Below is the derivation of the sentence, *The woman who sings in the choir is my sister*:

9

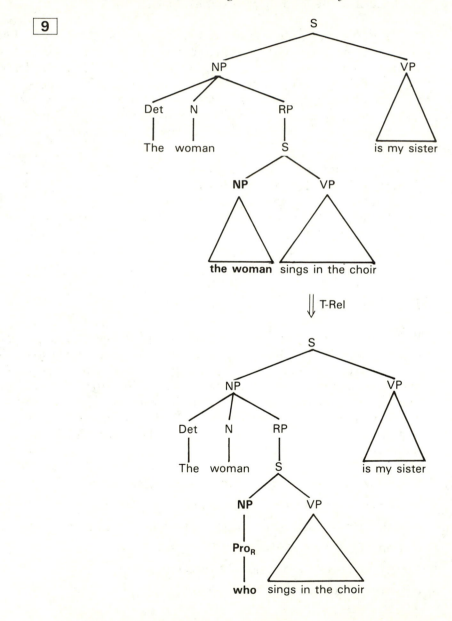

Just as we used the symbol CompP *to refer to complement clauses, we use* **RP** *to refer to relative clauses. The* P *in both symbols stands for "phrase." We label all groupings, including clauses, as phrases. In later chapters we will encounter instances where a* CompP *or an* RP *can be a simple phrase rather than a complete clause.*

Derivation 9 makes a number of interesting claims—ones that bear careful examination. Notice that our derivation assumes that the deep-structure form of the relative clause is a complete sentence (*the woman sings in the choir*). This clause is embedded in the main clause (*the woman...is my sister*). The embedded clause follows and modifies the subject of the main clause (*the woman*), providing additional information about it (in this case, telling us which woman is meant). In the deep structure, the embedded clause contains a noun phrase that is identical to the noun phrase being modified (*the woman*). A transformation replaces that noun phrase with a relative pronoun (*who*) in the surface structure.

So far at least, the explanation makes sense. When we read *who sings in the choir,* we understand *who* to refer to the woman. As usual, the deep structure represents the concept that we understand.

To account for our analysis, we must include in our grammar revised phrase-structure rules (10) and a new transformational rule (11):

10 NP → (Det) (AdjP)⁺ N (PP) **(RP)** (CompP)

RP → S

11 **Relative-Clause Transformation (T-Rel):** A relative clause is formed as follows:

a. If a noun phrase is modified by a clause that contains a noun phrase identical to the one being modified, the noun phrase within that clause is replaced by the appropriate relative pronoun.
b. That noun phrase is then moved to the beginning of the clause (if it is not already there).

Notice carefully how these rules were applied in derivation 9. The reason for step *b* in the transformational rule is demonstrated by the derivation in 12 of *The shirt that Amy wore was pink.*

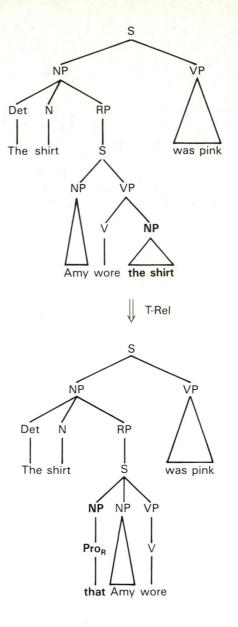

12

In the deep structure of **12** the identical noun phrase *the shirt* is the direct object, not the subject, of the lower clause. The transformational rule not only changes *the shirt* to *that,* but it also moves it to the front of the clause. Now you can see the reason for part *b* of rule 11.

Exercises

1. For each of the following surface sentences, underline the relative clause. Then write the deep-structure sentence below it, with the embedded clause placed within brackets:

   a. Clark knew the woman <u>whom Martin married</u>.
      Deep structure: Clark knew the woman [Martin married the woman]
   b. Clark knew the woman who married Martin.
      Deep structure:
   c. The veterinarian who cured the racehorse received a handsome fee.

   d. The clothes that suited Archie repelled Sidney.

   e. Harry owned the poster with the design which Gretchen admired.

      Sentence e above might be considered ambiguous. How would the deep-structure trees differ for the two readings: (1) when the relative clause means that Gretchen admired the design and (2) when it means that she admired the poster?

2. Draw the derivations of sentences 1a–1e.

3. In the NP phrase-structure rule 10, *CompP* is listed as occurring after *RP*. Both types of clauses can occur within the same noun phrases, as in this example:

   The proposal which she made that I marry her. . .

   But the reverse order seems possible as well:

   The proposal that I marry her which she made. . .

   Both examples are certainly awkward, but they can occur, at least in casual conversation. How can we account for both of them? For example, should we claim that complement clauses and relative clauses both belong to some larger category (which we might give a name such as "noun-modifying clauses")?

Possessive Relative Clauses

In the following derivation, notice how the relative-clause transformation applies to derive sentence 8d, *Don paid the lady whose car Ed rented*. The relative pronoun *whose* replaces a possessive noun phrase.

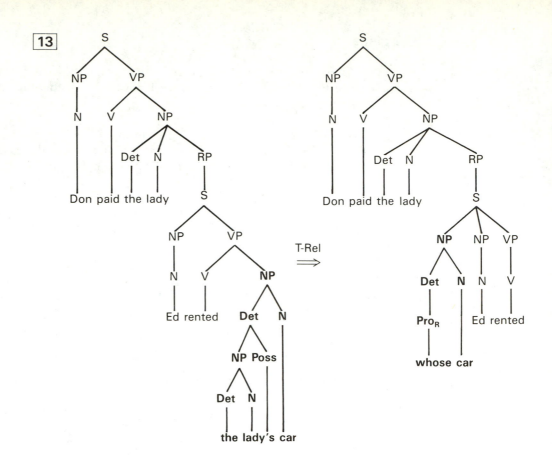

13

T-Rel ⟹

This derivation is interesting for at least two reasons: First, notice that *whose* is the possessive form of the relative pronoun, which replaces the possessive noun phrase *the lady's*. Second, notice that not just the relative pronoun but the entire noun phrase *whose car* was moved by T-Rel. This is precisely what the transformational rule 11b directs us to do.

Exercises

1. For each of the following surface sentences, first underline the relative clause. Then write the deep-structure sentence below it, with the embedded clause placed within brackets:

a. An intruder whose rudeness shocked the audience interrupted the meeting.

b. The committee awarded the job to a man whose application they rejected previously.

2. Draw the derivations for exercise sentences 1a and 1b above.

3. In Chapter 6 we listed the possessive pronouns (*my, our, your, her,* and so on) in the grammar's lexicon as determiners. Since then, however, we have derived the personal, reflexive, and relative pronouns from underlying noun phrases by transformations. Does it make sense that possessive pronouns would also be derived from underlying possessive nouns, perhaps in much the same way that possessive relative pronouns are derived? If so, write a transformational rule—call it **T-Pro$_S$**—that would allow the grammar to derive possessive pronouns, and then use your rule to draw the derivations of these sentences:

a. Loretta celebrated her birthday.
b. The couple lost their possessions in the fire.
c. His success surprised Douglas.

The Relative Pronoun as the Object of a Preposition

As a final example of relative clauses, let us consider the last two sentences in 8, where the relative pronoun replaces a noun phrase that is the object of a preposition. T-Rel can apply in two different ways to the deep structure to produce two alternative surface structures. Shown in 14 is the derivation of sentence 8e, *Marvin reached a decision which Jo agreed with*.

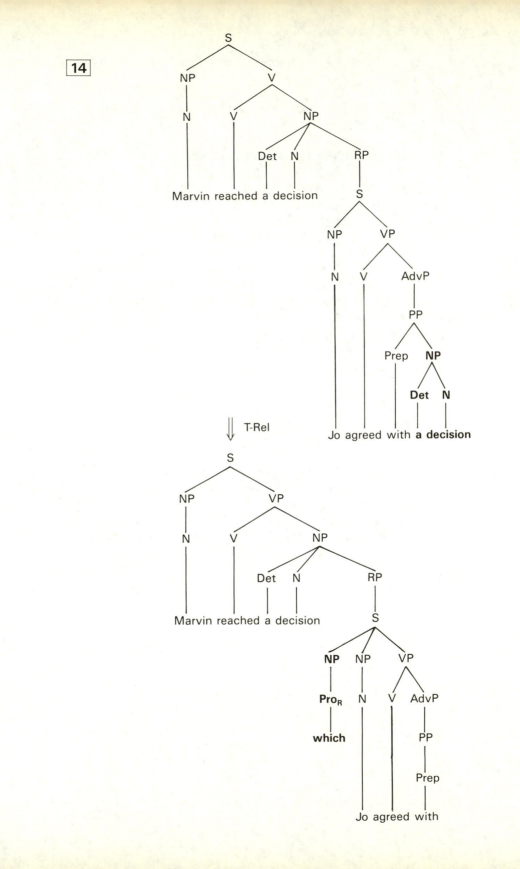

14

In 14 the derivation has proceeded according to the transformational rule by moving only the noun phrase that contains the relative pronoun *which*. But the deep structure of 14 can also be transformed into a different surface structure, that of sentence 8f, *Marvin reached a decision with which Jo agreed*:

15

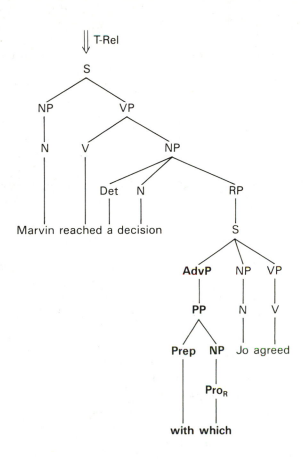

In this option, not just the relative pronoun but the entire prepositional phrase is moved to the front of the relative clause. We will have to revise 11b, the second provision of T-Rel, to make it more general:

16 **A phrase that contains the relative pronoun is moved (if necessary) to the beginning of the relative clause.**

The term *a phrase* allows us to move either a noun phrase, as in 14, or an entire adverbial phrase, as in 15.

Exercises

1. For each of the following surface sentences, write the deep-structure sentence below it, with the embedded clause placed within brackets:

   a. Ella was the person to whom Stevie gave the award.

   b. Cancer was the enemy that the scientist fought against.

   In the next two sentences, you will find relative clauses embedded within other relative clauses:

   c. Jan scolded the orator whose speech aroused the crowd that began the riot to which the police responded.

   d. The junior found the book that the sophomore who lived in the dorm lost.

2. Draw the derivations for exercise sentences 1a–1d.

3. We have seen the word *that* function as a demonstrative modifier (*that man*), as a complementizer (*I know that he prefers tea*), and now as a relative pronoun (*The drink that the man prefers is tea*). When a clause is introduced by *that*, you may sometimes find it difficult to tell whether it is a complement clause or a relative clause. One simple test is whether the word *that* can be replaced by another relative pronoun such as *which* or *who*. If it can (*The drink which the man prefers is tea*), then *that* is a relative pronoun. If not (**I know which he prefers tea*), then *that* is a complementizer. You will remember that, unlike the relative pronoun *that*, the complementizer *that* does not replace a noun phrase, and a complement clause is generated directly by the phrase-structure rules, not by means of a transformation.

   For each of the following sentences, decide whether the embedded clause is a complement clause or a relative clause.

   a. Peter bought the pastry that Sadie liked.
   b. Peter knew that Sadie liked pastry.
   c. The fact that you wore funny hats surprised us.
   d. The funny hats that you wore surprised us.
   e. We believe the theory that Mona proposed.
   f. We believe the theory that flowers feel pain.
   g. I borrowed the book that Judy recommended that I read.

4. Draw the derivations for the sentences above.

5. The following represent deep structures for sentences with relative clauses. What surface sentences are derived from them?

   a. The noise [Winthrop heard the noise] came from the attic.
   b. Merlin owns an owl [the owl's screech shatters glass].
   c. The organization [Byington resigned from the organization] has high standards.
   d. The color [the woman [you married the woman] prefers the color] is hot pink.

6. At times we have the option of omitting a relative pronoun. Instead of 8b, for example, we can say *The shirt Amy wore was pink*. But we cannot omit *who* in 8a: *The woman sings in the choir is my sister*. Examine the sentences of 8 and the other sentences with relative clauses in this exercise and note which of them have relative pronouns that can be omitted. Can you state a general principle for when a relative pronoun can and cannot be omitted? Is it similar to the principle for when a complementizer can be omitted in complement-clause sentences (see pages 65–66)? Why do you think our language has such principles? Do they help us to avoid confusion?

Clauses with Relative Adverbs

Instead of relative pronouns (such as *who*, *which*, and *that*), some relative clauses begin with **relative adverbs** (**Adv$_R$**) such as *where*, *when*, and *why*.

17
   a. We visited the house *where Mozart lived*.
   b. They remember the day *when Cliff came home*.
   c. She explained the reason *why the prices rose*.

Relative adverbs function in relative clauses in the same way as relative pronouns, but whereas relative pronouns replace deep-structure noun phrases, relative adverbs replace adverbial phrases. The sentences of 17 derive from the following deep structures:

18
   a. We visited the house [George lives *in the house*].
   b. They remember the day [Cliff came home *on the day*].
   c. She explained the reason [the prices rose *for the reason*].

In 17a, the relative adverb *where* replaces the adverbial phrase *in the house*. In 17b, *when* replaces *on the day*. And in 17c, *why* replaces *for the reason*.

Exercises

1. See if you can draw tree diagrams to show how the deep structures in 18a–18c are transformed into sentences 17a–17c. Formulate the necessary addition to the transformational rule 11.

2. State the deep structures for the following sentences with relative clauses that are introduced with relative adverbs. Draw the derivations.

    a. The map shows the cave where the pirates hid the gold.
    b. The reason why he was late was a faulty alarm clock.
    c. The gremlins await the time when the goblins are asleep.

Some Notes on Usage

Of the relative pronouns, *who* and *whom* are used for people, *which* is used for things, and *that* and *whose* are used for both people and things. At times you may hear it said that *that* should only be used for things, but such a claim is not supported by actual usage: *the person that I most admire*, for example, is a perfectly acceptable phrase. Another persistent claim is that a sentence may not end with a preposition. However, not only is the sentence *Marvin reached a decision which Jo agreed with* standard English, but it is created by T-Rel in exactly the same way that 8a–8d were created. Contrary to the claim, a preposition is a part of speech that educated speakers and writers frequently end their sentences with.

Because the word *whom* seems to be growing obsolete, an increasing number of people find the distinction between *who* and *whom* puzzling. The distinction is no longer part of the subconscious knowledge of most speakers of English; in order to know it, they must learn it consciously. Traditionally, *who* has been the nominative form, used to replace a subject noun phrase (*the man who saw me*), whereas *whom* has been the objective form, used to replace a direct object (*the man whom I saw*) or an object of a preposition (*the man whom I looked at*). Increasingly, however—especially in speech—*who* is being used for objective as well as nominative forms, with *whom* appearing consistently only when it directly follows a preposition (*the man at whom I looked*). This is consistent with the centuries-old trend of the English language to lose its inflected forms.

11 Restrictive and Nonrestrictive Clauses and Phrases

Restrictive and Nonrestrictive Relative Clauses

Although the italicized relative clauses in the following two sentences look similar, they function in very different ways:

1
a. Natalie dislikes all men *who dip snuff*.

b. Natalie dislikes John, *who is my best friend*.

Sentence 1a tells us which men Natalie dislikes. The relative clause *who dip snuff* is an essential part of the noun phrase. If it were omitted (*Natalie dislikes all men*), the original meaning of the sentence would be lost.

On the other hand, the relative clause is not essential to the main idea of sentence 1b. It provides only supplemental information about John; if it were omitted (*Natalie dislikes John*), the main idea of the sentence would be left intact.

As another demonstration of their difference, we could appropriately insert a phrase such as *by the way* or *incidentally* after the relative pronoun in 1b, but we could not do so in 1a; there is nothing incidental about the relative clause in that sentence:

2
a. *Natalie dislikes all men who (by the way) dip snuff.

b. Natalie dislikes John, who (by the way) is my best friend.

Relative clauses such as the one in 1a, which are essential to complete the idea of the noun phrase, are called *restrictive clauses*. Relative clauses such as the one in 1b, which provide supplementary information, are called *nonrestrictive clauses*.

Not only are the two types different in function but there are also some differences in the way they are spoken and written. Unlike a restrictive clause, a nonrestrictive clause—when spoken—is separated from the rest of the sentence by short pauses, and—when written—by commas, dashes, or parentheses. Read the following pairs of sentences aloud, pausing at the commas in the nonrestrictive sentences and noting the difference in function between the two types of clauses. Notice that the phrase *by the way* could appropriately be inserted before the relative pronouns in the nonrestrictive sentences but not in the restrictive sentences.

3 a. She wanted a watch which also acts as a calculator.   *–Restrictive*

b. She bought a new watch, which also acts as a calculator.

–Nonrestrictive

4 a. He likes people who always smile.   *–Restrictive*

b. He likes the twins, who always smile.   *–Nonrestrictive*

5 a. The ancient Chinese who invented gunpowder were smart people.

–Restrictive

b. The ancient Chinese, who invented gunpowder, were smart people.

–Nonrestrictive

The restrictive clauses in 3a and 4a tell us what kind of watch she wanted and what kind of people he likes. The nonrestrictive clauses in 3b and 4b, in contrast, tell us additional information about her watch and about the twins. In 5a, only some particular Chinese—those who invented gunpowder—are described as smart. But in 5b, the ancient Chinese as a whole are called smart people.

Exercises

Some of the relative clauses in the following sentences are restrictive, some are nonrestrictive, and some are ambiguous—that is, they could be either. Underline each relative clause and decide what type of clause it is. Insert commas to separate each nonrestrictive clause from the rest of the sentence.

1. The song which she wrote became a huge hit.

Four tests can be performed to determine whether a relative clause such as which she wrote *is restrictive or nonrestrictive:*

   a. *The* which *test: Is the purpose of the relative clause to tell us* which *song became a hit? If so, the clause is restrictive.*
   b. *The* that *test: Can* that *be substituted for the relative pronoun in the sentence (. . . the song that she wrote . . .)? If so, the clause is restrictive, since* that *is used only in restrictive relative clauses.*

---

    c. The by-the-way *test: Can the phrase* by the way *be appropriately in-serted after the relative pronoun (. . . which, by the way, she wrote . . .)? If so, the clause is nonrestrictive.*

    d. The pause test: When you read the sentence aloud, do you pause briefly on either side of the clause (before which *and after* wrote*)? If so, the clause is nonrestrictive.*

These tests can also be applied to the relative clauses in the following sentences.

2. My brother who is a baseball fan lives in Toronto.

3. He baked the lasagna which the family ate with gusto.

4. Our horse which we treated like a member of the family never won a race.

5. Irwin visited the cottage in which Wordsworth lived.

Accounting for Nonrestrictive Clauses

Heretofore we have assumed that different sentences—even ambiguous sentences with similar surface structures—should be represented differently in their tree diagrams. Because the sentences in 5 are very different sentences even though they have identical wording in their surface structures, they must have different derivations, and we need to represent them in different ways when we diagram them.

    By now, it should be evident that syntax is not a subject where the student has little to do but accept and memorize a body of unquestioned truths. It is, in fact, more like a puzzle that all of us—teachers and students alike—have a hand in trying to solve. As here, we are often presented with specific problems that we must use insight and ingenuity to resolve. Just how, we must now ask, can we account in our grammar for the differences between restrictive and nonrestrictive clauses so as to reflect their different functions and to capture our intuitions about their structures? The following represents one of several possible hypotheses.

    Since restrictive clauses seem to be essential parts of the noun phrases they modify, we will continue to diagram them as we did in Chapter 10—as direct constituents of the noun phrases. Nonrestrictive clauses, however, seem to have an existence separate from the noun phrases that precede them, and we must devise an appropriate structure to represent this fact. Consider the hypothetical derivations, shown in 6, of the subject noun phrases in 5.

6   **a. *Restrictive clause:***

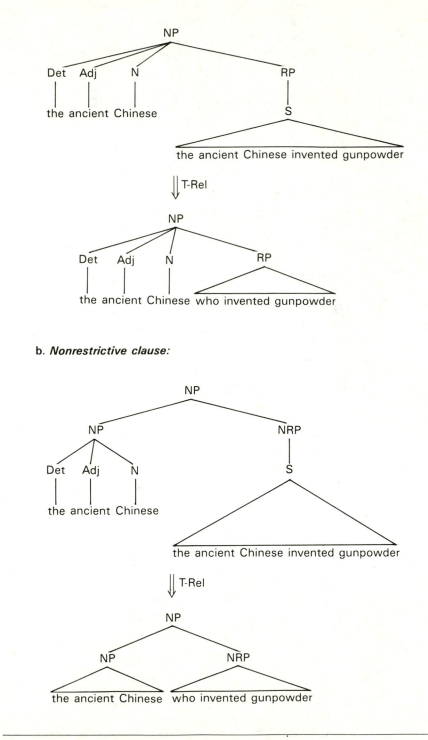

b. *Nonrestrictive clause:*

In the restrictive example, 6a, the relative clause is a direct constituent of the noun phrase. But in the nonrestrictive example, 6b, the NP label is repeated so that the noun phrase *the ancient Chinese* is treated as a complete unit, separated from the relative clause. Notice that a new category, ***nonrestrictive phrase*** (abbreviated ***NRP***), has also been introduced.

In the previous chapter, the R in the abbreviation RP *was said to stand for "relative." Since we now see that there can be both restrictive and nonrestrictive relative clauses and since we are using* RP *exclusively for the restrictive variety, let us reinterpret* ***RP*** *as standing for* ***restrictive phrase***.

Our grammar now generates restrictive and nonrestrictive clauses through these revised phrase-structure rules:

7   NP → $\begin{Bmatrix} \text{(Det)} & \text{(AdjP)}^+ & \text{N} & \text{(CompP)} & \textbf{(RP)} \\ & & \text{NP} & \textbf{NRP} & \end{Bmatrix}$

   RP → S

NRP → S

The relative-clause transformation applies in both sentences in 6 to replace the noun phrase *the ancient Chinese* with a relative pronoun.

Exercises

1. Show the derivations of these sentences with nonrestrictive relative clauses:

   a. Olivia served fresh prawns, which tickle Hiram's palate.
   b. Toby, whom Wanda supported, won the nomination.

2. Draw the derivations of the five sentences in the exercise on pages 138–139. If any of the sentences is ambiguous—that is, if its relative clause could be either restrictive or nonrestrictive—draw derivations for both of the interpretations.

Relative Clauses that Modify Sentences

Nonrestrictive relative clauses generally modify noun phrases, but sometimes we use them to modify entire clauses, as in *The chimps mimicked the trainer, which amused the audience.* In that sentence the relative clause modifies not just the noun phrase, *the trainer*, but the entire main clause, *The chimps mimicked the trainer*. We can account for this if we claim that entire clauses as well as noun phrases can have nonrestrictive modifiers:

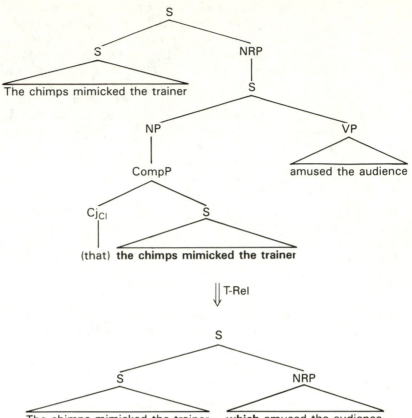

Note that in **8** it is not a noun phrase but an entire clause (*The chimps mimicked the trainer*) that is being modified by an NRP. That same clause is also found within the NRP — as a sentential complement. T-Rel replaces the identical clause with a relative pronoun, *which*.

We have now seen nonrestrictive clauses modify not just noun phrases but also entire S-clauses. You may remember a similar situation in Chapter 5 where we discovered that coordinating conjunctions could join together pairs of noun phrases and also pairs of sentences. In fact, *all* types of phrases can be joined by conjunctions, and so we devised a general rule to account for coordination (XP → XP Cj$_{Cl}$ XP).

Can a similar generalization be made about nonrestrictive clauses? That is, can all types of phrases be modified by nonrestrictive clauses? The following examples show that they can:

9   a. Miles *studied hard*, which is good, but *failed the exam*, which is bad.
                                                    —VPs with NRPs

b. The man *without shoes*—which is an odd way to dress—attracted stares.   *–PP with NRP*

c. Kit fought *fiercely*, which is the best way to fight an alligator.
–AdvP (specifically, an adverb) with NRP

Instead of many specific phrase-structure rules (such as the second option in the NP rule in 7), our grammar will contain a single general rule for generating all nonrestrictive clauses:

10 XP → XP NRP

Exercises

1. Use phrase-structure rule 10 to show the derivations of these sentences:
   a. The message, which Ludwig wrote in code, baffled the spies.
   b. Brad shaved his head, which horrified his mother.
   c. The baritone bowed grandly, which the audience appreciated.
   d. The comet appeared in July, which the astronomer predicted.

   Use your ingenuity to draw the derivation of this sentence:

   e. The comet appeared before August, which was early.

2. The following sentence is ambiguous:

   Pauline claimed that Ziggy tamed lions, which was foolish.

   Draw two derivations of the sentence—first when it means that Pauline's claim was foolish and again when it means that Ziggy's lion-taming was foolish.

Apposition

An *appositive* is a noun phrase that immediately follows and further explains another noun phrase. Like relative clauses, appositives can be either restrictive or nonrestrictive, as in these examples:

11 a. My brother *Claude* lives in Idaho.   *–Restrictive appositive*

b. My brother, *a chinchilla rancher*, lives in Idaho.
–Nonrestrictive appositive

In 11a, *Claude* is a noun phrase in apposition with the noun phrase *my brother*. It is restrictive because it tells us which particular brother the speaker means. In 11b, however, *a chinchilla rancher* is a nonrestrictive appositive, since the speaker assumes that the hearer already knows which brother is meant and is providing only supplementary information about him. Just as with nonrestrictive relative clauses, speakers pause briefly both before and following a nonrestrictive appositive; in writing, these pauses are represented by commas. On the other hand, speakers do *not* pause before and following restrictive appositives nor are commas usually used when restrictive appositives are written.

As an option, however, commas are sometimes used, especially with multiword restrictive appositives. Notice that both appositives in the following sentence (which is spoken without pauses) are restrictive: My brother, the rancher, is smarter than my brother, the auctioneer.

The two appositives in 11 can be diagrammed as follows:

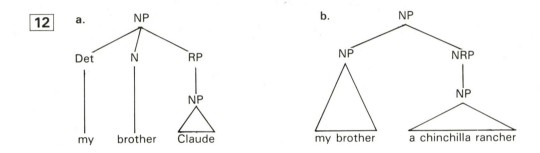

12

Restrictive and Nonrestrictive Adjectival Phrases

Adjectival phrases can also follow noun phrases, either restrictively or nonrestrictively, as in these examples:

13 a. A person *angry with the world* makes a poor neighbor.
    —*Restrictive AdjP*

  b. Cicely, *weary after her long journey*, arrived safely home.
    —*Nonrestrictive AdjP*

We have seen that not only a relative clause but also an appositive noun phrase and an adjectival phrase can follow a noun phrase as either a restrictive or a nonrestrictive modifier. We can account for these options within our phrase-structure rules:

14 a.
$$RP \rightarrow \left\{ \begin{array}{c} S \\ NP \\ AdjP \end{array} \right\}$$

b.
$$NRP \rightarrow \left\{ \begin{array}{c} S \\ NP \\ AdjP \end{array} \right\}$$

Exercises

1. Underline the restrictive and nonrestrictive modifying phrases in the following sentences (commas have been omitted). Identify them as either relative clauses, appositive noun phrases, or adjectival phrases—and as either restrictive or nonrestrictive. Supply commas where appropriate.

   a. The tourists visited Oslo the capital of Norway.
   b. Nigel cannot pronounce the word "ptisan."
   c. Milton a millionaire lived in a shack fit for a pauper.
   d. Daphne happy and carefree married Dominic a misanthropic hermit.
   e. The games Rex enjoys bore Alexandra who has fine taste.

2. Show the derivations of the sentences above.

3. Identify and describe each phrasal RP and NRP in the following sentences:

   a. Maxwell forgot the password—a disastrous blunder.
   b. The Bard (Shakespeare) had an enormous vocabulary.
   c. A person at peace with the world has little anxiety.
   d. The train, usually on time, arrived late on Thursday.

4. In addition to following the phrases they modify, nonrestrictive phrases can also precede them:

   a. *Curious but rude*, the intruder barged through the door.
   b. *A man without tact*, George insulted Christine.

   In previous instances where the same constituent could appear in several positions, we assumed that a transformational rule was responsible for moving the constituent. Here too we can assume the existence of a transformational rule, which we can call *NRP Movement* or *T-NRP*. Formulate that rule, and then use it to draw the derivations of sentences *a* and *b* above.

5. In Chapter 9 we examined reflexive pronouns such as *myself* and *themselves*. The same words that act as reflexive pronouns can also act in a different function—as *intensive pronouns* (abbreviated Pro_i). Intensive

pronouns are appositives whose function is to reinforce (or "intensify") the noun phrases that they follow, as in these examples:

a. I *myself* have no fear of goblins.
b. Blanche's best friend is Blanche *herself*.

Are intensive pronouns restrictive or nonrestrictive? Can you formulate an intensive-pronoun transformation (**T-Pro**$_i$)? How would you use it to derive sentences *a* and *b* above?

An Alternate Analysis of Restrictive and Nonrestrictive Phrases

Restrictive and nonrestrictive modifiers, we have seen, can be relative clauses, but they can also be phrases such as noun phrases and adjectival phrases. Another location in a sentence where both of those two phrases can occur, we can recall, is following a linking verb:

$$\boxed{15} \quad VP \rightarrow V_L \left\{ \begin{matrix} NP \\ AdjP_L \end{matrix} \right\}$$

This fact may be more than a coincidence. As the following examples show, for each appositive noun phrase or adjectival phrase there also exists a corresponding relative clause with a linking verb:

$\boxed{16}$
a. Jorge, the leader of the uprising, . . .   *–Nonrestrictive appositive*
b. Jorge, who was the leader of the uprising, . . .
                                    –Nonrestrictive relative clause

$\boxed{17}$
a. My friend the insurance adjustor . . .   *–Restrictive appositive*
b. My friend who is the insurance adjustor . . .
                                    –Restrictive relative clause

$\boxed{18}$
a. Noreen, happy with the arrangements, . . .   *–Nonrestrictive AdjP*
b. Noreen, who was happy with the arrangements, . . .
                                    –Nonrestrictive relative clause

$\boxed{19}$
a. A cupboard full of food . . .   *–Restrictive AdjP*
b. A cupboard that is full of food . . .   *–Restrictive relative clause*

The similarity between the pairs of examples has led some grammarians to speculate that phrasal modifiers—such as in the first example of each pair—are derived from deep-structure clauses with linking verbs. This hypothesis claims, for example, that both noun phrases in **16a** and **16b** are derived from this same deep structure:

20

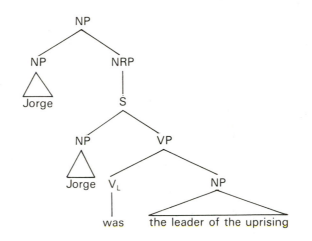

Either the relative-clause transformation can apply to this deep structure to produce **16b**, or else, according to this hypothesis, another transformation applies to remove the subject and linking verb from the appositive clause, thereby producing **16a**. We might call such a transformation *Relative-Clause Reduction*:

21 **Relative-Clause Reduction (T-RelRed):** An appositive is derived from a relative clause under these conditions:

a. the subject of the relative clause is identical to the noun phrase that the clause modifies, and

b. the verb of the relative clause is a linking verb.

The appositive is formed by deleting the subject and verb from the relative clause.

We now have two analyses to choose from. Appositives such as *the leader of the uprising* in **16a** are derived either directly from a phrase-structure rule with multiple options (**14b**) or else from a simpler rule (NRP → S) and a transformation (relative-clause reduction). I will leave it to you to decide which hypothesis better reflects the way we produce restrictive and nonrestrictive phrases.

Exercises

In addition to noun phrases and adjectival phrases, adverbial phrases can also follow linking verbs. Does the following sentence provide evidence that would help you decide whether appositive phrases are derived by T-RelRed?

The guests, *here at last*, apologized for the delay.

12 Verb Inflections

Present and Past Tenses

Until now in our study of grammar, we have ignored the different verb tenses and other verb inflections. In this chapter we will examine the way verbs are formed.

Tense is frequently described as the property that relates to the time a verb's action is performed. In traditional grammar study, verbs in English are said to take twelve tenses. Here, for example, are the traditional tense forms of the verb *go* in the indicative mood:

1

TRADITIONAL ANALYSIS OF ENGLISH VERB TENSES	
Common Forms	
Present Tense:	I go, you go, she goes, we go, they go
Past Tense:	I went, you went, . . .
Future Tense:	I will go, . . .
Present Perfect Tense:	I have gone, . . .
Past Perfect Tense:	I had gone, . . .
Future Perfect Tense:	I will have gone, . . .
Progressive Forms	
Present Progressive Tense:	I am going, . . .
Past Progressive Tense:	I was going, . . .
Future Progressive Tense:	I will be going, . . .
Present Perfect Progressive Tense:	I have been going, . . .
Past Perfect Progressive Tense:	I had been going, . . .
Future Perfect Progressive Tense:	I will have been going, . . .

This traditional analysis can be misleading, however, because it does not reflect the way in which verb inflections in English are actually formed. In English, unlike many other languages, verbs by themselves have only two distinct tense forms, present and past. All the other "tenses" in list 1 are formed by using auxiliary (or helping) verbs such as *have* or *will*. In this chapter we will examine how the grammar produces these verb forms.

Every English verb has a present and a past form. For the majority of verbs, known as ***regular*** (or ***weak***) ***verbs***, the past is formed by adding *-d* or *-ed* to the present form. Examples of the two tenses for regular verbs are *talk/talked*, *bake/baked*, and *need/needed*. In contrast, ***irregular*** (or ***strong***) ***verbs*** form the past tense in irregular ways: *do/did*, *have/had*, *take/took*, and *go/went*. Linking verbs are even less regular, with multiple forms in both present tense (*am, are, is*) and past tense (*was, were*).

We can assume that the grammar has some way of marking each verb's tense and assigning to it the proper spoken form. We can represent this in our model of the grammar by incorporating into the verb phrase a new element to hold tense information. We will call this element an ***auxiliary*** or ***Aux***. Our revised grammar will include these phrase-structure rules:

2   VP → **Aux**   V   (NP)   (AdvP)⁺

Aux → Tense

Tense → $\left\{ \begin{array}{c} \text{Present} \\ \text{Past} \end{array} \right\}$

According to this hypothesis, the grammar produces the following deep structure in order to derive the sentence, *Pete went to Chicago*:

3

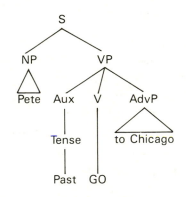

Notice that the verb *GO* is written in capital letters. You will remember that in earlier chapters we wrote certain deep-structure elements in capital letters to indicate that they represented concepts and not the words as actually spoken in the surface structure. In deep structure 3, the spoken form of the verb has not yet been assigned, and so, to show that, we list the verb in its basic form (also called its ***infinitive form***), written in capital letters.

Given this deep structure, a transformational rule will then assign the proper form of the verb in the surface structure. The various forms a word takes are called its *inflections*, so we will call this rule the *inflection-assigning transformation* or *T-Infl*.

In diagramming sentence derivations, we have always drawn a second tree to show the operation of a transformational rule. We could do so here, but instead we will adopt a simpler, more convenient method: we will not recopy the entire tree but instead will show just the operation of T-Infl. We will draw the surface-structure changes underneath the deep-structure tree, separated from it by a broken line. Here then is the entire derivation of *Pete went to Chicago:*

4

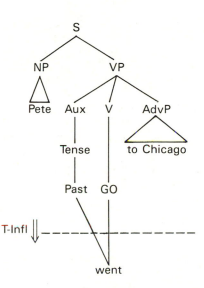

Speakers of English know the past tense of *GO* because we store information about the various forms of verbs in our memories—which is another way of saying in our mental lexicons. Derivation 4 does nothing more complicated than demonstrate that the grammar assigns the proper surface form to the verb. We could describe what happens here by saying that T-Infl sees that the past tense of the verb *GO* is called for, and it supplies the proper form to the surface structure—namely, *went*.

For an example of a sentence with a verb in the present tense, consider the derivation of *Ingrid loves anchovies* in 5.

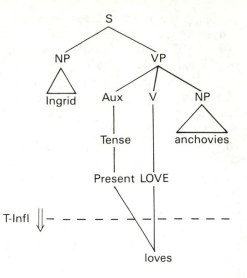

In addition to reading the auxiliary tense marker and the verb, T-Infl must take note of the subject as well. Since *Ingrid* is a third-person-singular noun (see page 47 for a discussion of person and number), the form *loves* is assigned to the verb. On the other hand, if the subject had been in the first person (that is, if the subject had been *I*), T-Infl would have assigned the form *love* instead.

Exercises

1. Using derivations 4 and 5 as your models, show how the following sentences are derived:

    a. Arthur hates okra.
    b. Bethany captured a lemming.
    c. The anthropologists puzzled the chimpanzees.
    d. I sleep soundly.

2. We usually think of the present tense as describing actions taking place at the present time and of the past tense as describing past actions. This is sometimes, but by no means always, the case. For the following sentences, identify the tense of each italicized verb and note whether the time it describes is the present, the past, the future, or an ongoing time.

    a. Tomorrow I *drive* to Cincinnati.
    b. Your disguise *fooled* me.
    c. "So then this big oaf *walks* up to me and he *says*, '*Beat* it, buster!'"
    d. A gentleman never *wipes* his mouth on his sleeve.
    e. I *wonder* what I would do if he *spoke* to me.
    f. Lefty *winds* up. He *delivers*. McGraw *swings*. He *misses*. The game *is* over.

Modal Auxiliaries

Although we sometimes use the present tense to describe future actions (see the preceding exercise 2a), usually we indicate the future by using the words *will* or *shall*, as in *We will go* or *They shall sing*. *Will* and *shall* are sometimes called "helping verbs." They are better described as ***modal auxiliaries*** (abbreviated ***M***). In addition to *will* and *shall*, there are other modal auxiliaries in English. Here are modals in their present- and past-tense forms:

6

MODAL AUXILIARIES	
PRESENT	*PAST*
will	would
shall	should
can	could
may	might
must	(no past tense form)

Let us place the modal auxiliary as an optional constituent of the auxiliary category. The Aux rule in 2 will then need to be revised to include it:

7 Aux $\rightarrow$ Tense (M)

$$M \rightarrow \left\{ \begin{array}{c} \text{WILL} \\ \text{SHALL} \\ \text{CAN} \\ \text{MAY} \\ \text{MUST} \end{array} \right\} \emptyset$$

The *null* symbol ∅ indicates that the verb that follows a modal will not take an inflectional ending in the surface structure but will instead remain in its uninflected form. With these rules, we can now derive sentences with modal auxiliaries, such as 8a, *Myra will retire*, and 8b, *Gordon might need a bandage*.

a.

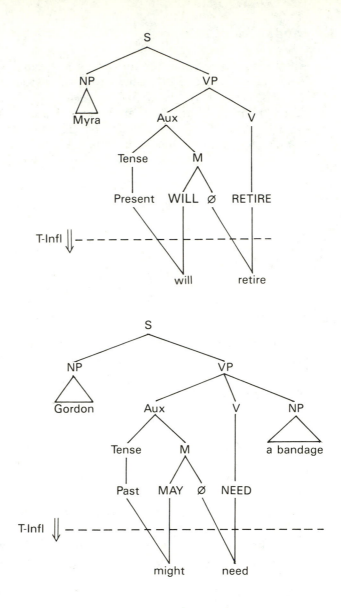

b.

In these examples, T-Infl is used to form both the modals and the main verbs. The diagrams show that the main verbs *retire* and *need* take the infinitive form because they follow modal auxiliaries.

Our experience in the derivations in 8 will now allow us to state the inflection-assigning transformation more specifically:

9 **Inflection-assigning Transformation (T-Infl):** Starting with the tense marker and moving to the right, pair off all the constituents of the *Aux* and *V* categories, and then assign to each pair the appropriate surface verb form.

Let us review the operation of T-Infl in the diagrams in 8. Following the rule, *Present* and *WILL* are paired in 8a to produce the surface form *will*. The null marker is then paired with *RETIRE*, indicating that the verb will retain its uninflected form *retire* in the surface structure. Similarly, in 8b, *Past* and *MAY* are paired to produce *might*, and Ø and *NEED* are paired to produce the uninflected form, *need*.

You may have remarked that you do not usually think of *will* as being in the present tense nor of *might* as being the past form of *may*. Nevertheless, those labels provide the best classification of these forms. As we have seen, tense is best described as a category that determines which form of a verb will be spoken; it only loosely indicates the time at which the action of the sentence is performed. As is often the case in grammar, the concept of tense can be described more accurately in terms of structure than in terms of meaning.

Exercises

1. Underline the modal auxiliaries and show the derivations of the following sentences:

    a. Audrey can ski expertly.
    b. Jeremy could be the boss.
    c. The children must take baths.
    d. The restaurant may hire Candace as a cook.
    e. The medics would assist the surgeons in an emergency.

2. In addition to the modals in chart 6, certain two-word combinations also perform the same function as modals. These **quasi-modals** include *have to, had to, used to,* and *ought to*. Although written as two words, they act as single words in modern English and are even pronounced like single words in normal, rapid speed (*hafta, hadda, useta, oughta*). Show the derivations of the following sentences; treat the quasi-modals like single words.

    a. Young Clampett ought to learn proper manners.
    b. Trains used to be a popular form of transportation.
    c. The marines had to march in a straight line.

    Note that *had to* in sentence *c* serves the function of the nonexistent past form of *must*.

3. In some parts of the United States, it is possible in informal speech to have more than one modal auxiliary in a verb phrase (*I might can go, We used to could sleep late*). Are such forms possible in your dialect? How may the rules of 7 be different for dialects that allow these expressions?

Perfect and Progressive Auxiliaries

In addition to the modal auxiliaries, there are other auxiliaries that can precede verbs, such as forms of *HAVE* and *BE*. Thus we have verb phrases such as *is taking* and *have taken*, not to mention those with combinations of auxiliaries such as *could have been taking*.

In order to understand how the system of verbs works in our language, we need to discover when and how these various auxiliaries occur. To do so, we will find it useful to have a body of data to examine. The following exercise can help us discover more about how English verbs are used.

Exercises

The noun phrase *He* can be combined with any of the auxiliaries in the second column and with any of the verb phrases in the third column to form a sentence:

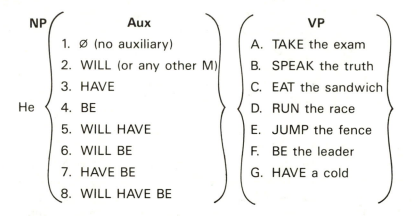

NP	Aux	VP
	1. Ø (no auxiliary)	A. TAKE the exam
	2. WILL (or any other M)	B. SPEAK the truth
	3. HAVE	C. EAT the sandwich
He	4. BE	D. RUN the race
	5. WILL HAVE	E. JUMP the fence
	6. WILL BE	F. BE the leader
	7. HAVE BE	G. HAVE a cold
	8. WILL HAVE BE	

Create as many sentences from the chart as you can. In each case, combine one item from each column and assign the appropriate forms to the auxiliaries and to the main verb. Do not draw trees; simply write down the surface forms of the sentences. For example, the surface sentence for combination 6A is *He will be taking the exam*. The sentence for 3C is *He has eaten the sandwich*, and the form for 1F is *He is the leader*. Clearly you know subconsciously what forms to use in each situation. Our goal is to see if we can state this knowledge in a conscious way. Try all the possible combinations of auxiliaries and verbs in this chart and then see if you can draw any conclusions from the data you have assembled. Can you discover what principles allowed you to choose the various forms of the verbs that you did? The chart lists eight possible combinations of auxiliaries. Are any other combinations possible (such as *BE WILL* or *BE HAVE WILL*)?

The data from this exercise may seem hopelessly confusing, a jumble beyond our capacities for comprehending. If, however, we analyze our data carefully and systematically, we can begin to find order where at first seemed only chaos.

We have already noted the two forms that verbs can take when they occur without any preceding auxiliaries: the present-tense form (such as *take/takes*) and the past-tense form (*took*). In addition, we now see that verbs that are preceded by auxiliaries can have other inflected forms such as *taken* and *taking* as well. These are called the **perfect** and the **progressive** forms respectively. From the sample sentences in the exercise, we can now list the various forms that each verb can take:

10

VERB INFLECTIONS				
UNINFLECTED Ø-ending	PRESENT	PAST	PERFECT -en ending	PROGRESSIVE -ing ending
TAKE	take(s)	took	taken	taking
SPEAK	speak(s)	spoke	spoken	speaking
EAT	eat(s)	ate	eaten	eating
RUN	run(s)	ran	run	running
JUMP	jump(s)	jumped	jumped	jumping
BE	am/is/are	was/were	been	being
HAVE	have/has	had	had	having

From the exercise it also seems that there are three classes of auxiliaries that can precede a verb. These can occur alone or in combination. One class is the **modal auxiliaries** (such as *WILL, CAN, MAY*, etc.). Another consists of forms of the verb *HAVE* (known as the **perfect auxiliary**). The third consists of forms of the verb *BE* (known as the **progressive auxiliary**).

You may also have noticed that each of these auxiliaries causes the verb that follows it to take a certain ending. First, modals are always followed by verbs in their uninflected (or "basic") form, as in *can take* or *shall jump*. In our diagrams we will represent this form with the null symbol (Ø), since uninflected verbs add no ending at all. Second, the perfect auxiliary *HAVE* is always followed by a perfect verb form, as in *have taken* or *has jumped*. We will represent the perfect form by the symbol **-en**, since many (but not all—see chart **10**) perfect verbs end in those letters. Finally, the progressive auxiliary *BE* is always followed by a progressive verb form, as in *is taking* or *am jumping*. We will represent the progressive form by the symbol **-ing**.

One further discovery from the data in our exercise is that any or all of the three types of auxiliary verbs can occur together in a verb phrase, but when they do so, they must occur in a certain order. When they occur together, modals come before perfect and progressive auxiliaries, and perfects come before progressive auxiliaries. This knowledge now allows us to write phrase-structure rules that will produce grammatical combinations of auxiliaries and verb endings. As a result, they model the rules you observe as you produce these same grammatical forms.

11   VP → Aux   V   (NP)   (AdvP)+

Aux → Tense   (M)   (Perf)   (Prog)

Tense → $\begin{Bmatrix} \text{Present} \\ \text{Past} \end{Bmatrix}$

M → $\begin{pmatrix} \text{WILL} \\ \text{SHALL} \\ \text{CAN} \\ \text{MAY} \\ \text{MUST} \end{pmatrix}$ ∅

Perf → HAVE -en

Prog → BE -ing

Generating the deep structures of verb phrases from these phrase-structure rules and deriving surface forms using T-Infl, we can now account for sentences with auxiliary verbs, such as *The gamblers had been cheating Sam:*

12
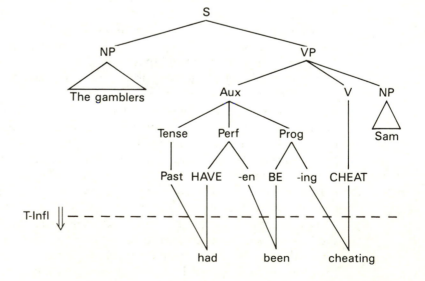

T-Infl pairs the elements of the Aux and V categories: *had* is the *Past* tense of *HAVE*; *been* is the -en form of *BE*; and *cheating* is the -ing form of *CHEAT*. This solution is elegant, and as you will see in the following exercise, it works every time. Our analysis of auxiliaries is an impressive demonstration of the effectiveness of transformational grammar in describing the rules we observe as we use our language.

Exercises

Follow the rules of 11 to show the derivations of the following sentences. Your trees will resemble that of 12.

1. Joel could have done the work.
   > *–Remember: Not every perfect verb form ends in the letters* -en.
2. Pamela is trying eagerly.
3. Colin may be the winner.
   > *–Note: Here* BE *is the main verb, not an auxiliary.*
4. Daisy may be leaving soon.
5. The girls had been laughing.
6. The cooks will have been working for an hour.
7. I must have a car.   *–Hint: See the note following sentence 3.*
8. The snow should have ended.
9. We would have recognized you.
10. You must have been dreaming.

The Emphatic Auxiliary

Some verbs that act as auxiliaries in certain sentences can act as main verbs in other sentences. Both *HAVE* and *BE* can be auxiliaries (*He has eaten, She is coughing*) as well as main verbs (*He has a pencil, She is a gourmet*). Another verb that can act as either a main or an auxiliary verb is *DO*.

The auxiliary *DO* is called the **emphatic auxiliary** (abbreviated **Emph**) because its purpose is to emphasize the statement being made, as in *I do respect you* and *You did try hard*. Unlike the modal, perfect, and progressive auxiliaries, which can occur together in combinations, the emphatic auxiliary cannot occur with other auxiliaries (**We do will go*, **They did have asked*).

A verb following the emphatic auxiliary *DO* takes the uninflected form. Here is the derivation of *Wanda did make an effort*:

13

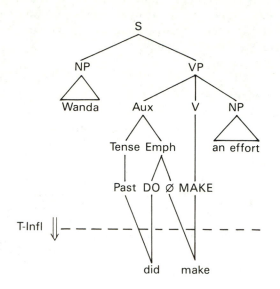

Exercises

1. Write the additional phrase-structure rules necessary to generate 13.

2. Draw the derivations of the following sentences with emphatic auxiliaries:
   a. Loud stereos do annoy Maurice.
   b. The outfit did cause a sensation.
   c. Brigid does do her homework faithfully.

3. Invent three additional sentences with combinations of auxiliary verbs and show their derivations.

13 Negatives and Questions

Negative Sentences

For each sentence that makes a positive statement there can also be a corresponding negative sentence that contains the word *not*. For example, corresponding with the positive sentence, *Howard will write letters*, there is the negative sentence, *Howard will not write letters*. Obviously the word *not* is added to form such sentences, but how and where? In order for us to answer these questions, we need more data to examine.

Negatives of Sentences with Auxiliary Verbs

Let us see what various sentences with negatives look like. The following tree shows the deep structure for a sentence with different combinations of auxiliary verbs. We would like to discover what the negative version of each of these seven combinations would be.

1

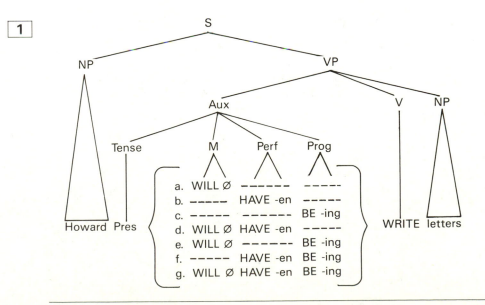

In this chart, *a* represents the deep structure of *Howard will write letters; e* of *Howard will be writing letters;* and *g* of *Howard will have been writing letters.*

Exercises

1. For each of the seven positive sentences in 1, supply the corresponding negative sentence. For example, the negative of *a* is *Howard will not write letters.*

2. Can you state a generalization about how we form the negative for a sentence with one or more auxiliary verbs? Does your generalization also apply to the past-tense versions of sentences in 1?

You undoubtedly noticed that the negative is formed by placing *not* immediately after the first auxiliary, as in *Howard has not been writing letters.* We can state this observation about the structure of negative sentences in the form of a transformational rule:

2   **Negative Transformation (T-Neg):** Following the operation of T-Infl, the first auxiliary verb is moved so that it precedes *not.*

Rule 2 presupposes that *not* is already a part of the deep structure, and if we continue to assume that the deep structure represents the essential concept or meaning of a sentence, then indeed the negative element must be present in the deep structure of a negative sentence. We can capture this by including negation as an optional element in the auxiliary category:

3   Aux → **(Neg)** Tense (M) (Perf) (Prog)

Neg → not

These revised rules allow us to show the derivations of negative sentences. Tree 4 gives the derivation of *Howard has not been writing letters.*

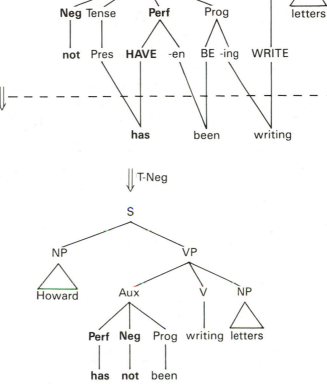

After T-Infl has supplied the verb forms in 4, T-Neg then moves the first auxiliary, *has*, so that it precedes *not*.

Exercises

1. For each of the following positive sentences, write the corresponding negative sentence:

    a. Ginny has been losing sleep lately.

b. Tyrone can speak Hungarian.
c. Seth would have remembered my birthday.
d. The workers are taking a break.
e. Their parents have worried about them.
f. The book is losing its cover.
g. The assassin could have been posing as a cop.
h. Melanie and Frederick had been wasting time.

2. Draw the derivations for the negative sentences corresponding to 1a–1h.

3. When an auxiliary such as *has* is followed by *not*, the two words are usually combined in speech to form a **contraction**, such as *hasn't*. We could say that an optional transformational rule (which we may call **T-Cont**) can apply following T-Neg to produce the contracted forms. State the contracted negative versions of sentences 1a–1h.

4. Rule 2 correctly describes the structure of negative sentences with auxiliary verbs. But what if a sentence lacks an auxiliary, such as *Howard writes letters*? How do you form the negative of such a sentence?

Negatives of Sentences without Auxiliary Verbs

Several centuries ago, it was possible to form the negative of a sentence with no auxiliaries in the same way as a sentence with auxiliaries—by moving the verb to precede *not*, as in *Howard writes not letters*. The English language is constantly changing, however, and in our century such sentences are no longer grammatical. If a negative sentence lacks an auxiliary verb in deep structure, one must be supplied. For this purpose, the **supporting auxiliary DO** is used, as in *Howard does not write letters*. This is a different role for *DO* from its role as an emphatic auxiliary. Here it is simply a device to allow negation; it does not emphasize the action.

We can state this observation in the form of a transformational rule:

5.   **DO-Support Transformation (T-Supp):** If a negative sentence lacks an auxiliary verb in deep structure, the supporting auxiliary (*DO* + Ø) is supplied following the tense marker.

In order, then, to derive a sentence whose deep structure lacks an auxiliary verb, such as *Howard does not write letters*, the supporting auxiliary *DO* must first be supplied. We could draw a new tree to show the operation of T-Supp, but it is simpler to do what we have done with T-Infl—that is, we can use the broken-line method to show the changes made by the transformation. We can draw a dotted line beneath the deep structure and show the insertion of the supporting auxiliary *DO* underneath the line:

6

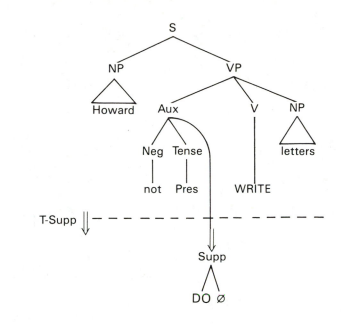

After T-Supp has supplied the supporting auxiliary *DO* (notice that we label it *Supp* rather than *Emph* since its purpose is not emphatic in this sentence), T-Infl then provides the proper forms of the verbs, and finally T-Neg moves *does* into the proper position. The complete derivation of *Howard does not write letters* is shown in 7.

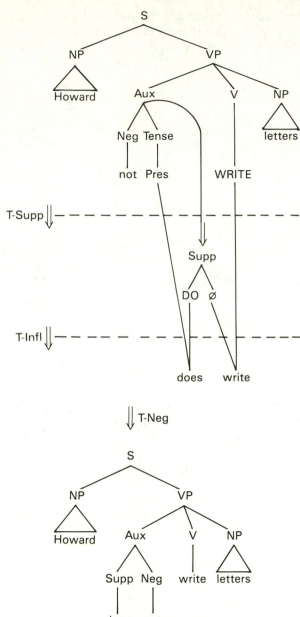

7

In a lengthy-looking derivation such as **7**, the grammar can appear very complex—and, in a real sense, it is. The very least you will gain from this course is an appreciation of the remarkably complex tasks our minds constantly (and easily) perform as we use language. On the other hand, we should not allow these derivations to seem any more complicated than they are. For example, writing a transformational rule like T-Neg is simply another way of showing that we put the first auxiliary before *not* when we speak. Having to draw a separate tree in our diagram to show this simple step makes it look complicated, but that is only a limitation of our model—and especially of our need to represent it in a visual diagram. If, however, you understand what these derivations are really showing, they will seem straightforward and reasonable.

Exercises

1. State the corresponding negative sentence for each of the following positive sentences:
   a. Meg likes spicy foods.
   b. Politics bored Alphonse.
   c. The mountaineers use ropes.
   d. The bright lights dazzled Stella.

2. Draw the derivations for the negative sentences corresponding to exercise sentences 1a–1d.

Questions

Yes/No Questions

For each declarative sentence, there also corresponds a question that calls for a yes or no answer. For example, the question form of *Howard will write letters* is *Will Howard write letters?* In order to discover how yes/no questions are formed, we need once again to assemble a body of data to examine.

Exercises

1. For each of the sentences in 1a–1h of the exercise on pages 163–164, state the corresponding yes/no question.

2. For each of the seven deep structures in 1 on page 161, state the corresponding yes/no question. Then state the yes/no question corresponding to *Howard writes letters*.

3. From this data, can you describe how yes/no questions are formed for sentences with auxiliaries in their deep structures? For sentences with no auxiliaries in deep structure? For negative sentences?

The similarity between the rules for forming negatives and for forming yes/no questions is evident. In both cases the supporting auxiliary *DO* must be added if the sentence lacks an auxiliary verb in deep structure. In both cases the first auxiliary is then moved. For the negative sentence, it is moved to precede the negative element *not*. For the question, it is moved to precede the entire sentence.

In order for our grammar to represent what we have discovered about questions, it first needs a way of denoting in the deep structure that the sentences are questions (interrogative sentences) rather than statements (declarative sentences). In other words, the mood of the sentence needs to be noted. We can alter our phrase-structure rules as follows:

8 Aux → **Mood** (Neg) Tense (M) (Perf) (Prog)

$$\text{Mood} \rightarrow \begin{cases} \text{Dec} \\ \text{Q} \\ \text{Imp} \\ \text{Subj} \end{cases}$$

These rules add a mood marker to the auxiliary category to designate each sentence as *declarative* (abbreviated **Dec**), *interrogative* (**Q**), *imperative* (**Imp**), or *Subjunctive* (**Subj**).

In addition, the grammar must have a transformational rule (which we can call **T-Q**) to move the auxiliary in forming questions. We can derive yes/no questions such as *Has Howard been writing letters?* as shown in **9**.

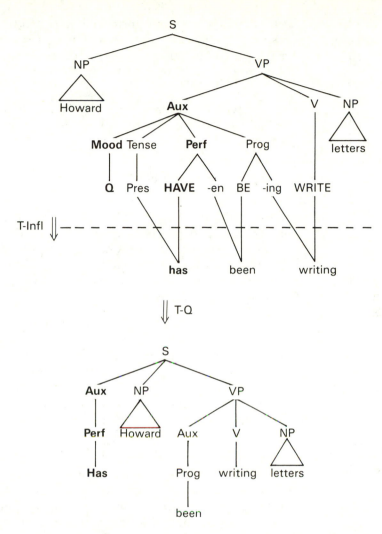

In this derivation, T-Q has moved only the first auxiliary verb, *has,* to the front of the sentence. The other auxiliary, *been,* stays in its original position. We will wait until we have examined some other kinds of questions before we formally state the question transformation T-Q.

Note: It is not necessary to retain either the mood or tense markers in drawing the surface-structure trees.

Exercises

1. Show the derivations of the yes/no questions that correspond with sentences 1a–1d from the exercise on pages 163–164.

2. Revise the *DO*-Support Transformation (5) so that it applies to yes/no questions as well as to negative sentences. Using your revised transformation, show the derivations of the questions corresponding with 1a–1d in the exercise on page 167.

3. The contraction transformational rule is usually applied when we form questions from negative sentences. Show the derivations of these questions:

   a. Won't Gertrude be coming?
   b. Doesn't Andy work here?

4. Every declarative sentence can be followed by a **tag question**, can't it? The phrase *can't it?* at the end of the previous sentence is an example of a tag question. If sentence 1a in the exercise on page 163 were followed by a tag question, it would become: *Ginny has been losing sleep lately, hasn't she?* The negative version of that sentence, followed by a tag question, becomes: *Ginny has not been losing sleep lately, has she?*

   a. Restate sentences 1a–1h from the exercise on pages 163–164, adding the appropriate tag questions. Add tag questions to sentences 1a–1d from the exercise on page 167.
   b. State the negative versions of those sentences, with tag questions added.
   c. Examine the data that you have produced and describe the series of operations your mind had to have performed in order for you to have produced the appropriate tag question for those sentences. How many steps (transformations) are required?

   Your answer to *c* must surely have impressed you. A very great many steps are required for us to produce tag questions, and yet you can state the correct tag question for any given sentence almost instantaneously, can't you? The operation of the grammar in your mind is truly a wondrous thing. You can also understand, from the complexity of forming tag questions, why most three-year-olds have not yet learned how to produce them. Tags are, in fact, among the last grammatical skills that children master as they learn English.

5. The rules of **8** assume that deep-structure trees must have a way of specifying the sentence's mood. Why is or isn't this a worthwhile assumption? Using these rules, draw the derivations of the following two sentences. Do they help you to answer the previous question?

   a You study hard.   –*Statement*
   b. Study hard.   –*Command*

Wh-Questions

The questions we have so far examined are requests for yes or no answers. Other types of questions call for more substantial replies. These questions are called *wh-questions*, because (with one exception) they begin with words whose first two letters are *wh* (*who, whom, what, when, where, why, how, which,* and *whose*). The following are all *wh*-questions:

10
a. Who bought a computer?

b. What has Eloise bought?

c. When will Eloise be using the computer?

d. Where did she get such a bargain?

e. Why didn't she buy a printer too?

f. How could she afford it?

g. Which model did Eloise get?

h. Whose software is she borrowing?

Interrogative Pronouns

Of the *wh*-words, *who, whom,* and *what* are ***interrogative pronouns*** (abbreviated Pro_Q). Interrogative pronouns take the place of noun phrases in the deep structure, just as these same words do when they act as relative pronouns. An interrogative pronoun replaces an *indefinite noun phrase*, an unidentified someone or something whose identity is being sought. We can use the abbreviation *SME* to represent an indefinite item in the deep structure. Here, in 11, for example, is the derivation of *Who bought a computer?*

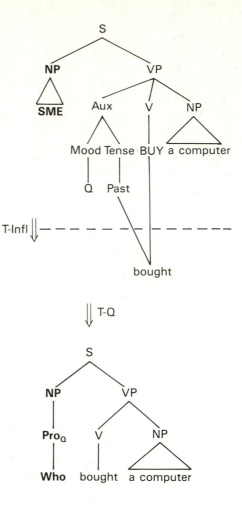

The indefinite element *SME* in the deep structure represents the unknown quantity, the someone or something whose identity is being asked for by the question. When *SME* is the subject noun phrase in the deep structure, it is simply changed into the appropriate interrogative pronoun, as derivation 11 demonstrates. However, an additional step is involved when the *SME* occurs later in the sentence. For example, the question *What has Eloise bought?* is derived from *Eloise bought SME*. The indefinite *SME* is replaced by the interrogative pronoun *what*, and both *what* and *has* are moved to the beginning of the sentence, as shown in 12.

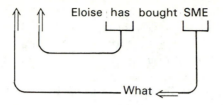

12

Here is the complete derivation of *What has Eloise bought?*

13

(tree diagram)

S

NP   VP

Eloise   **Aux**   V   **NP**

Mood   Tense   **Perf**   BUY   **SME**

Q   Pres   **HAVE**   -en

T-Infl

has   bought

T-Q

S

NP   **Aux**   NP   VP

Pro$_Q$ **Perf**   Eloise   V

What   **has**   bought

When the indefinite element *SME* follows the verb, both the interrogative pronoun (which replaces *SME*) and the first auxiliary are moved to the beginning of the sentence. We can now state the question transformation so that it accounts for both yes/no and *wh*-questions:

14 | **Question Transformation (T-Q):** When a sentence is marked as a question (that is, when it has the mood marker *Q* in its deep structure), it is transformed as follows:

a. If the sentence does not contain the indefinite element *SME*, it is formed into a yes/no question: The first auxiliary verb (as well as *not*, if the sentence is negative) is moved to the beginning of the sentence.

b. If the sentence has the indefinite element *SME*, it is formed into a *wh*-question: *SME* is changed to the appropriate *wh*-word; if *SME* occurs in the subject noun phrase, no further changes are made; if *SME* occurs anywhere else, the phrase in which it occurs and the first auxiliary verb (as well as *not*, if the sentence is negative) are moved to the beginning of the sentence.

Exercises

1. Show the derivations of the following questions:
   a. What caused the commotion?
   b. Who should have unlocked the cabinet?
   c. What might Sheila have been plotting?
   d. Whom has Chloris been dating lately?

2. When *SME* occurs within a prepositional phrase, either the *SME* by itself or else the entire prepositional phrase can be moved to the front of the sentence. Show the derivations of these questions:
   a. What has Morey sat on?
   b. With whom will Tammy elope?

3. When the deep structure lacks an auxiliary verb, one is supplied by T-Supp. Show these derivations:
   a. Whom did Marguerite admire?
   b. What does Charles expect?

   But note that T-Supp is not needed when *SME* is the deep-structure subject:
   c. Who admired Marguerite?

Interrogative Adverbs

The question words *when, where, why,* and *how* are **interrogative adverbs** (abbreviated **Adv_Q**). Each replaces an adverbial phrase that contains the indefinite element *SME. When,* for example, replaces a deep-structure phrase whose approximate meaning is "at some time." Deep structures, of course, represent concepts, not the words that are actually spoken, and we will represent the deep-structure adverbials in capital letters. Here is the derivation of *When will Eloise be using the computer?*

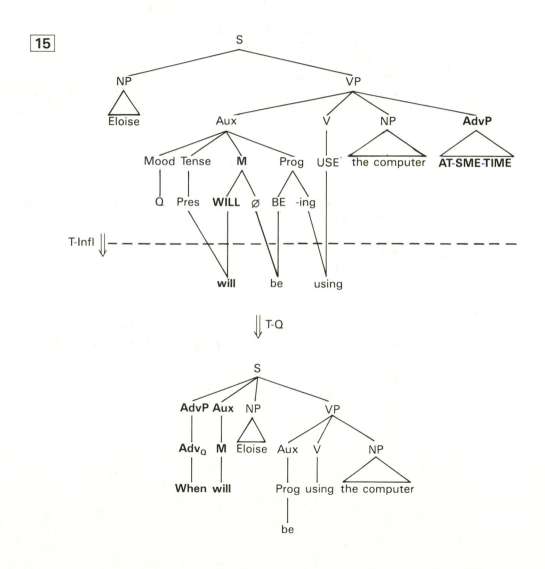

The adverbial concept *AT-SME-TIME* becomes the interrogative adverb *when*, and it is moved (together with the auxiliary *will*) to the beginning of the sentence. In other sentences, such as 10d–10f, *where* would replace *AT-SME-PLACE*, *why* would replace *FOR-SME-REASON*, and *how* would replace *IN-SME-MANNER*.

Exercises

1. Show the derivations of these questions:

   a. Where has Mitch stored the supplies?
   b. How can we repay you for your kindness?
   c. When is the boat sailing?
   d. Why did Josh insult those thugs?

2. Does the question transformation (14) need to be revised in order to account for questions with interrogative adverbs, or is it adequate as it is stated?

Interrogative Determiners

Which, what, and *whose* act as **interrogative determiners** (abbreviated **Det$_Q$**), as in these three questions:

16
   a. Which
   b. What   } car should Bernie wash?
   c. Whose

Each of these *wh*-words replaces an indefinite determiner in the deep structure. For example, 17 is the derivation of *Which car should Bernie wash?*

17

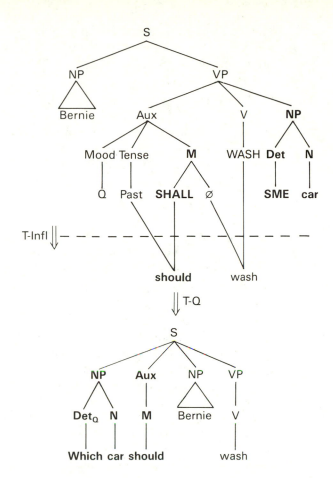

In this derivation the indefinite determiner *SME* becomes the interrogative determiner *which,* and the entire noun phrase is moved to the beginning of the sentence.

Exercises

1. Show the derivations of these questions:
   a. What movie did Cecil admire?
   b. Which actor won an Oscar?
   c. In what theater has Frankie been selling popcorn?

2. The interrogative determiner *whose* replaces an indefinite possessive determiner (*SME's*) in the deep structure. (See the discussion of possessive noun phrases on pages 74–76.) Show the derivations of these questions:

   a. Whose watch tells the date?
   b. Whose birthday are they celebrating?

3. Questions that ask for information are called ***direct questions***. All the questions we have examined so far have been direct questions. When a sentential-complement clause is introduced by a *wh*-word, it is called an ***indirect question***, as in these examples:

   a. I wonder *who is kissing her now.*
   b. We know *what we like.*
   c. Jerry asked *when the show will start.*
   d. The women knew *which box held the treasure.*
   e. *What damages the jury would award* remained a mystery.

   Unlike direct questions, indirect questions are not requests for information. What differences do you notice between the ways direct and indirect questions are formed? In particular, how are auxiliaries affected in the two kinds of questions? From your experience with sentential-complement clauses in Chapter 5, with relative clauses in Chapter 10, and with *wh*-questions in this chapter, see if you can determine how these indirect questions are formed. Draw the derivations of the five sample sentences.

4. The sample sentences in exercise 3 can all be called ***wh- indirect questions***, since the clauses are introduced by *wh*-words that replace *SME* in the deep structure. Can ***yes/no indirect questions*** also be formed? Consider the following data: For every declarative sentence, there is a corresponding yes/no direct question. For example, the yes/no question corresponding to the sentence *The rain will end* is *Will the rain end?* Can a yes/no indirect question be formed from the following deep structures? Must any word(s) be added to form them?

   a. I wonder [the rain will end]
   b. The children asked [the museum charges admission]

   Draw the derivations of these sentences. Finally, formulate an ***indirect-question transformation*** (abbreviated **T-IQ**) that will account for both yes/no and *wh*- indirect questions.

14 The Passive Voice

Active and Passive Voice

Verbs can occur in either the active or the passive voice. The difference between the two voices is best described in terms of meaning. When a verb is in the *active voice*, the subject of the sentence performs the action. When the verb is in the *passive voice*, the subject receives the action. Note the following examples:

1
a. Olga *ate* the apple.   –*Active voice*

b. The apple *was eaten* by Olga.   –*Passive voice*

As you examine these two sentences, you can make several observations about them. Both sentences describe the same event and communicate the same information. In 1a, however, greater attention seems to be paid to Olga, whereas in 1b focus is placed on the apple. In the active sentence, 1a, the subject noun phrase *Olga* performed the action—that is, she was the one who did the eating. In the passive sentence, 1b, the subject *the apple* received the action—that is, it didn't eat but got eaten. *The apple*, which is the receiver of the action in both sentences, is the direct object in 1a but the subject in 1b. The doer of the action, *Olga*, is the subject of the active sentence but is the object of the preposition *by* in the passive sentence. Finally, we can observe that although the action occurred in the past in both sentences, the past form of the verb is used in the active sentence but not in the passive, where the past form of *BE* is used, followed by the *-en* form of the verb.

Verbs in both tenses, with or without auxiliaries, can have active and passive versions. Here are some further examples:

2
  a. Veronica prefers soft drinks.   *—Active, no auxiliary verbs*

  b. Soft drinks are preferred by Veronica.   *—Passive, no auxiliary verbs*

3
  a. Marlene can mow the lawn.   *—Active, with modal auxiliary*

  b. The lawn can be mowed (or mown) by Marlene.
          —Passive, with modal auxiliary

4
  a. The workers are repairing the potholes.
          —Active, with progressive auxiliary

  b. The potholes are being repaired by the workers.
          —Passive, with progressive auxiliary

5
  a. The taxi should have picked up Charles by now.
          —Active, with modal and perfect auxiliaries

  b. Charles should have been picked up by the taxi by now.
          —Passive, with modal and perfect auxiliaries

For each pair of sentences, notice carefully the differences between the two sentences. In particular, be certain that you understand why the *a* sentence is active and the *b* sentence is passive.

Exercises

Identify each of the following sentences as active or passive. If it is active, state also the corresponding passive version. If it is passive, state its active counterpart. Make certain that the two versions have the same tense and the same auxiliaries. But note: A form of the auxiliary *BE* must be added as you transform an active into a passive sentence and removed as you do the reverse.

1. The tomato was sliced by Willie.
2. Jill could have fired Greg.
3. The committee was debating the merits of the new constitution.
4. Common courtesy is observed by all members of this crew.
5. The actors had performed a play by Shakespeare.
6. The decorations will astound you.

7. The joke might have been appreciated by a more sophisticated audience.

8. The boys were being punished by their parents.

9. Evelyn was told a lie by Barney.

10. Tallulah looks up to Marjean.

Deriving Passive Sentences

In each pair of active and passive sentences that you have examined, the two sentences focus on different noun phrases, but they have the same essential meaning. We can assume that both sentences are derived from the same deep structure. But what is that structure? From the very beginning of this book we have assumed that deep structures were active sentences, and that assumption seems reasonable. Active sentences occur far more frequently than passive sentences; they are simpler—for example, sentence 1a has two fewer words than its passive counterpart, 1b; and most people have the intuitive feeling that the word order *performer-verb-receiver* is more "natural" and "basic" than *receiver-verb-performer*.

For these reasons let us assume that the performer of the action is the deep-structure subject. The form of the passive sentence is derived from the active version by a transformational rule. Several steps are required, which we will state as parts of a single rule:

6   **Passive Transformation (T-Pass):** To form the passive version of a sentence, the following operations are performed:

     a. The subject noun phrase in the deep structure is replaced by the noun phrase that follows the verb.

     b. The passive auxiliary (*BE* + *−en*) is added as the final constituent of the auxiliary.

     c. The position vacated by the noun phrase that followed the verb in the deep structure is left empty (∅).

     d. A prepositional phrase, consisting of the preposition *by* and the subject noun phrase from the deep structure, is added at the end of the verb phrase.

With this rule we can show the derivation of the passive sentence *The treasure might have been hidden by the pirates*. This sentence has the same deep structure as the active sentence *The pirates might have hidden the treasure*. In effect we can say that the passive sentence is derived from the active sentence by the passive transformational rule as in 7.

7   The pirates might have hidden the treasure.   *–Active version*

⇓ T-Pass

The treasure might have been hidden by the pirates.   *–Passive version*

The four steps of T-Pass can be shown in detail through a tree diagram:

8

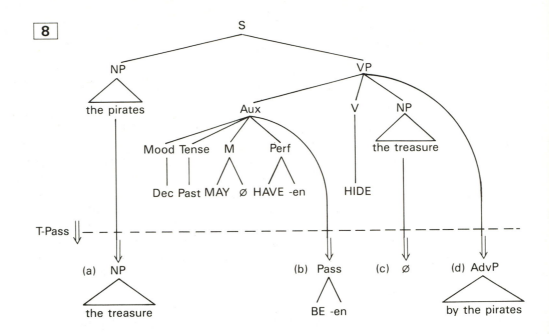

The operation of T-Pass is shown below the broken line. In step *a* the deep-structure subject noun phrase *the pirates* is replaced by the object noun phrase *the treasure*. In step *b* the passive auxiliary is added. In *c* the direct-object slot becomes vacant (symbolized by Ø). In *d*, the original subject noun phrase *the pirates* becomes the object of a prepositional phrase, preceded by *by*. We can now show T-Infl supplying the appropriate verb forms. The entire derivation of the sentence is shown in **9**.

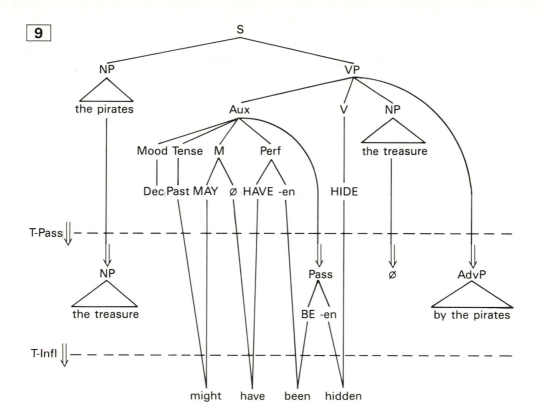

Exercises

Show the derivations of the following passive sentences. Passive derivations may seem difficult, but they will be less so if you follow the rules step by step. You may find it helpful to begin the exercise by stating the active counterpart of each sentence.

1. Lancelot was banished by the prince.
2. The roses must have been sent by a secret admirer.
3. The mice are being exterminated by the piper.
4. The fortress should have been overrun by the barbarians.

Passive Sentences with Indefinite Agents

Not every passive sentence names the agent or performer of the action in a *by*-phrase. That is step *d* of the transformation is omitted if the deep structure has the indefinite subject *SME* (which represents an unspecified "someone" or "something"). Here, for example, is the derivation of the passive sentence *Horseplay is forbidden*:

10

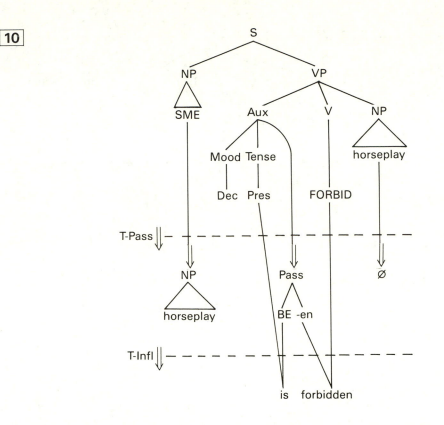

Since the subject is not specified in the deep structure of **10**, no *by*-phrase is spoken in the surface structure.

Exercises

1. Revise the passive transformational rule, **6**, to account for sentences with indefinite agents.

2. Show the derivations of the following passive sentences:
   a. Soup is served in bowls.
   b. That insult should have been avenged.
   c. The children may be excused.

3. In exercise 1, you revised the passive transformational rule so that it deletes the indefinite subject *SME* in forming the passive sentence. But sentences such as the following also occur: *That insult should have been avenged by someone.* In addition to being deleted, *SME* can also be replaced by an ***indefinite pronoun*** (abbreviated **Pro**$_{SME}$), such as *someone*. Other indefinite pronouns include *some, something, somebody, any, anyone, anything,* and *anybody.* Write the ***indefinite-pronoun transformation*** (abbreviated ***T-Pro***$_{SME}$), and use it to draw derivations of these sentences:

   a. Somebody ate my lunch.
   b. My lunch was stolen by someone.

   Is T-Pro$_{SME}$ an optional transformation, or is it sometimes obligatory? Which indefinite pronouns could serve as replacements for *SME* in the following sentences?

   c. Gary likes SME.
   d. Gary doesn't like SME.

   Are there certain circumstances when we use pronouns beginning with *some-* and when we use those beginning with *any-*? Do they have different meanings?

Passive Sentences with Indirect Objects

As you recall from Chapter 8, the transformational rule T-IO can move an indirect object so that it directly follows the verb. Sentence 11b has an indirect object, *Gina*, that has been moved by T-IO:

11 a. Arnold told a secret to Gina.
   b. Arnold told Gina a secret.

T-Pass affects the first noun phrase following the verb. That is, applied to 11a, it moves the direct object *a secret*, thereby producing the passive sentence 12a. Applied to 11b, in which T-IO has already operated, it moves the indirect object, *Gina*, producing 12b:

12 a. A secret was told to Gina by Arnold.
   b. Gina was told a secret by Arnold.

Tree 13 shows the derivation of 12b.

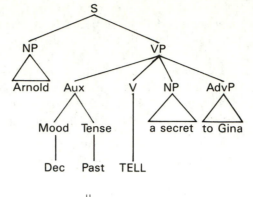

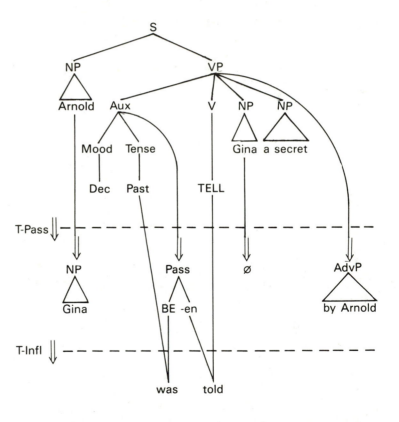

Three transformational rules apply to derive surface structure 12b.

Exercises

1. Show the derivations of the following sentences:

   a. The finder is being offered a reward by the owners.
   b. Kathleen will be promised a job.
   c. Donnie has been shown the secret by the wizard.
   d. A secret has been shown to Donnie by the wizard.

2. T-Pass moves the noun phrase that follows the verb, whether it is the direct or indirect object. Can it also apply to other noun phrases in that position? Consider the following sentence:

   The chair was sat upon by a giant.

   What is the active counterpart of this sentence? Notice that the noun phrase that follows the verb in the deep structure is the object of a preposition. Nevertheless, step *a* of T-Pass applies to it as well. Show how this passive sentence is derived.

15 Infinitives

Infinitive Verb Forms

The *nonfinite* (or *infinitive*) *form* of a verb is its basic form, without any inflectional changes. *Have, look, do,* and *be* are all nonfinite forms. In contrast, *has, looked, doing,* and *were* are examples of the many *finite* (or *inflected*) *forms* of those verbs. In our tree diagrams, we have been using nonfinite forms, written in capital letters, to represent the deep–structure concepts of verbs.

An *infinitive phrase* is a verb phrase in which the nonfinite form of a verb is preceded by the word *to*. For example, an infinitive phrase is italicized in the following sentence:

1. Ruth's proudest achievement was *to pass the exam*.

Sentences with infinitive phrases are among the most interesting and unusual sentences in the English language. We will devote this chapter to examining them.

Sentential-Complement Infinitives

The word *to* in 1 is a different word from the preposition *to* in a sentence like *Ruth went to the movies*. In 1 *to* has no meaning of its own, serving only to alert us that an infinitive phrase is being introduced. For that reason, this *to* can be called an *infinitive marker*, or **IM**. That part of an infinitive phrase that consists of the verb plus the infinitive marker *to* is called an *infinitive*. In 1, *to pass* is an infinitive.

Analyzing the meaning of 1 can give us a clue to its deep structure. We can ask who is the subject of the infinitive in that sentence—that is, who passed the exam? The answer is Ruth herself. Or to put it another way, what was Ruth's proudest achievement? The answer: the fact that she passed the exam. The underlying meaning—or deep structure—of 1 can therefore be represented as in 2, with a complete sentential-complement clause underlying the infinitive phrase.

To simplify our trees in this section, I will not show the complete auxiliary category with its mood and tense markers.

2

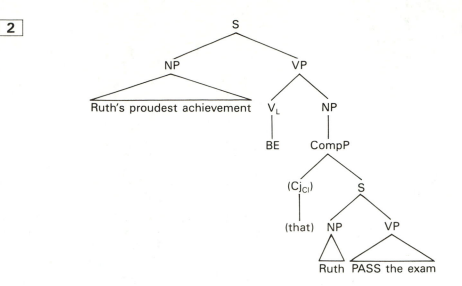

Surely this is the meaning that we understand when we read sentence 1. We know that it is Ruth, and not some other person, who she hopes will pass the exam.

Deep structure 2 underlies not only the infinitive sentence 1 but also the complement-clause sentence 3:

3   Ruth's proudest achievement was that she passed the exam.

In Chapter 5 we assumed that the complementizer that *is already present in the deep structures of sentences with complement clauses. An alternative analysis is to assume that the complementizer is not a part of the deep structure but is added by a transformational rule (which we might call **T-Comp**) used to form complement clauses. In deep structure 2, I placed the complementizer in parentheses; I will no longer represent it in diagramming the deep structures of such sentences.*

It is appropriate for sentences 1 and 3 to have a common deep structure since they are *paraphrases* of each other — that is, they are two different sentences that have the same underlying meaning. When we intend the meaning of 2, we can choose to form either of the two possible surface sentences. Since the infinitive in 1 derives from a sentential-complement clause, we will call it a *sentential-complement infinitive*.

If we choose to produce the infinitive form 1, an optional transformational rule creates the desired surface structure. The rule, which we can call **T-Inf**, deletes *Ruth* from the embedded clause in 2 and inserts the infinitive marker *to* at the front of the verb phrase, as shown in 4.

4

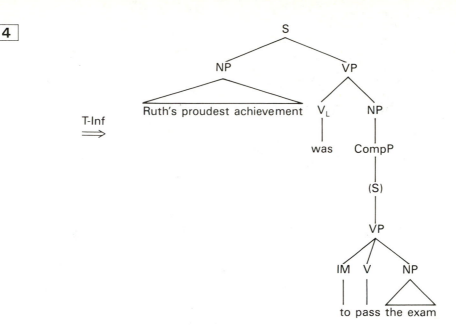

T-Inf
⟹

We can either delete the embedded S-label or else place it within parentheses to show that the infinitive phrase is no longer a complete sentence.

*You may have noticed that I did not show the operation of **T-Infl** in the derivation. I haven't forgotten about it; I am simply taking the liberty of assuming its operation — for example, changing BE to was—without taking the time and space to show this step. Simplifying the tree here allows us to focus our attention on what is new. But it is important to remember that a complete derivation would show all the steps.*

Unlike the infinitive in 1, not every infinitive has the same subject as does the main sentence. Consider sentence 5:

5 Ruth's fondest hope is *for Hiram to pass the exam.*

This sentence talks about Hiram, not Ruth, doing the exam passing. Consequently, *Hiram* is the subject of the embedded clause in the deep structure of 5. The precise structure of surface sentence 5, however, is debatable, and we need to speculate about what its tree should look like. Tree 6 shows one possible representation of the derivation of 5.

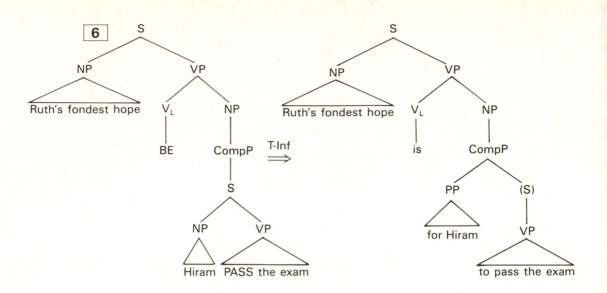

6

A number of problems present themselves in our discovery of the appropriate structure for sentence 5. What role does the word *for* play, for example, and where in the tree should we put the NP *Hiram*? There is evidence to support the claim that *for* is used here as a preposition. For example, verbs such as *hope* and *pray* which are often followed in simple sentences by the preposition *for* can also be followed by infinitive phrases beginning with *for*. Consider these sentences:

7 a. Elise hopes for rain.
b. Elise hopes for the rain to end.

8 a. He prayed for guidance.
b. He prayed for the Cubs to win the pennant.

If we decide that *for* is a preposition in all four of these sentences , we will then need to decide what is the object of the preposition in the infinitive sentences. In 5, for example, is it simply the noun phrase *Hiram*—as assumed in 6—or is the object of the preposition the entire phrase *Hiram to pass the exam*?

While *Hiram* is clearly the subject of the complement clause in the deep structure, its role in the surface structure is less clear. Does *Hiram* remain the subject of an embedded clause or is it removed from that clause and made into an object—perhaps the object of the preposition *for*, as derivation 6 assumes? There is strong evidence to support the latter claim. Consider these two sentences:

---

9 a. Ruth's fondest hope is *for him* [not **he*] *to pass the exam*.

b. Ruth's proudest achievement was *for herself* [not **she*] *to pass the exam*.

The fact that the pronoun *him* is used in 9a—and not *he*—shows that this noun phrase is in the objective, not the nominative, case. If so, it cannot still be the subject of the lower clause (since subjects are in the nominative case). In 9b, *herself* is a reflexive pronoun that refers back to *Ruth*. Since a pronoun can only be reflexive if it occurs in the same clause as the noun phrase it refers to, *herself* must no longer be in the lower clause at all. For these reasons we will assume that 6 represents the derivation of sentence 5.

Having derived sentences 1 and 5, we can tentatively formulate the infinitive transformation:

10 **Infinitive Transformation (T-Inf):** An embedded complement clause can become an infinitive phrase as follows:

a. The infinitive marker *to* is attached to the front of the verb phrase.
b. The verb retains the nonfinite form.
c. If the subject of the embedded clause is identical to a noun phrase in the main clause (or if it is the indefinite noun phrase *SME*), it is deleted.
d. If the subject of the embedded clause is not identical to a noun phrase in the main clause, it is removed from the embedded clause and placed before the clause as the object of the preposition *for*.

Exercises

Use the infinitive transformation to show the derivations of the following sentences:

1. Pearl attempted to swim around Manhattan.

2. To write a best-seller is the dream of the young novelist.

3. Sigmund tried to swindle Esther.

4. The farmers prayed for prices to rise.

5. For Elmo to apologize is a rare occurrence.

6. Pedro and Ann failed to amuse themselves.

Use *SME* to represent the indefinite subject in the deep structures of the following sentences:

7. To understand grammar is a lifelong satisfaction.

8. To neglect to try is to waste an opportunity.

Sentential-Complement Infinitives without "For"

The infinitive phrases that we have seen are derived from the same underlying structures as sentential-complement clauses. Sentences 1 and 3, we claimed, share a common deep structure. The infinitive sentences are derived from that deep structure by rule 10. But the rule as we have written it is not entirely adequate. If T-Inf were applied to the deep structures underlying the following sentences, what would be the resulting infinitive versions?

11
a. Josie believes *that the earth is flat*.

b. Casper expects *that Cosmo will disappear*.

If step 10d of T-Inf were applied as written, the results would be ungrammatical:

12
a. *Josie believes *for the earth to be flat*.

b. *Casper expects *for Cosmo to disappear*.

Instead, as every speaker of English is aware, the correct infinitive versions of 11a and 11b are these:

13
a. Josie believes *the earth to be flat*.

b. Casper expects *Cosmo to disappear*.

The deep-structure subjects of these embedded clauses are not preceded by *for*. If we collected a wide variety of sentences with infinitive clauses, we would find those with *for* following certain verbs (such as *pray, wish, hope,* and *ask*) and those without *for* following certain other verbs (such as *believe, expect, understand,* and *require*). We need to revise the infinitive transformation to allow for these latter cases.

Steps *a–c* of rule 10 need no changes. Step *d*, however, needs to be revised as follows:

14 *Revision of 10d:*

d. If the subject of the embedded clause is not identical to a noun phrase in the main clause, one of the following steps occurs:

1. Following main-clause verbs of the *PRAY* type (or forms of *BE*), the subject is removed from the embedded clause and placed before that clause as the object of the preposition *for*.

2. Following main clause verbs of the *BELIEVE* type, the embedded subject is placed before that clause as a simple noun phrase.

Sentence 13a, then, is derived as follows:

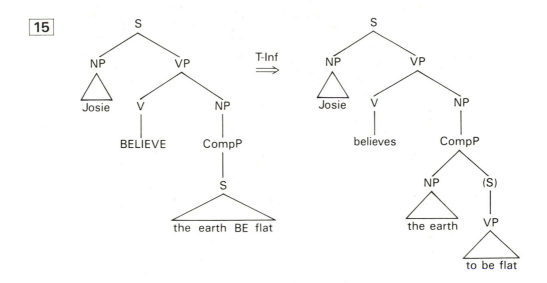

15

Notice that here again the noun phrase *the earth* is removed from the embedded S-clause and made in effect a part of the main S-clause. As evidence for this claim, consider how the passive transformation can apply to 13a. In its operation, *the earth* is indeed treated as a part of the main clause:

16 The earth is believed by Josie to be flat.

Remember that according to the passive transformational rule (as formulated on page 181), the noun phrase following the verb in the active version becomes the subject of the passive version. If *the earth* has been raised to be a part of the main clause—that is, if T-Inf has operated as in 14d2—then T-Pass can apply to produce the passive sentence 16, as shown in 17.

17

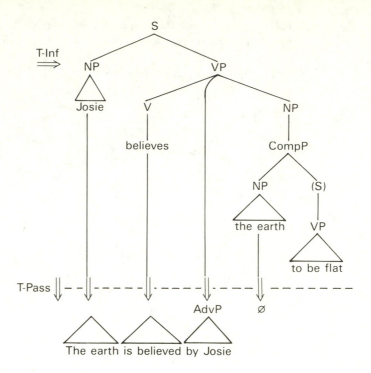

The most interesting and impressive examples of how T-Pass and T-Inf can operate together in a derivation are sentences such as in **18**, in which the same noun phrase can be moved several times, finally ending up in a very different position from where it began in its deep structure:

18 a. The song was thought by the critics to have been composed by a lunatic.

b. Jo is known by Ed to be dated by Al.

In each of these sentences, both the main-clause verb and the infinitive phrase are in the passive voice, so T-Pass has operated on two different parts of the deep structure. It is interesting to compare the deep and surface structures of these sentences. The sentential-complement sentences that correspond to the deep structures of 18a and 18b are as follows:

19 a. The critics thought that a lunatic composed the song.

b. Ed knows that Al dates Jo.

Here, in abbreviated form, is the derivation of sentence **18b**, *Jo is known by Ed to be dated by Al*. Notice the amazing path of the noun phrase *Jo*, shown in **20**, as it is moved with each successive transformation.

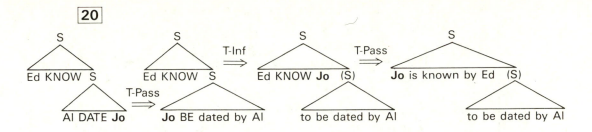

20

The original position of *Jo* in the deep structure is as the direct object of the lower clause. T-Pass then applies to that clause, moving *Jo* to the subject position. Then T-Inf raises it to an object position in the upper clause. And finally T-Pass applies to that clause, moving *Jo* once more, this time to the upper subject position. In short, the lower object (the last word in the deep structure) ends up as the upper subject (the first word in the surface structure). The workings of our grammar are strange and wondrous indeed.

Notice too that all three transformations in 20 are optional. If we had stopped the derivation at any stage, the result would have been a grammatical surface structure. The four possible sentences that can be derived from the one deep structure—all paraphrases of each other—are as follows:

21

a. Ed knows that Al dates Jo.   *—No transformations*

b. Ed knows that Jo is dated by Al.   *—T-Pass on lower clause*

c. Ed knows Jo to be dated by Al.   *—T-Pass followed by T-Inf*

d. Jo is known by Ed to be dated by Al.
   —T-Pass on lower clause, T-Inf and T-Pass on upper clause

Derivation 20 also illustrates the *cyclic operation of transformations*. That is, transformational rules operate one at a time and in a set order, applying first to the lowest clause in a tree. When they have finished with that clause, they move up the tree to the next lowest clause and the cycle begins again. The cycle concludes with the main clause. In a sentence such as 20 with two clauses, T-Pass operates first on the lower clause during the first cycle and again later on the upper clause during the second cycle.

Exercises

1. Show the derivations of the following sentences:
   a. Casper expects Cosmo to disappear.
   b. Sherlock suspected the evidence to be false.
   c. George understood cherries to grow on trees.

2. Show the derivations of these passive sentences:
   a. Water is known by physicians to cure thirst.
   b. Plants are supposed to lack language.
   c. The song was thought by the critics to have been composed by a lunatic.

3. It might be argued that the following sentences are derived not by step 14d2 of T-Inf, but by step 14d1 and an additional step that then deletes the preposition *for*:
   a. Portia wanted the jury to show mercy.
   b. The gorilla likes his trainer to tickle him.

   According to this hypothesis, exercise sentences 3a and 3b are different from the sentences such as in 13a and 13b. What arguments could you give to support or deny this claim?

4. It could also be argued that the following sentence is derived, not by step 14d2 of T-Inf, but by T-IO and step 10c of T-Inf:

   Portia asked the jury to show mercy.

   What arguments could you give to support or deny this claim?

Nominal-Complement Infinitives

Infinitive phrases, we have seen, are often associated with complement clauses. Sentence 1 with an infinitive phrase, for example, has the same deep structure as sentence 3 with a sentential-complement clause.

Nominal-complement clauses, in which the clause follows (or "complements") a noun phrase (see pages 66–67) can also be associated with infinitive phrases. The following is an example of a nominal-complement clause and a related *nominal-complement infinitive phrase*:

22
a. Clancy has a desire *that she prove herself*.

–*Nominal-complement clause*

b. Clancy has a desire *to prove herself*.

–*Infinitive phrase as nominal complement*

The same deep structure underlies both sentences. The derivation of sentence *b* appears in 23.

23

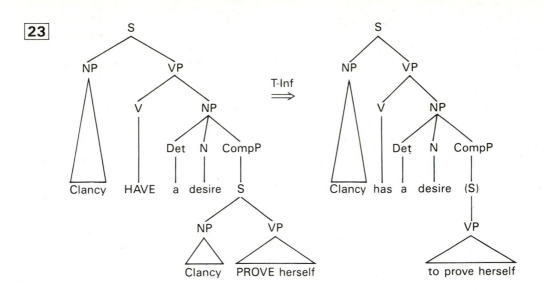

The infinitive transformation applies to the deep structure to produce the infinitive phrase. Had we not chosen to apply T-Inf, that same deep structure would have produced the complement-clause sentence 22a.

Exercises

Show the derivations of the following sentences with nominal-complement infinitives:

1. Christina has the gumption to persevere.
2. The junta issued a plea for the rebels to surrender.
3. A reluctance to handle slimy objects was the biologist's undoing.
4. The mechanic had the ability to fix the car.

Adverbial (Pseudo-Sentential-Complement) Infinitives

We have observed infinitives in three patterns so far, which are typified by these three examples (optional elements are in parentheses):

24
  a. Margo prayed for Les to lead the parade.
  b. Margot prayed (for herself) to lead the parade.
     —Sentential-complement infinitives with "for"
  c. Margot PRAY [Les/Margot LEAD the parade]   *—Deep structure*

25
a. Margot expected Les to lead the parade.

b. Margot expected (herself) to lead the parade.
—Sentential-complement infinitives without "for"

c. Margot EXPECT [Les/Margot LEAD the parade]   *—Deep structure*

26
a. Margot expressed a wish for Les to lead the parade.

b. Margot expressed a wish (for herself) to lead the parade.
—Nominal-complement infinitives

c. Margot EXPRESS a wish [Les/Margot LEAD the parade]
—Deep structure

Another infinitive pattern is the *adverbial* or the *pseudo-sentential-complement infinitive*. Consider how the following sentences differ from the previous patterns:

27
a. Margot selected Les to lead the parade.

b. Margot selected herself to lead the parade.
—Adverbial (pseudo-sentential-complement) infinitives

One evident difference between this and the three previous patterns is that in **27** the reflexive pronoun *herself* cannot be omitted from sentence *b*. This pattern also differs in another way from that of **25**, the sentential-complement pattern without "for," which it most closely resembles in its surface form. Whereas **25a** has a corresponding sentential-complement-clause sentence (*Margot expected that Les would lead the parade*), there is no such corresponding sentential-complement-clause sentence for **27a** (**Margot selected that Les would lead the parade*). In fact, whereas in **25a** it was the whole clause that Margot expected (*Les LEAD the parade*), it is just the single noun phrase *Les*—not the entire clause—whom Margot selected in **27a**. If we had to state the meaning of **27a** in clause form, it would be something like this: *Margot selected Les so that he (Les) might lead the parade*. That is, the infinitive phrase *to lead the parade* corresponds to an adverbial clause.

Les appears twice in this paraphrase, and we can assume it also appears twice in the deep structure. We can assume that *Les* and not an entire clause is the direct object of the deep structure. We can further assume that the clause *Les LEAD the parade* is an adverbial clause.

28
Margot SELECT Les/Margot [(so that) Les/Margot LEAD the parade]
—Deep structure for 27

The derivation of *Margot selected Les to lead the parade* is therefore as follows:

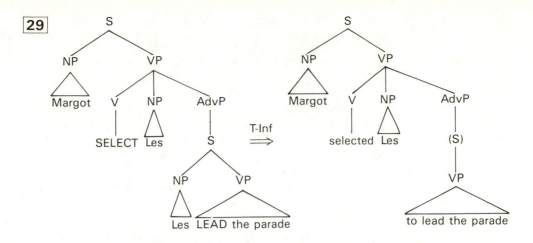

29

The second occurrence of *Les* is deleted by step 10c of the T-Inf rule. Because the surface structure of the adverbial pattern outwardly resembles the sentential-complement pattern (but is actually derived from an adverbial-clause deep structure), it can also be called the *pseudo-* (meaning "not authentic") *sentential-complement pattern*.

Exercises

1. Show the derivations of the following sentences with adverbial-clause infinitives:

    a. The mayor appointed Grendelson to run the police department.
    b. The faculty singled out Ankleford to receive special honors.

2. For each of these sentences decide whether it has the nominal-complement pattern or the adverbial pattern. How did you decide?

    a. The bricklayers elected Vidoni to lead their union.
    b. Everyone supposed Marina to be happy.
    c. The mob expects Francis to drive the getaway car.
    d. The mob tabbed Francis to drive the getaway car.

    The following sentence presents a more difficult decision:

    e. The mob forced Francis to drive the getaway car.

3. We saw in Chapter 10 that adverbial clauses can be moved to the beginning of sentences by T-AdvP. Can any of the infinitive phrases in exercise 2 also be moved to begin the sentence?

4. How might the infinitive phrases in the following sentences be derived?

    a. Joanie walked to school to save money.

    b. To impress girls, Wigglesworth grew a moustache.

Our analysis at this point may seem terribly complex to you, and I admit it is true: There is no denying that infinitives are devilishly tricky (and so, for lovers of syntax, devilishly intriguing). It is worthwhile here to pause and reflect on what we have been doing. Although, at first glance, infinitive phrases seem on the surface rather simple and similar, we are finding them to derive from rather complex and diverse deep structures. For each type of sentence involving an infinitive we have asked what that sentence means. For each type, we have tried to state the structure of that meaning (in other words, the sentence's deep structure). We have decided, for example, that when we hear sentences 25a and 25b, we understand the meaning represented by 25c. On the other hand, when we hear sentences 27a and 27b, we understand a meaning whose structure is represented by 28. Before continuing on, you may wish to review or reread the preceding parts of this chapter so that it is clear what we have discovered so far about infinitives.

Adjectival-Complement Infinitives

Just as nominal-complement clauses have associated infinitive phrases, so too do adjectival-complement clauses (in which a clause follows or complements an adjective—see pages 69–70). The following are examples of an adjectival-complement clause and a related infinitive phrase:

30 a. Stanley is happy *that he has a job*.   *–Adjectival-complement clause*

    b. Stanley is happy *to have a job*.

                                      –Infinitive phrase as adjectival complement

Here are additional examples of sentences with *adjectival-complement infinitives* and their deep structures:

31 a. Margot is eager for Les to lead the parade.

    b. Margot is eager (for herself) to lead the parade.

                                  –Adjectival-complement infinitives

    c. Margot BE eager [Les/Margot LEAD the parade]   *–Deep structure*

We can assume that 30b, *Stanley is happy to have a job*, has the derivation in 32.

32

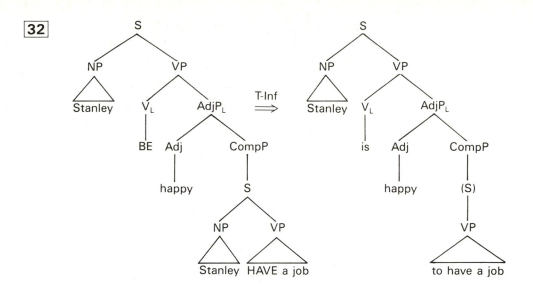

Exercises

Show the derivations of the following sentences with adjectival-complement infinitives:

1. Martina is eager to enter the tournament.
2. Dasher was unwilling for Rudolph to join the team.
3. The mechanic was able to fix the car.
4. Our competitors were unprepared to match our prices.

Pseudo-Adjectival-Complements and Extraposed Complements

Infinitives, we have seen, are formed in some unusual ways, and the surface structures of sentences with infinitives can sometimes be deceiving. The following sentences look at first as if they contain adjectival-complement infinitives, but a closer examination shows that they are very different from the sentences in the preceding section:

33 a. Our prices were impossible for our competitors to match.
    b. The lawn is fun to mow.

On the surface, the structural pattern of these sentences is identical to that of sentence 30b. Sentences 30b, 33a, and 33b all have this surface arrangement: NP + V$_L$ + Adj + CompP. Nevertheless, in other respects these two types behave very differently, leading us to conclude that they come from deep structures of a very different sort.

One difference is that, unlike the adjectival-complement sentence in 30b, the sentences in 33 could not have been produced by T-Inf from a deep structure such as that of 32. If they had been, such a deep structure would also produce the following adjectival-complement clauses:

34
a. *Our prices were impossible that our competitors will match.

b. *The lawn is fun that the lawn mows.

Sentences such as those in 33 must have a deep structure other than one that would produce these nonsensical sentences. We must look elsewhere to discover what that deep structure might be.

Sentences such as those in 33 are among the most extraordinary in the English language. Notice that the adjectives in these sentences do not directly describe the subject noun phrases. In 33a, for example, it is not the *prices* that were impossible but the *matching* of the prices. Likewise, 33b does not mean that the *lawn* is fun but that *mowing it* is fun. Since we expect deep structures to reflect the sense of what the sentence actually means, we may assume that the adjectives did not occupy their surface positions in the deep structures. Because the infinitives in 33a and 33b are not the adjectival complements that they first appear to be, we can call them ***pseudo-adjectival-complement infinitives***.

We can gain clues to the deep structures of the sentences in 33 by examining sentences that paraphrase them. The following, for example, are identical in meaning to 33a and 33b:

35
a. For our competitors to match our prices was impossible.

b. To mow the lawn is fun.

Moreover, there is still a third set of sentences with the same meaning:

36
a. It was impossible for our competitors to match our prices.

b. It is fun to mow the lawn.

Perhaps the *a* and *b* sentences of 33, 35, and 36 have identical deep structures. We already know what the deep structure of sentential-complement sentences such as in 35 look like. In 37, for example, is the deep structure of 35a.

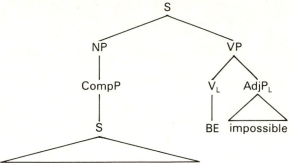

37

According to our hypothesis, not just **35a** but also **33a** and **36a** derive from this single deep structure.

If T-Inf is applied to deep structure **37**, surface sentence **35a**, with a sentential-complement infinitive, is produced:

38

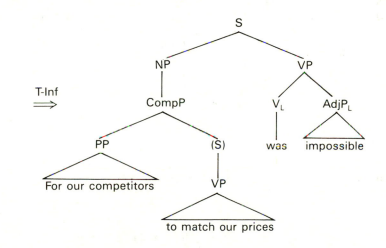

If sentences **33a** and **36a** are also derived from deep structure **37**, it must be by different means. As you can observe, several changes must occur for **37** to be transformed into **36a**. We will give these changes the name *extraposition*, which can be described in the following transformational rule:

39 **Extraposition Transformation (T-Extra):** When a sentential-complement clause acts as the subject of a sentence with a linking verb, the clause can be extraposed as follows:

  a. The embedded CompP is removed from the subject noun phrase and placed in a complement position at the end of the main clause.

b. If the subject noun phrase is now empty, the expletive *it* is inserted in its place.

If T-Extra and T-Inf are applied to 37, the result is as shown in 40:

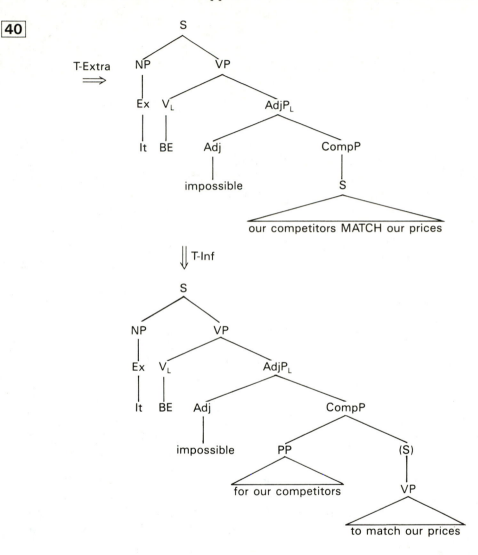

40

In **39b** *the word* it *that begins an extraposed sentence was called an* **expletive** *rather than a pronoun. Notice that* it *here acts differently from a conventional pronoun in that it does not "mean" or "stand for" a noun phrase. It has no meaning. It is simply a place-filler, a dummy marker used to fill the position of the vacated* *subject.* It *also has similar place-filling uses in sentences like* It is foggy *and* It is wintertime.

Finally, we can derive the pseudo-adjectival-complement sentence 33´a if we apply one further transformational rule to the final tree of 40:

41 **Raising from an Extraposed Infinitive Phrase (T-Raise/Ex):** After T-Extra and T-Inf have applied, the object of the extraposed phrase can be raised to take the place of the expletive *it* in the main clause.

Applied to the output of 40, this rule moves the noun phrase *our prices* out of the embedded infinitive phrase and makes it the subject of the main clause:

42

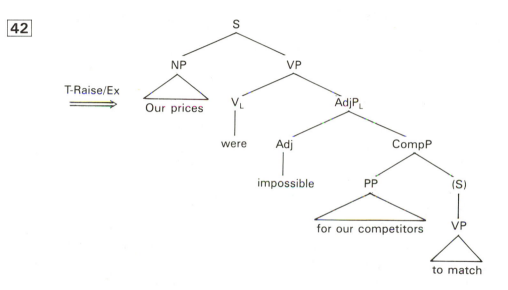

We can summarize what we have discovered in this section. Tree 37 is the deep structure for all of the following sentences:

43   a. For our competitors to match our prices was impossible.
                              –Sentential-complement infinitive

b. It was impossible for our competitors to match our prices.
                              –Extraposed infinitive

c. Our prices were impossible for our competitors to match.
                              –Pseudo-adjectival-complement infinitive

We can derive sentence 43a from deep structure 37 by applying a single transformational rule, T-Inf. If T-Extra and T-Inf are applied to 37, the result is the extraposed sentence 43b. And if T-Extra, T-Inf, and T-Raise/Ex are applied to 37, the result is the pseudo-adjectival-complement sentence 43c.

Exercises

1. Show the derivations of the following sentences with extraposed infinitives:

   a. It is unfortunate that Maria lost her voice.
   b. It is unusual for Eudora to smile.

2. Show the derivations of the following sentences with pseudo-adjectival-complement infinitives:

   a. The lawn is fun to mow.
   b. Virginia is pleasant to talk to.

3. Decide whether the infinitive phrases in each of the following sentences are true adjectival complements or are pseudo-adjectival-complements derived by T-Raise/Ex:

   a. These oysters are impossible to pry open.
   b. Maxwell is keen for the competition to begin.
   c. I will be sad to reach the end of this class.
   d. Infinitives are sometimes hard to comprehend.

4. In addition to pseudo-adjectival-complement infinitives, very similar phrases exist which might be called *pseudo-nominal-complement infinitives*, such as in these examples:

   a. The lawn was a pleasure to mow.
   b. The book was a struggle for me to finish.

   How do these examples differ from true nominal-complement infinitives? Using our discussion of pseudo-adjectival-complements as a model, determine how these sentences are derived. Show their derivations.

5. In addition to *it*, the word *there* can also act as an expletive. Speculate about the derivations of the following sentences with the expletive *there* and about the transformational rule needed to derive them:

   a. There are homemade cookies on the counter.

b. There is a storm coming.

c. There should have been more security guards on hand.

Note that *there* can be an expletive, as in the previous sentences, but it can also be a place adverb, as in *There (not here) is where he lives*. Identify each occurrence of *there* in the following sentences as either an expletive or an adverb:

d. There is a cow over there.

e. There is a celebration on the Fourth of July.

f. There go the fireworks.

Restrictive-Phrase Infinitives

All infinitive phrases are derived from embedded clauses, but not all are derived from complement or adverbial clauses. Consider the infinitives in these sentences:

44 a. Kathleen is the person for you to emulate.

b. The manager to replace Filsner is Drimble.

These *restrictive-phrase infinitives* are derived not from complement clauses but from relative clauses. Sentences 44a and 44b have the same deep structures as do sentences 45a and 45b:

45 a. Kathleen is the person whom you should emulate.

b. The manager who should replace Filsner is Drimble.

Both sets of sentences can be derived from the same deep structures. The infinitive phrases are derived by the application of T-Inf, shown in 46.

46 a.

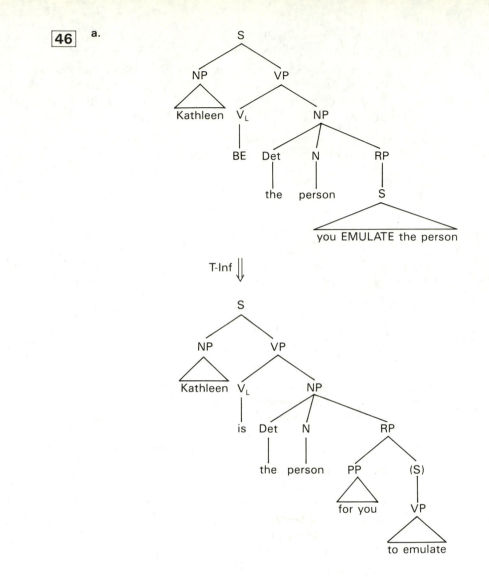

T-Inf

b.

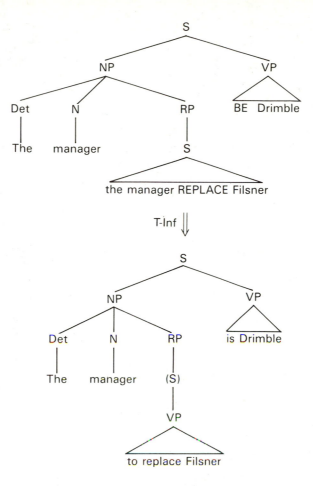

Had the relative-clause transformation (T-Rel), instead of T-Inf, been applied to the deep structures of 46, the sentences of 45 would have been produced.

Exercises

1. Draw trees to show the derivations of these sentences with restrictive-phrase infinitives:

   a. Chrissy bought a magazine for Tim to read.
   b. I have a report to write.
   c. A man to admire is Rupert.
   d. The data for us to memorize for the exam is in the textbook.
   e. Corinne is the very person to persuade the committee.

2. The following sentence is very similar to the pseudo-adjectival-complement sentence 33b, *The lawn is fun to mow*, and the pseudo-nominal-complement sentence in the previous exercise 4a, *The lawn was a pleasure to mow*:

   Our yard was a fun lawn to mow.

Here again it is not the lawn but the mowing of it which was fun. What do you think would be the deep structure of this sentence? What steps would its derivation entail? Are any new transformational rules necessary? For a hint about the derivation, see the pattern in 56 for *restrictive-phrase infinitives with raised adjectives*.

Summary of Principal Infinitive Patterns

We have examined infinitives in greater detail than any other construction— and we have found in them far greater variety and complexity. At this point you may wish to review and sum up the principal infinitive patterns that we have examined. Here are the derivations of sample sentences in each pattern:

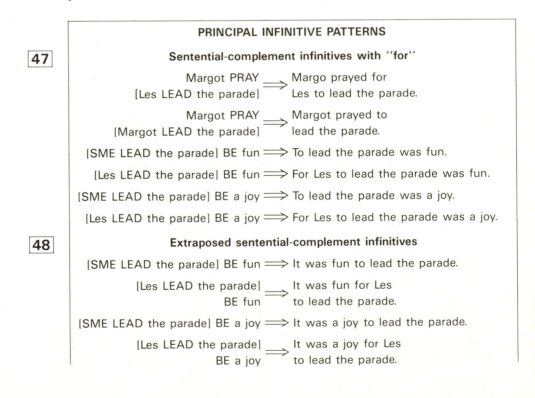

PRINCIPAL INFINITIVE PATTERNS

47

Sentential-complement infinitives with "for"

Margot PRAY ⟹ Margo prayed for
[Les LEAD the parade]   Les to lead the parade.

Margot PRAY ⟹ Margot prayed to
[Margot LEAD the parade]   lead the parade.

[SME LEAD the parade] BE fun ⟹ To lead the parade was fun.

[Les LEAD the parade] BE fun ⟹ For Les to lead the parade was fun.

[SME LEAD the parade] BE a joy ⟹ To lead the parade was a joy.

[Les LEAD the parade] BE a joy ⟹ For Les to lead the parade was a joy.

48

Extraposed sentential-complement infinitives

[SME LEAD the parade] BE fun ⟹ It was fun to lead the parade.

[Les LEAD the parade] ⟹ It was fun for Les
BE fun   to lead the parade.

[SME LEAD the parade] BE a joy ⟹ It was a joy to lead the parade.

[Les LEAD the parade] ⟹ It was a joy for Les
BE a joy   to lead the parade.

49

Pseudo-adjectival-complement infinitives

[SME LEAD the parade] BE fun $\Longrightarrow$ The parade was fun to lead.

[Les LEAD the parade] $\Longrightarrow$ The parade was fun for
BE fun   Les to lead.

50

Pseudo-nominal-complement infinitives

[SME LEAD the parade] $\Longrightarrow$ The parade was a joy
BE a joy   to lead.

[Les LEAD the parade] $\Longrightarrow$ The parade was a joy for
BE a joy   Les to lead.

51

Adjectival-complement infinitives

Margot BE eager $\Longrightarrow$ Margot was eager for
[Les LEAD the parade]   Les to lead the parade.

Margot BE eager $\Longrightarrow$ Margot was eager to
[Margot LEAD the parade]   lead the parade.

52

Nominal-complement infinitives

Margot EXPRESS a wish $\Longrightarrow$ Margot expressed a wish for
[Les LEAD the parade]   Les to lead the parade.

Margot EXPRESS a wish $\Longrightarrow$ Margot expressed a wish
[Margot LEAD the parade]   to lead the parade.

53

Sentential-complement infinitives without "for"

Margot EXPECT $\longrightarrow$ Margot expected Les
[Les LEAD the parade]   to lead the parade.

Margot EXPECT $\longrightarrow$ Margot expected to
[Margot LEAD the parade]   lead the parade.

54

Adverbial (pseudo-sentential-complement) infinitives

Margot SELECT Les $\Longrightarrow$ Margot selected Les
[Les LEAD the parade]   to lead the parade.

Margot SELECT Margot $\Longrightarrow$ Margot selected herself
[Margot LEAD the parade]   to lead the parade.

Margot PAY a bribe $\Longrightarrow$ Margot paid a bribe
[Les LEAD the parade   for Les to lead the parade.

Margot PAY a bribe $\Longrightarrow$ Margot paid a bribe
[Margot LEAD the parade]   to lead the parade.

55

Restrictive-phrase infinitives

Les BE the person $\Longrightarrow$ Les was the person
[the person LEAD the parade]   to lead the parade.

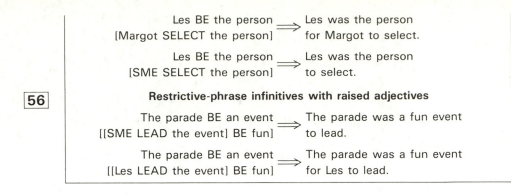

Les BE the person
[Margot SELECT the person] $\Longrightarrow$ Les was the person
for Margot to select.

Les BE the person
[SME SELECT the person] $\Longrightarrow$ Les was the person
to select.

56   **Restrictive-phrase infinitives with raised adjectives**

The parade BE an event
[[SME LEAD the event] BE fun] $\Longrightarrow$ The parade was a fun event
to lead.

The parade BE an event
[[Les LEAD the event] BE fun] $\Longrightarrow$ The parade was a fun event
for Les to lead.

Exercises

1. This exercise calls on you to use all the information you have learned in this chapter, as well as your insight and ingenuity. The sentences in each of the following five pairs are very similar in their surface structures, but they may be derived from very dissimilar deep structures. Describe their deep structures and account for their derivations.

   a. 1. Daphne is eager to please.
      2. Daphne is easy to please.

   b. 1. Carla expected Gladys to leave.
      2. Carla promised Gladys to leave.

   c. 1. The Warthogs are the team to win.
      2. The Warthogs are the team to watch.

   d. 1. We prayed for the song to end.
      2. We prayed for a song to dance to.

   e. 1. The denture salesman encountered a difficult person to sell to.
      2. The denture salesman encountered a toothless person to sell to.

2. Infinitives, as you have seen, are a complex and fascinating topic—perhaps even a bit too complex and fascinating for your tastes. You may be discouraged—or delighted—to learn that we have not exhausted the subject. If you care to, you can speculate on the derivation of this sentence:

   The students lacked the strength to continue.

A Further Note on Usage: Split Infinitives

In the eighteenth century, certain grammarians decided that then-current English usage was both slipshod and improper, and they took it upon themselves to prescribe rules of proper English usage. Many of their rules had no basis in the language as it was actually spoken or written. Some of their rules, however, have come over the years to be widely accepted, such as the condemnation of double negatives, as in *I don't have none*. Others have been deservedly forgotten, while still others continue to be proclaimed as prescriptive rules by people who consider themselves language purists, even though these rules are ignored in actual usage.

One such prohibition is that against "split infinitives." This rule of usage held that it is improper in an infinitive phrase to place an adverbial phrase between the infinitive marker *to* and the verb. The following sentences contain such "split" infinitives:

57 a. The company's goal is *to sharply increase* sales next year.

b. *To always speak* properly is Simon's goal.

Such sentences are widely spoken, however, and split infinitives are frequently used by literate and well-educated writers. Most modern stylists object to split infinitives only when they are awkward, as in this example:

58 She tried *to as quickly as possible finish* her dinner.

Judgments of awkwardness are, of course, subjective, and student writers are best advised to trust their own good sense and their ears for language, rather than relying on any general "rule" about split infinitives.

16

Gerunds, Participles, and Absolutes

Grammatical forms such as infinitives that are derived from verbs by a transformational rule are called *verbals*. In addition to infinitives, two other types of verbals are *gerunds* and *participles*.

Gerunds

A *gerund phrase*, like an infinitive phrase, can act as a noun phrase. We have already seen that noun phrases can take many different forms. As the italicized phrases in 1 demonstrate, a noun phrase can be (among other options) a simple noun, an entire clause, or an infinitive phrase:

1. a. *Exercise* is important.   **–Noun**
   b. *That one gets exercise* is important.   **–Complement clause**
   c. *To get exercise* is important.   **–Infinitive phrase**

We will now consider yet another option that speakers of English have for filling the NP category, namely, a gerund phrase, as in this example:

2. *Getting exercise* is important.   **–Gerund phrase**

A *gerund* consists of the basic form of the verb plus the *-ing* ending. In 2 , *getting* is a gerund; *getting exercise* is a gerund phrase. Like complement clauses and infinitive phrases, gerund phrases are derived from embedded sentences in the deep structure, as, for example, in 3.

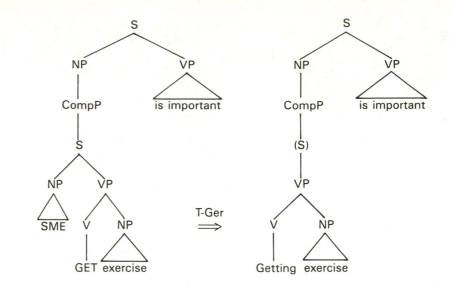

3

The deep structure in **3** is the same deep structure that underlies both the complement-clause sentence 1b and the infinitive-phrase sentence 1c. The different surface structures are produced, depending on which transformational rule is applied to this deep structure.

The deep structure of **3** has the indefinite subject *SME*, which does not appear in the surface structure. But like sentences with complement clauses and infinitive phrases, gerund phrases can also be derived from underlying sentences with actual subjects. Consider these examples:

4

a. *That Meg volunteers her time* is impressive.   *–Complement clause*

b. *For Meg to volunteer her time* is impressive.   *–Infinitive phrase*

c. *Meg's volunteering her time* is impressive.   *–Gerund phrase*

As we can see from **4c**, the subject of the embedded clause in the deep structure (*Meg*) becomes a possessive noun phrase (*Meg's*) in the surface structure of a sentence with a gerund phrase, as shown in **5**.

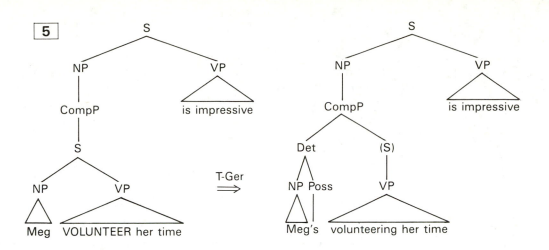

Having seen how the gerund transformation operates, we can now write the rule:

6 **Gerund Transformation (T-Ger):** A complement clause in deep structure can become a gerund phrase as follows:

a. the verb is changed to the *-ing* form;
b. if the clause has an unspecified subject (*SME*), it is deleted;
c. if the embedded clause has a specified subject, it takes on the posses-sive form and is moved to precede the clause.

Exercises

1. For each of the following deep structures, state both the sentence with a complement clause (some of these may be awkward) and the sentence with a gerund phrase that could be derived from it:

   a. [SME TAKE vitamins] prevents illnesses.
   b. [Viola RECEIVE a scholarship] relieved her parents.
   c. We resented [Lillian not INVITE us to her party].
   d. The worst crime is [SME MURDER a fellow human].

2. Draw trees to show the derivations of these sentences:

   a. Wearing a purple tuxedo attracts notice.
   b. Having a hippo for a pet causes problems.
   c. Buying a house requires getting approval for a mortgage.
   d. The legislation outlawed driving a car without wearing a seatbelt.
   e. Everett's bursting into the room disrupted the party.
   f. We admired Sonia's doing the right thing.

g. The landlord's increasing the rent led to the tenants' circulating a petition.

3. Our gerund transformational rule 6 states two possibilities for treating underlying subjects in the embedded clause: 6b and 6c. Actually there is a third case to be considered as well. For each of the following sentences, state the deep-structure sentence. In particular, consider what must be the subject of the embedded clause in the deep structure.

a. Fred enjoys owning a yacht.

–Consider: who is it who owns the yacht?

b. Losing her driver's license dismayed Cornelia.

c. Ramona made a fortune by selling encyclopedias.

d. Injuring themselves kept Bob and Sally from entering the marathon.

Now revise the gerund transformational rule 6 to account for sentences such as these. Notice the similarity between this provision and the conditions under which the personal-pronoun transformation T-Pro$_P$ can operate (see page 117).

Participles

Whereas gerunds are verbals that function like nouns, **participles** are verbals that function like adjectives. They are used to modify nouns. ***Participial phrases*** are italicized in the following examples:

7   a. The man *walking the dog* witnessed the burglary.

       b. The sonnets *written by the poet* describe his cat.

In 7a, *walking* is an **active participle** (often inaccurately called a *present participle*). It is used to modify the noun phrase *the man*. In 7b, *written* is a **passive participle** (often inaccurately called a *past participle*). It is used to modify the noun phrase *the sonnets*. In Chapter 11 (pages 146–147), we speculated whether an appositive phrase (as in *Darwin, a botanist*) is derived from a relative clause (*Darwin, who is a botanist*). If so, the appositive is derived by a transformational rule, which we named *relative-clause reduction* (abbreviated T-RelRed). Strong evidence in support of this hypothesis comes from the fact that the rule can also be used to derive active and passive participial phrases:

8   a. The man [the man **BE walking** the dog] witnessed the burglary.

              ⇓ T-RelRed

   The man **walking** the dog witnessed the burglary.

---

b. The sonnets [the poet **WRITE** the sonnets] describe his cat.

⇓ T-Pass

The sonnets [the sonnets **BE written** by the poet] describe his cat.

⇓ T-RelRed

The sonnets **written** by the poet describe his cat.

Participles can be formed from embedded sentences that contain a form of the verb *BE*. These include active sentences with progressive verbs such as *BE walking* in 8a, and passive sentences, such as *BE written* in 8b. Here is a revised formulation of T-RelRed, which accounts for the derivation of participles, as well as of appositives:

9 | **Relative-Clause Reduction (T-RelRed):** An appositive or participial phrase can be formed from an embedded relative clause under the following conditions:

a. the embedded clause must modify a noun phrase;
b. the subject of the embedded clause must be identical with the noun phrase being modified;
c. the first verb in the embedded clause must be a form of *BE*.

If these conditions are met, the embedded clause is changed into an appositive or participial phrase as follows:

d. the subject of the embedded clause and *BE* are deleted.

Note that condition *c* applies to *BE* whether it is an auxiliary or a linking verb. Note too that if conditions *b* and *c* are not met, as in the deep structure of 8b, T-Pass can apply to move the identical noun phrase *the sonnets* to the beginning of the embedded sentence and to supply the auxiliary verb *BE*.

The formation of participial phrases can be represented by tree diagrams, as shown in 10.

a.

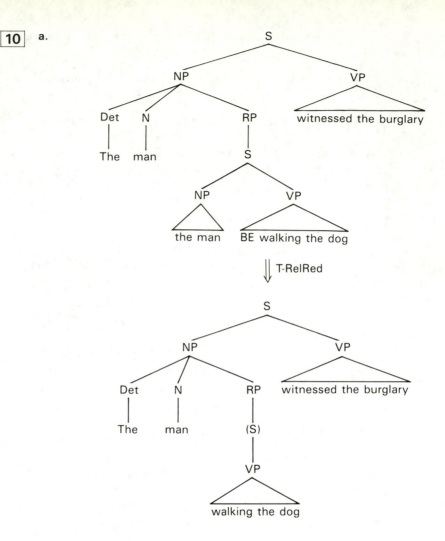

b.

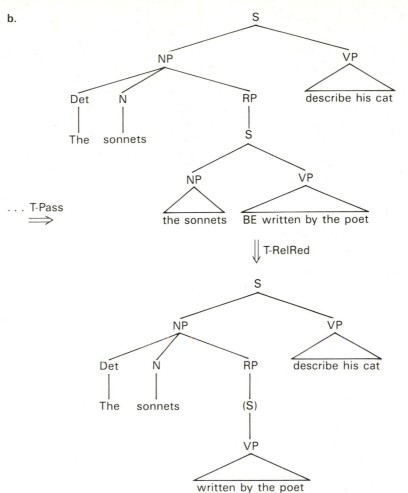

Adjectival phrases that follow the nouns they modify are similar to participial phrases:

<blockquote>

11 People *eager for glory* joined the crusade.

</blockquote>

The italicized adjectival phrase in 11 is also derived by T-RelRed from an embedded sentence:

<blockquote>

12 People [people **BE eager** for glory] joined the crusade.

⇓ T-RelRed

People **eager** for glory joined the crusade.

</blockquote>

For this reason, such phrases can be called ***participial adjectival phrases***.

Exercise

1. Underline the participial phrases in the following sentences and identify them as either active or passive:

    a. The box sitting on the desk contains chocolates.
    b. We met a man wearing pajamas in public.
    c. The records played by the station were oldies.
    d. The fish caught by the boys was a trout weighing three pounds.
    e. The weapon found near the body was a pistol made in Europe.

2. Show the derivations of the sentences in exercise 1.

3. State the deep structure for each of the following sentences with participial adjectival phrases:

    a. Eyes red from fatigue need rest.
    b. People sick with the flu should stay in bed.
    c. We drove on a road full of potholes and covered with leaves.

Restrictive and Nonrestrictive Participial Phrases

Notice that the underlying structures of 10a, 10b, and 12 could also be used to derive relative–clause sentences if T-Rel were applied instead of T-RelRed:

13

    a. The man *who was walking the dog* witnessed the burglary.

    b. The sonnets *that are written by the poet* describe his cat.

    c. People *who were eager for glory* joined the crusade.

All three of these sentences contain restrictive relative clauses, and so their participial counterparts 7a, 7b, and 11 could be called *restrictive participial phrases*. Nonrestrictive relative clauses also have their participial counterparts:

14

    a. Missy, *drawing sketches in her notebook*, passed the time quietly.

    b. Meg's husband, *consumed by jealousy*, spied on her at work.

    c. The children, *happy and carefree*, played in the treehouse.

The italicized phrases in 14 are *nonrestrictive participial phrases.*
   Nonrestrictive participles, like nonrestrictive relative clauses, provide additional information about the nouns they modify. Unlike a restrictive participial phrase, a nonrestrictive participial phrase, such as those in 14a–14c, is not essential to the meaning of the main sentence; if it is removed, the

---

sentence's essential meaning remains intact. The main clause of 14a, for example, retains its meaning if the nonrestrictive participial phrase is removed:

15 | Missy passed the time quietly.

In contrast, note how meaning would be affected if the italicized restrictive phrase were removed from this sentence:

16 | Only a lunatic would drink water *mixed with turpentine*.

Another difference is that nonrestrictive phrases, unlike restrictive phrases, are set off from the rest of the sentence by brief pauses in speech, which are represented by commas in writing. Note the difference in punctuation between the sentences of 7 and 14.

Participles in Other Positions

Moving Nonrestrictive Participles

A nonrestrictive participial phrase can be moved to the beginning of a sentence. For example, the participial phrases in 14 can be moved as follows:

17 | a. *Drawing sketches in her notebook*, Missy passed the time quietly.
b. *Consumed by jealousy*, Meg's husband spied on her at work.
c. *Happy and carefree*, the children played in the treehouse.

Nonrestrictive participles can also be moved to the end of sentences:

18 | a. Missy passed the time quietly, *drawing sketches in her notebook.*
b. Meg's husband spied on her at work, *consumed by jealousy.*
c. The children played in the treehouse, *happy and carefree.*

The rule that moves these phrases has already been introduced as T-NRP in an exercise on page 145. We can now formulate that rule:

19 | **Nonrestrictive-Phrase Movement (T-NRP):** If a nonrestrictive phrase that has been derived by T-RelRed modifies a noun phrase that begins the sentence, the nonrestrictive phrase may be moved to precede that noun phrase. It may also be moved to the end of the sentence.

Although participial phrases can sometimes be moved away from the noun phrases that they modify—as in 18—the resulting surface structures can cause confusion if the phrases are moved next to other noun phrases. In such cases, they are called *dangling participles*, as in these examples:

20   a. *Opening the door to the room*, the sight that I saw surprised me.

       b. Larry accosted Tony, *eager for a fight*.

       c. *Being forgetful about the time*, the steak burnt to a crisp.

The deep-structure subject of the participial phrase in 20a is *I*, not *the sight*. While not ungrammatical, sentences such as 20a and 20b are criticized by many stylists, particularly when they are ambiguous. You can decide whether it is clear in 20a who opened the door or in 20b who was eager to fight. Stylists are much more critical of dangling participles whose deep-structure subjects are entirely absent from the surface structure, as in 20c. Note that such sentences are formed in violation of provision 9b of the T-RelRed rule. A sentence such as 20c can easily be amended so that the participle does not dangle: *Being forgetful about the time, I let the steak burn to a crisp.*

Moving Restrictive Participles

Movement of restrictive participles is quite different. A restrictive participle (but not a complete participial phrase) can be moved to a position before the modified noun—that is, it can act as an adjective. Compare the participial phrases in 21 with the single participles in 22:

21   a. A baby *crying for its mother* needs attention.

       b. Schildkraut is an artist *neglected by everyone*.

       c. Hell hath no fury like a woman *scorned*.

22   a. A *crying* baby needs attention.

       b. Schildkraut is a *neglected* artist.

       c. A *scorned* man can also become furious.

A new transformational rule is needed to account for the movement of restrictive participles:

23   **Restrictive-Phrase Movement (T-RP):** If a restrictive phrase that has been derived by T-RelRed contains a single participle or adjective (but not a multi-word participial phrase), that participle or adjective may be moved into an adjectival position preceding the noun it modifies.

Exercises

1. Underline the participial phrases in the following sentences and describe them as restrictive or nonrestrictive. State the deep structure for each sentence.

    a. A warbling mockingbird distracted the poet.
    b. Wallace, miffed by a perceived snub, refused to perform.
    c. Giggling uncontrollably, the couple ran from the theater.
    d. Burton enjoys a steak cooked over an open campfire.

2. Which of the participles in exercise 1 were moved by either T-RP or T-NRP? Show the derivations of the four sentences.

Inflection of Participles

In addition to the simple active form of the participle (for example, *seeing*) and the simple passive form (*seen*), participles can also take other forms with auxiliary verbs. The following is a chart of the various indicative forms of the verb *SEE* and their corresponding participial forms:

24

INDICATIVE AND PARTICIPIAL VERB FORMS		
Active Voice		
	INDICATIVE FORMS	PARTICIPIAL FORMS
Simple (no auxiliary):	*see/saw*	*seeing*
Modal forms:	*can/could see*, etc.	no participle forms
Perfect:	*has/had seen*	*having seen*
Progressive:	*is/was seeing*	*seeing*
Perfect Progressive:	*has/had been seeing*	*having been seeing*
Passive Voice		
	INDICATIVE FORMS	PARTICIPIAL FORMS
Simple (no auxiliary):	*is/was seen*	*seen*
Modal forms:	*can/could be seen*, etc.	no participle forms
Perfect:	*has/had been seen*	*having been seen*
Progressive:	*is/was being seen*	*being seen*
Perfect Progressive:	*has/had been being seen*	*having been being seen*
	(rare)	(rare)

Note that no participial forms are possible with modals (*coulding see, *canning be seen, *coulding have been seen, etc.). The perfect progresive passive forms occur only rarely, if at all.

Exercises

1. Underline each participial phrase in the following sentences and state which form the participle takes. State also the corresponding deep-structure sentence.

   a. Having lost our map, we asked for directions.
   b. The tomatoes being sold today are not fresh.
   c. The fish caught by Ernest was a blue marlin.
   d. The shopper staring at the display was shocked at the prices written on the tags.
   e. Having been trying for years to join the club, Pangborn was overwhelmed by the letter accepting him as a member.
   f. The rebels, having been caught in a withering crossfire, raised a white flag.
   g. Seeing no cars coming, Ashley crossed the street.

2. Of the participial forms listed in chart 24, not all can occur in both restrictive and nonrestrictive participial phrases. For each of these forms, attempt to compose a sentence using it in a restrictive participial phrase and another using it in a nonrestrictive participial phrase. What limitations do you find on where some of these forms can be used?

3. The data from chart 24 indicates that our statement of the rule for forming participles in 9 is not adequate, because it cannot account for the derivation of all participial forms. For example, a participial phrase such as *having seen the show* cannot derive from a relative clause such as *who is having seen the show*, since no such verb form exists. It appears that, in order to form participles, a special participial supporting auxiliary (*BE + -ing*) is added at the beginning of verb phrases that do not already begin with *BE*. See which of the participial forms from chart 24 require this auxiliary in order to be formed from the corresponding indicative forms. Finally, revise rule 9 in order to reflect this change.

4. Like participles, gerunds too can occur in a number of active and passive forms. Which of the participial forms in 24 could also occur as gerunds? Is our gerund transformational rule, as stated in 6, adequate to account for them?

5. Some sentences with verbals are ambiguous. Can you see two readings of the following sentence?

   a. The FBI caught the terrorists threatening the embassy.

   One of these readings has the corresponding passive form *The terrorists threatening the embassy were caught*, whereas the passive form for the other is *The terrorists were caught threatening the embassy.* Can you speculate on the derivations of these two readings? You may also wish to consider the ambiguity of the following three sentences:

b. Visiting relatives can be boring.
c. Mickey watched the man climbing the ladder.
d. Dolly found the money missing from the till.

Absolutes

An *absolute construction* consists of a noun phrase and a modifying participial or appositive phrase. An absolute is separated from the rest of the sentence by a pause in speech and by a comma in writing. Absolutes are italicized in these examples:

25   a. *The buses being unreliable,* Werner drove his car to work.

b. They resorted to violence, *all attempts at peaceful settlement having failed.*

c. The rollercoaster roared down the tracks, *its passengers screaming with terror and delight.*

An absolute such as *the buses being unreliable* is not a part of the main clause, *Werner drove his car to work*. Like all absolutes, it is derived from an underlying sentence that is related to the main sentence by a subordinating conjunction such as *because*. The sentences of **25** are equivalent in meaning to the following sentences; both may be said to derive from the same deep structures:

26   a. *Because* the buses were unreliable, Werner drove his car to work.

b. They resorted to violence *after* all attempts at peaceful settlement had failed.

c. The rollercoaster roared down the tracks, *while* its passengers screamed with delight.

Adjectival participial phrases and appositive phrases are also possible in absolute constructions, as in 27a and 27b:

27   a. *Her hands blue from the cold*, Morgan fumbled with her mittens.

b. *His unexpected sortie a complete success*, the general pressed his advantage.

Exercises

1. For each of the following sentences, invent an appropriate absolute construction to take the place of the dots:

   a. . . ., the pirates boarded the captured vessel.
   b. The runner, . . ., crossed the finish line and collapsed.
   c. The motorcycle sped down the hill out of control, ...

2. You may wish to explore in greater detail the derivation of sentences with absolute constructions such as 25a–25c. Draw the deep structures for sentences 26a–26c (see the discussion of adverbial clauses in Chapter 10) and consider how the sentences of 25 can be derived from them. Formulate any revisions of existing transformational rules (or entirely new transformational rules) that are needed.

17 Abbreviating Sentences: Ellipsis and Pro-Forms

In several of the constructions we have examined, an element that is present in the deep structure is not spoken in the surface structure. For example, the command *Open the door* is understood to mean *HEARER OPEN the door*. The deep-structure subject *HEARER* is eliminated by T-Imp, the imperative transformation. In other sentences, the indefinite element *SME* is eliminated. For example, the surface sentence *Smoking is forbidden* derives from the deep structure *SME FORBID SME SMOKE*. The *SME*s are omitted when the transformational rules T-Ger and T-Pass are applied. The elimination of a deep-structure element from a surface sentence by a transformation is called *ellipsis*.

Ellipsis

Ellipsis can occur in other circumstances as well. When elements occur more than once in a sentence or in adjacent sentences, all but one occurrence of the identical elements can sometimes be omitted from the surface structure. In each of the following examples, a sentence with an ellipsis is followed by the same sentence in which the missing elements have been retained:

1. a. Travis votes Democratic; Olivia Republican.

   b. Travis votes Democratic; Olivia *votes* Republican.

2. a. If we get the breaks, we will win; if not, we will lose.

   b. If we get the breaks, we will win; if *we do* not *get the breaks*, we will lose.

3. a. First we noticed Pamela's gloves on a chair and then Christine's on the floor.

   b. First we noticed Pamela's gloves on a chair, and then *we noticed* Christine's *gloves* on the floor.

Ellipsis can also occur in conversation, where one speaker omits elements spoken by a previous speaker.

4 | a. "Who made this mess?" "Julie."

b. "Who made this mess?" "Julie *made this mess.*"

In examples 1–4, ellipsis occurs when an element appeared twice or more in the deep structure. Ellipsis can also occur when the missing element is obvious, even though it occurs only once in the deep structure, as in this example:

5 | a. I am expected for dinner at my parents'.

b. I am expected for dinner at my parents' *house.*

The concept *house* is understood by the hearer without its being spoken; the hearer has no difficulty reconstructing the deep structure.

The omission of obvious elements also occurs frequently in posted notices (*Smoking strictly forbidden on assembly line*) and in newspaper headlines (*UFO Sighted by Beauty Queen*).

We can state the principle behind these ellipses as a transformational rule:

6 | **Ellipsis Transformation (T-Ell):** When an element occurs twice or more in a deep structure (either in one sentence or in adjacent sentences), the latter occurrences of that element can be omitted in the surface structure. Similarly, when an element is obvious to the hearers, it can be omitted.

Of course, this rule has many restrictions and exceptions (for example, the second occurrence of the article *the* in a sentence cannot be omitted). Rule 6 is a general rather than a precise statement of the principle of ellipsis.

Exercises

1. Each of the following sentences has an ellipsis. Supply the missing element(s):

   a. Although sick of traveling, we packed our bags one more time.
   b. Mildred enjoys shrimp whether boiled or fried.
   c. The tourists have seen all the sights they could.
   d. Fergus became a lawyer and Vladimir a journalist.
   e. We admired Trollope's novels as well as Smollett's.
   f. I have my favorite pastimes; you yours.
   g. If ready, begin; if not, hold your fire.
   h. When in doubt, get advice.
   i. The children should have been preparing for bedtime, and the adults for a long night of work.
   j. Although we should have, we did not pay our taxes on time.
   k. Complaints About NBA Referees Growing Ugly
      –*Headline in the* Chicago Sun-Times, *23 May 1979*

l. "Has the concert started?" "Not yet."

m. See you after New Year's.

2. Consider the hypothesis that the italicized phrase in each of the following sentences is an infinitive phrase, even though the infinitive marker *to* is not present:

a. Chuck's storytelling made the time *fly by*.

b. Patrick heard the car *backfire*.

c. The family saw the building *burn*.

d. What Tricia did was *take a vacation*.

According to this hypothesis, the infinitive marker *to* has been deleted in the surface structure. Do you agree that these phrases are infinitive phrases? As data to consider in making your decision, answer these two questions: Can T-Pass apply to exercise sentences 2a–2c? If so, what are the passive versions?

Objective Complements

Sentences with *objective complements* are also assumed to be derived through ellipsis. In such sentences, a verb is followed either by two noun phrases or else by a noun phrase and an adjectival phrase. The final noun phrase or adjectival phrase in such sentences is called an objective complement. Objective complements are italicized in the following examples:

7

a. The Lodge considered Humphrey *a loyal Moose*.

b. Real men prefer their milk *ice cold*.

c. Ventriloquism made Gigi *the life of the party*.

d. The bureaucrats declared the directive *inoperative*.

In 7a and 7c the objective complements are noun phrases; in 7b and 7d they are adjectival phrases. How can we determine the appropriate analysis of such sentences?

One factor that we can consider is the existence of similar sentences in which those same noun phrases and adjectival phrases occur within infinitive phrases:

8

a. The Lodge considered Humphrey *to be a loyal Moose*.

b. Real men prefer their milk *to be ice cold*.

c. Ventriloquism made Gigi *(to) be the life of the party*.

d. The bureaucrats declared the directive *to be inoperative*.

Because we recognize the sentences of 7 and 8 to be paraphrases of each other, we can assume they are derived from the same deep structures. The derivation of 7a is therefore as shown in 9.

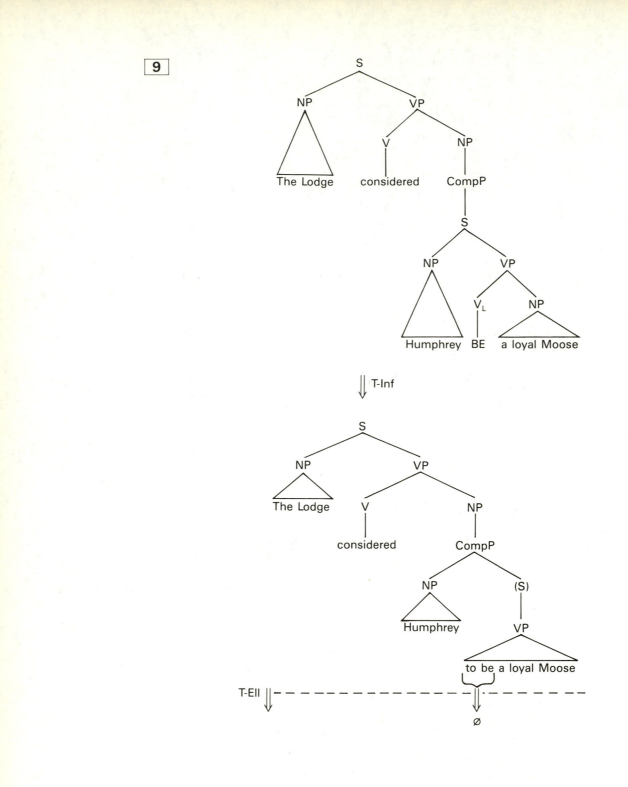

According to our analysis, an objective complement is derived from a sentential-complement infinitive phrase with a linking verb. The infinitive *to be* is then deleted by the ellipsis transformation.

Exercises

1. Show the derivations of sentences 7b–7d.

2. Show the derivations of these sentences:
   a. Binney found square dancing a bore.
   b. New circumstances rendered the plans useless.
   c. The examiners believed the proposal without merit.
   d. A cheerful attitude made the job easy.

3. The objective complements in exercises 1 and 2 are derived from sentential-complement infinitive phrases. The objective complements in the following sentences are derived from pseudo-sentential-complement infinitive phrases (see pages 199–201). Show their derivations.
   a. The Dickinsons named the baby Emily.
   b. The Lodge elected Humphrey the new Grand Moose.
   c. Winston scrubbed the floor clean.

Ellipsis in Comparisons

Another circumstance in which ellipsis can occur is in a comparison, where an element in one clause is compared to an element in another clause. Each of the following is a comparative sentence with an ellipsis (followed in each case by the same sentence with the elliptical elements restored). In sentences 10–12, the adjectives *nervous, older,* and *angry* are the bases for the comparisons:

10
   a. Yvette was less nervous than Lawrence.

   b. Yvette was less nervous than Lawrence *was nervous*.

11
   a. Lee is older than Duane.

   b. Lee is older than Duane *is old*.

12
   a. Adrian is as angry as I am.

   b. Adrian is as angry as I am *angry*.

In sentences 13 and 14, the adverbs *better* and *loudly* are the bases for the comparisons:

13 a. Nan likes fiction better than nonfiction.

   b. Nan likes fiction better than *Nan likes* nonfiction.

14 a. Jerry snores less loudly than Artie.

   b. Jerry snores less loudly than Artie *snores*.

T-Ell has applied to produce the ellipsis in each of these five sentences.

A Closer Examination of Comparison

Since we have not yet studied constructions involving comparison, a closer examination of them is in order.

Comparison of adjectives and adverbs is expressed through sequences such as *more . . . than, less . . . than, as . . . as,* and *(not) so . . . as.* The introductory elements *more, less, as,* and *so* can be classified as degree modifiers (you may wish to review our discussion of degree modifiers on pages 82–84). The elements *than* and *as* that follow the adjective or adverb can be classified as a type of subordinating conjunction. More specifically, we will call them **comparative conjunctions** (abbreviated Cj_{Cp}).

When a compared adjective or adverb is a short word—usually one or two syllables—the degree modifier *more* can be replaced by the ending *-er.* Thus in the sentences of 11 and 13 we have the forms *older* and *better* instead of *more old* and *more well.* In fact, the former expressions can be said to derive from the latter ones by a transformation:

15

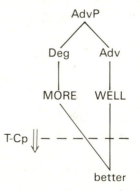

We can call the transformation that derives *better* from *MORE WELL* the **Comparative-Inflection Transformation** or **T-Cp**.

*Adjectives and adverbs are traditionally classified as having three forms: the **positive** or uncompared form (pretty, beautiful, well); the **comparative** form (prettier, more beautiful, better); and the **superlative** form (prettiest, most beautiful, best). T-Cp is also used to derive superlative forms such as* prettiest *and* best *from* MOST PRETTY *and* MOST WELL.

According to our analysis, sentence **10a**, *Yvette was less nervous than Lawrence*, is derived as follows:

16

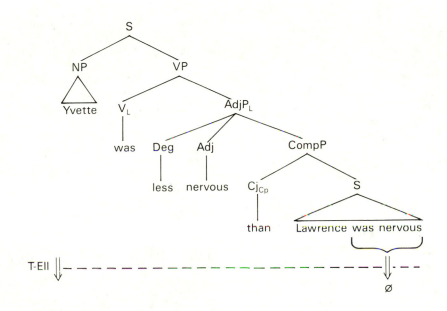

The derivations of **12a**, *Adrian is as angry as I am*, and of **13a**, *Nan likes fiction better than nonfiction*, are shown in 17 and 18.

17

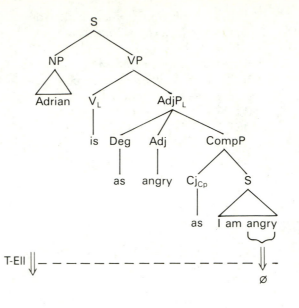

18

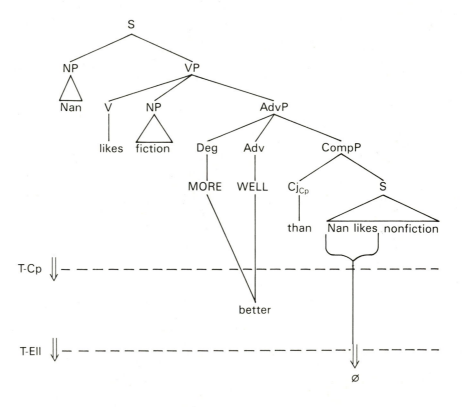

Derivation 18 makes the claim that adverbial phrases, as well as adjectival phrases, can take complements. This is in fact the case, as sentences 19 and 20 attest:

19 The jogger is so fanatical that she even runs during blizzards.

–Adjectival-complement clause

20 The jogger trains so fanatically that she even runs during blizzards.

–Adverbial-complement clause

Our transformational rules for adjectives and adverbs can be modified to account for comparatives and for *adverbial-complement clauses*:

21 $\text{AdjP}_\text{L} \rightarrow (\text{Deg}) \quad \text{Adj} \quad (\text{CompP})$

$\text{AdvP} \rightarrow (\text{Deg}) \quad \text{Adv} \quad (\text{CompP})$

$\text{CompP} \rightarrow \left\{ \begin{matrix} \text{Cj}_{\text{Cl}} \\ \text{Cj}_{\text{Cp}} \end{matrix} \right\} \text{S}$

Exercises

1. Show the derivations of the following comparative sentences:
    a. Gretel is smarter than Hansel.
    b. Raymond plays the saxophone more expertly than Gene.
    c. Raymond plays the saxophone more expertly than the tuba.
    d. You are as pretty as a picture.
    e. More than ever Abraham likes peace and quiet.
    f. Spenser will try harder than Marlowe will.

2. In the surface structure of exercise 1f, the auxiliary *will* was retained in the comparative clause, even though T-Ell deleted the rest of the verb phrase. Notice that when a comparative clause lacks an auxiliary, the supporting auxiliary *DO* can be supplied:

    Spenser tries harder than Marlowe does.

    Revise the DO-Support transformation (T-Supp) on page 164 to account for sentences such as this one.

3. An adjectival phrase that contains a comparative clause, such as *less nervous than Lawrence* in 10a, occurs following a linking verb. When a comparative adjectival phrase precedes a noun, that noun may also be followed by a comparative clause, as in this example:

Yvette was a less nervous person than Lawrence.

Moreover, in addition to acting as degree modifiers before adjectives and adverbs, *more* and *less* can also act as quantifiers before nouns (*more people, less room*). A noun preceded by these quantifiers can be followed by a comparative clause, as in this example:

Lawrence experienced more anxiety than Yvette.

How might our grammar account for such sentences?

4. Can we compare prepositional phrases that act as adjectival or adverbial phrases? Consider such prepositional phrases as *in love, on time, in tune*, and *like a professional*, as well as such prepositional phrases as *with enthusiasm* and *in a good mood*. Can adverbial clauses also be compared? Consider the following sentence:

He made a donation more because he felt guilty than because he felt generous.

Revise the rules of 21 to account for this data.

5. In addition to the determiner (or "attributive") possessive pronouns (*my, your, her,* and so on) which can replace possessive noun-phrase modifiers (*Mary's old car* $\Longrightarrow$ *her old car*), there also exist **nominal** (or "substantive") **possessive pronouns** (*mine, yours, hers,* and so on) which can replace not just the possessive modifiers but the entire noun phrases (*Mary's old car* $\Longrightarrow$ *hers*). How might our grammar account for a sentence such as the following with a nominal possessive pronoun?

Mary's car has less rust on its body than mine has.

Pro-Forms

Pronominal Determiners

In the preceding exercise 5, we observed that for each possessive pronoun that acts as a determiner (such as *my, our,* and *their*), there also exists a corresponding possessive pronoun that acts as a noun phrase (*mine, ours, theirs*). Other types of determiners also have corresponding forms that act as noun phrases and so can be called pronouns (the "pro" in *pronoun* is the Latin word meaning "for"; pronouns stand for nouns). These determiners include demonstratives (*this, that, these, those*), quantifiers (*many, some, no, every*), and possessive noun phrases (*Anne's, the king's*). Here are examples of corresponding pronominal forms:

22	a. I like *this*.
	b. *That* surprised me.
	c. *These* outperform *those*. **–Demonstratives as pronouns**

23	a. I want *some*.
	b. I don't need *any*.
	c. *None* look interesting.
	d. *Everyone* came. **–Quantifiers as pronouns**

24	The yacht is *Nelson's*. **–Possessive NP as pronoun**

You may wish to consider whether these examples are true pronouns—that is, whether they *replace* deep-structure noun phrases—or whether they are really examples of ellipsis—that is, whether T-Ell eliminated all constituents of deep-structure noun phrases except for the determiners. Under either hypothesis, the concepts (or deep structures) represented by sentences 22a, 23a, and 24 might be the following:

25	a. I like THIS WORK.
	b. I want SOME CORNFLAKES.
	c. The yacht is NELSON'S YACHT.

The question we are considering is whether in sentence 22a, *I like this*, the word *this* is a pronoun that replaces (by T-Pro) the concept *THIS WORK* or whether it is a determiner that is left behind after *WORK* has been eliminated (by T-Ell).

One factor to consider in choosing between hypotheses is the fact that the pronominal words are not always identical with their determiner equivalents. The determiners *my* and *your*, for example, are different from the corresponding pronouns *mine* and *yours*, and the quantifiers *no* and *every* differ from their corresponding pronoun forms *none/no-one/nobody/nothing* and *everyone/everybody/everything*.

Exercises

1. What other factors, including your intuitions, can help you choose between these two hypotheses? Do you prefer one of these hypotheses over the other? Do you have another hypothesis of your own?

2. Of all the determiners discussed in Chapter 6, we have discussed pronominal equivalents for all types except for the articles (*a*, *an*, and *the*). Noun

phrases with definite articles can be replaced by personal pronouns:

I met *the actress*. $\implies$ I met *her*.

I ate *the apple*. $\implies$ I ate *it*.

I found *the keys*. $\implies$ I found *them*.

What pronoun(s), if any, can replace noun phrases that are preceded by indefinite articles?

a. I wanted *a sports car*. $\implies$ I wanted _____.

b. He admired women from Minnesota, and he wanted to meet *some women from Minnesota*. $\implies$

c. She disliked men from Rhode Island, and she didn't want to meet *a man from Rhode Island*. $\implies$

Other Pro-Forms

We use pronouns as handy substitutes for longer noun phrases. In addition, other convenient substitutes (or *pro-forms*) are used to take the place of other types of phrases and concepts. Consider how the pro-form *so* is used in these examples. In each case, what element(s) does *so* replace?

26
a. I doubt Bartleby will be our new boss, but, if *so*, we will make the most of it.

b. She will believe that goblins exist if you say *so*.

c. She will go to college if you say *so*.

d. He wasn't fat before, but he has become *so* now.

e. She acted cheerfully then but less *so* now.

f. Charlotte stormed out. *So* ended the conversation.

g. Phillip picked up the money before Rose could *do so*.

h. Sean played James Bond in the movies, and Roger *did so* too.

In sentences 26a–26c, *so* substitutes for an entire clause. The deep structures of those sentences are approximately as follows:

27
a. I doubt Bartleby will be our new boss, but, if *Bartleby will be our new boss*, we will make the most of it.

b. She will believe that goblins exist if you say *that goblins exist*.

c. She will go to college if you say *that she should go to college*.

In examples 26d and 26e, *so* takes the place of an adjectival phrase and an adverbial phrase respectively:

28 a. He wasn't fat before, but he has become *fat* now.

b. She acted cheerfully then but less *cheerfully* now.

The pro-form *so* does not always take the place of a clearly specified phrase, however. In 26f, for example, *so* replaces an understood but unspecified concept—an adverbial phrase that may be represented as IN-THE-AFOREMENTIONED-MANNER:

29 Charlotte stormed out. The conversation ended *IN-THE-AFOREMENTIONED-MANNER*.

A separate transformation allows the word order to be reversed in the second sentence of 26f: So ended the conversation. *This transformation allows us to switch elements preceding and following a verb (except when a direct object follows the verb— can you see why?). Other examples of such reversals include* Up popped the toast; Cold were the nights we spent in Maine; Silently advanced the stalking adversary; A jolly old soul was he; *and* To the victor belong the spoils. *This transformation is a vestige from the days when English depended less heavily on word order to convey case information than it now does. Like other vestigial forms, it is now mostly used in "poetic" expressions.*

In 26g and 26h, *so* is used with the supporting auxiliary verb *DO* as a substitute for a verb phrase:

30 a. Phillip picked up the money before Ross could *pick up the money*.

b. Sean played James Bond in the movies, and Roger *played James Bond in the movies* too.

In addition to the various pronouns and the pro-form *so*, two other words, *then* and *there*, can also be regarded as pro-forms—namely **pro-adverbs**:

31 a. She will leave on Saturday, and I will leave *then* too.

b. He flew to Bombay, and I will fly *there* too.

Although we have not considered all possible pro-forms, we can summarize our findings about the ones we have examined:

32 **Pro-Form Transformation (T-Pro-Form):** Certain phrases whose meaning is understood by the hearer may be replaced by a pro-form: A phrase following a linking verb or an entire clause may be replaced by *so*. Other verb phrases may be replaced by *do so*. Adverbial phrases may be replaced by *so* when they describe manner, by *then* when they describe time, and by *there* when they describe place.

Exercises

1. The following sentences contain pro-forms. For each, state the phrase or concept which that pro-form replaces:
   a. They predict that spring will soon arrive, and I certainly hope so.
   b. I had heard that Korean food was spicy, and it is indeed so.
   c. "The check is in the mail." "So you say, but you've said so many times before."
   d. He was expected to play the trumpet like an angel, but I did not find that he played so.
   e. They told me to show no emotion, but I was unable to do so.
   f. I liked New Orleans when I was there in the summer of 1985, although it was very rainy then.

   In the following sentence, speculate on the derivation of *such*:

   g. I do not think that Winnie gave in, and, if such were the case, I would be surprised.

2. Words such as *however, therefore,* and *for example* are sometimes regarded as conjunctions, since they are used to join sentences. However, they may also be regarded as pro-forms—perhaps as **pro-adverbs**, like *then* and *there*. Speculate, therefore, on how such words (for example, when they occur within this very paragraph) are derived. What might be the concepts, or deep structures, that they represent?

3. In the following sentences, *each other* and *one another* are **reciprocal pronouns**:
   a. Benedick and Beatrice love each other.
   b. The brothers assist one another with their chores.
   c. The cousins borrowed each other's class notes.

   What function do reciprocal pronouns serve? How do they differ in meaning from reflexive pronouns?

Retrospective

In the course of these seventeen chapters, we have examined a variety of English constructions. It is time to bring together our discoveries in a final update of our model. Here are the latest versions of all the phrase-structure rules that we have formulated. The transformational rules in our model are listed on the inside back cover.

FINAL UPDATE OF OUR MODEL OF ENGLISH GRAMMAR

PS RULES

$$S \rightarrow NP \quad VP$$

$$NP \rightarrow \left\{ \begin{array}{l} (Det) \quad (AdjP)^+ \quad N \quad (PP) \quad (RP) \quad (CompP) \\ CompP \end{array} \right\}$$

$$VP \rightarrow Aux \left\{ \begin{array}{l} \left\{ \begin{array}{l} V_T \quad NP \\ V_I \end{array} \right\} \\ V_L \left\{ \begin{array}{l} NP \\ AdjP_L \\ AdvP_L \end{array} \right\} \end{array} \right\}$$

$$Det \rightarrow \left\{ \begin{array}{l} Art \\ Dem \\ Quant \\ NP \quad Poss \end{array} \right\}$$

$$AdjP \rightarrow \left\{ \begin{array}{l} (Deg) \quad Adj \\ (AdjP)^+ \quad N \end{array} \right\} \quad \text{—See note i following}$$

$$AdjP_L \rightarrow (Deg) \quad Adj \quad (CompP)$$

$$N \rightarrow \left\{ \begin{array}{l} N_C \\ N_P \end{array} \right\}$$

$$PP \rightarrow Prep \quad NP$$

$$XP \rightarrow XP \quad (Cj_C \quad XP)^+ \quad \text{—See note ii following}$$

$$XP \rightarrow XP \quad NRP$$

$$RP \rightarrow S$$

$$NRP \rightarrow S$$

$$CompP \rightarrow \left\{ \begin{array}{l} Cj_{Cl} \\ Cj_{Cp} \end{array} \right\} \quad S$$

$$(V_{T \text{ or } I} \rightarrow V \quad Prt)$$

$$Aux \rightarrow (Neg) \quad Mood \quad Tense \left\{ \begin{array}{l} (M) \quad (Perf) \quad (Prog) \\ Emph \end{array} \right\}$$

$$Mood \rightarrow \left\{ \begin{array}{l} Dec \\ Q \\ Imp \\ Subj \end{array} \right\}$$

$$Tense \rightarrow \left\{ \begin{array}{l} Pres \\ Past \end{array} \right\}$$

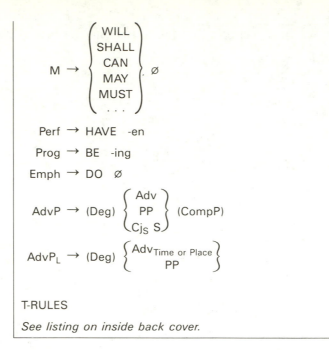

$$M \rightarrow \left\{ \begin{array}{c} \text{WILL} \\ \text{SHALL} \\ \text{CAN} \\ \text{MAY} \\ \text{MUST} \\ \ldots \end{array} \right\} \cdot \emptyset$$

$$\text{Perf} \rightarrow \text{HAVE} \quad \text{-en}$$

$$\text{Prog} \rightarrow \text{BE} \quad \text{-ing}$$

$$\text{Emph} \rightarrow \text{DO} \quad \emptyset$$

$$\text{AdvP} \rightarrow (\text{Deg}) \left\{ \begin{array}{c} \text{Adv} \\ \text{PP} \\ \text{Cj}_\text{s} \text{ S} \end{array} \right\} (\text{CompP})$$

$$\text{AdvP}_\text{L} \rightarrow (\text{Deg}) \left\{ \begin{array}{c} \text{Adv}_{\text{Time or Place}} \\ \text{PP} \end{array} \right\}$$

T-RULES

See listing on inside back cover.

Notes on the rules in 33:

i. In our discussion of adjective phrases in Chapter 6, we noted that noun phrases may modify other nouns (for example, wild horse *modifies* trainer *in the phrase* the wild horse trainer*). The formulation here,* AdjP → (AdjP) + N, *reflects the fact that such modifying noun phrases cannot include determiners, relative clauses, and the like.*

ii. This formulation allows multiple conjoined phrases, such as Anne and Bill and Cathy and . . . . *The ellipsis transformation may then delete all but the last conjunction.*

This model of grammar, which we have constructed through trial and error, is now capable of generating an enormous range of grammatical English sentences. Still, it is by no means a perfect model. You have undoubtedly encountered other constructions and variations of construction which we have not taken into account. The English language, as you are now fully aware, is an instrument of such remarkable complexity that our study in this book can only be called introductory.

But the incompleteness of our investigation need not dismay us. You have learned much about the structure of English, and—more important—you are prepared to explore the language further and to construct hypotheses to account for almost any new data you encounter. The English language and the human mental processes that allow us to create it are so intriguing that we can regard the unexplored territories before us as holding promise of on-going adventure.

There is still much to learn. Our focus in this book has been deliberately narrow. We have looked at sentences, but we have not considered how sentences derive from larger units of discourse. We have considered how we create language structures, but we have paid scant attention to how meaning is transformed in our minds into those structures. Our analysis of the language has of necessity ignored many of the complexities of advanced syntactic analysis. If in this course you have been captivated by the fascination of the subject, you should pursue it in further study. Your present understanding of the English language and of the techniques for investigating it have prepared you well for continuing inquiry.

In the final chapter, we will consider some practical applications for what you have learned. The discussion about teaching grammar has applications for future teachers and future parents as well.

Exercises

Test Grammar 33 by seeing if it can generate any English sentence that you can suggest. As a procedure for testing the grammar, you may wish to open a book or magazine at random, place your finger anywhere on the page, and see if the grammar is adequate to generate the sentence you encounter. Repeat the procedure several times. If you find gaps or problems with our grammar, test your own skill as a grammarian by seeing if you can adapt our grammar to account for the new data.

18 Grammar in the Schools

Few topics in education have been the subject of as much controversy over the past quarter-century as the teaching of grammar. Although grammar was once a central and unquestioned part of the curriculum (the elementary grades are still known as "grammar school"), its role is now very much debated. Past assumptions about the effectiveness of grammar teaching in the development of speaking, writing, and thinking skills have been called into question. Moreover, the introduction of modern scientific approaches to language study (most notably, transformational grammar) have challenged the validity of the grammar systems traditionally taught in the schools, while at the same time the complexity of those modern systems has raised questions about their own applicability and teachability in elementary and secondary classrooms. More than ever before, teachers and parents are uncertain and confused about how—and even whether—grammar should be taught.

A Brief History of Grammar Instruction

Although we think of instruction in English grammar as a traditional part of education, it is in fact a relatively recent phenomenon, and it has occupied a central place within the curriculum for only about the last hundred years. The changing role of grammar is in large part due to changing attitudes toward the language itself.

In the middle ages and in succeeding centuries, English and other vernacular languages (the national languages spoken in everyday life) were held in lower regard than the classical languages of Latin, Greek, and Hebrew. The modern notion of "progress" was an attitude quite alien to the time. Rather than progressing, knowledge and culture were thought to have declined from the days of classical antiquity. It was believed that the highest pinnacle of science, literature, and the arts had been achieved in that earlier age, and consequently the focus of education was on classical, not contemporary, studies. Latin retained its high status in Europe as the language of religion, law, and scholarship.

In English schools, the central subjects within the curriculum were Latin and Latin literature. From the earliest grades, students studied Latin grammar intensively, while English grammar was not studied simply because it was not thought worthy of study. Until very recent centuries, it was even questioned whether English had a grammar. (If that seems preposterous, remember that the same false attitude is widely held today about black English and other dialects.)

Over the past few centuries, however, the status of English gradually rose, and a grammatical model of our language was developed. Because of the pervasiveness of Latin studies, however, the model for English was contrived to resemble the Latin model as closely as possible. This unscientific, Latin-based model became the basis for school instruction, and its influence is still felt today. For generations, school children were taught many inexact notions: English, for example, was said to have eight parts of speech and a classification of verb tenses and noun cases akin to those of Latin. None of these notions has a basis in the actual structure of English.

The growth of the British Empire and the gaining of independence by the American colonies led to increased national pride within both the British Isles and the United States. One consequence was an increasing pride in the language. In America, the stature of English—and consequently of English studies in the schools—was unquestioned, and from the end of the last century the study of grammar occupied the central place in the language-arts curriculum. The concept of "grammar" was different from our use of that term in this book, encompassing Latin-based descriptions of syntax, prescriptive rather than descriptive rules based on logic (for example, "double negatives are ungrammatical because two negatives make a positive"), and rules of style ("awkward and unnecessary repetition of words and sounds should be avoided") and of punctuation ("the semicolon is used to separate items in a series when one of those items contains a comma within it"). The latter two topics, stylistic conventions and punctuation, are usually referred to as the study of *usage*, which is different from syntax, the study of how language is structured (the topic of this book). As practiced in many classrooms, language study was quite narrow, going little beyond "skill and drill" excercises.

In the twentieth century, while "traditional" grammar continued to hold sway in the schools, linguists were developing more scientific approaches that attempted to describe the actual structure of English, not the structure it might have if it were more like Latin or if it conformed to the wishes of the describers. ***Structural linguistics***, the dominant school of descriptive linguistics in the middle decades of this century, held that the syntax of a sentence should be studied without regard to the sentence's meaning. Confusing the two, it was claimed, resulted in imprecise definitions and analyses. Instead, as its name implies, this school concentrated on purely structural analysis. Our attempts in the early chapters of this book to define nouns and verbs based on their ability to fill certain slots in sentences shows the influence of structural grammar.

Since the late 1950s, when it was developed by Noam Chomsky, *transformational grammar* has replaced structuralism as the principal school of modern linguistic thought. Transformational syntax is interested in producing a model not just of sentences as they are actually produced (which transformationalists call *surface structures*) but also of the way speakers produce them. An important claim of transformational grammar is that sentences have a history: Surface sentences are the products of changes (or *transformations*) from more abstract underlying forms (or *deep structures*). Because deep structures are related to the concepts or ideas being communicated by sentences, transformational grammar is also more interested in meaning than is structural grammar.

Structural and transformational grammar have had an impact on grammar teaching in the schools. It is now widely recognized, for example, that English and all other languages constantly change and that correctness is determined not by logical or traditional rules but by the actual practice of those who speak and write the language. What is correct in formal written English is determined by the usage of literate writers. If they routinely begin sentences with conjunctions and end them with prepositions (as indeed they do), then such practices are part of standard English.

Not every attempt to introduce scientific concepts into the curriculum, however, has been successful. Part of the reason is the complexity of modern systems, which can make them inappropriate as teaching models, at least without modification. (As complex as you may have found the analyses in this book, they are in fact far simpler than they could be. In the interest of clarity, I made every effort to reduce complexity, but a glance at a recent issue of any linguistics journal will show you how intricate and abstract advanced syntactic analysis can be.)

Another cause of difficulty with introducing scientific grammar study into the schools has been the attempt to put it to uses for which it was never intended. Transformational grammar attempts to provide accurate descriptions of our subconscious knowledge about language. It assumes that conscious knowledge about language is quite separate from the subconscious knowledge that enables us to produce and understand language. Grammar instruction in the schools, however, is usually based on a quite opposite theory—namely, that better speaking and writing abilities will result from increased conscious knowledge about language. This latter theory has not been supported by studies into the effectiveness of grammar instruction.

Teaching Grammar Is Not Teaching Reading and Writing

The arguments traditionally given for the kind of grammar instruction that has dominated English studies for the last hundred years have been based on claims for grammar's utility. It was argued that by studying grammar, students would learn the makeup of the language and so be able to apply what they learned as better speakers, writers, and readers. Recent linguistic theory, however, is in conflict with this assumption, and numerous research studies have also failed to show a direct link between such study and improved language skills.

This claim—that the study of grammar does not help students to read and write better—may strike you as surprising and suspect. Like many students who prepare to teach English or elementary education, you may have always loved studying grammar. It may seem reasonable or even obvious to attribute your own success in reading and writing to your instruction in grammar. Nevertheless, the case against such a connection is extremely strong. The study of grammar is indeed valuable, as we will see, but there are solid reasons for questioning traditional goals and methods.

The principal theoretical objection to traditional arguments for teaching grammar derives from the difference between our conscious and our subconscious knowledge of language (see our discussion in Chapter 1). The subconscious faculty of the mind that directs our production and understanding of language is separate from the conscious faculty that is affected by grammar study. Conscious knowledge is not automatically transformed into subconscious knowledge. When we learn about language consciously, our ability to produce language is not necessarily improved. Learning about grammar has about the same effect on the ability to read and write as learning about leg muscles has on the ability to run.

What linguists have learned about *child language acquisition* (the way in which infants and children learn to use language) also supports this objection. The preceding seventeen chapters have attempted to describe the principles or rules that you and I use to produce English sentences. Most of them we acquired very early, since we were speaking grammatical English long before we were old enough to attend school. Obviously we did not learn these rules directly. Our parents did not tell us, for example, that a sentence must consist of a subject (or noun phrase) and a predicate (or verb phrase), and yet we were applying this rule before we were out of diapers. Nor did we learn by simple imitation: The speech of children is different in significant ways from the speech of adults. Rather, we were exposed to language, and from that exposure, we figured out the rules on our own.

Linguists believe that children are born with a capacity (we can call it an instinct if we like) for learning language. Children's minds are innately prepared to discover and then apply the rules of whatever language is spoken around them. Children learn these rules without specific instruction (making mistakes at first and overgeneralizing—saying, for example, "I eated.." and "she gots.."—but with further experience learning to refine their rules and to allow for exceptions). Direct teaching by parents *about* language does the child little if any good. Children learn language very much on their own, and while parents can provide a rich language environment that can aid children in learning, even children who are ignored still learn language, provided they are at least exposed to language spoken around them. Given the extraordinary complexity of the rules of language (as our analysis in this book has demonstrated to us), we must truly be impressed by the innate capacity of human children to learn language.

School children learn to read and write in similar ways. Most of what they learn about reading, for example, comes from their own experiences. Direct instruction plays a relatively minor part; exposure to the written word is far more important. Children who since infancy have been read to on their parents' laps become early readers. Schools that make frequent reading for study and pleasure (rather than phonics drills) the focus of their reading program have the best results.

Writing, too, is largely self-taught. The best predictor of the writing abilities of college students is the amount of reading and writing they have previously done—not the amount of instruction they have had in the rules of grammar or usage. To foster literacy, schools can offer an environment in which language skills can flourish; they can provide experiences which aid development; and they can promote attitudes that encourage learning—but they cannot teach those skills directly.

Modern composition theory is in accord with linguistic theory about the ineffectiveness of isolated grammar instruction in promoting writing ability. It rejects traditional arguments for a building-block model of acquiring writing skills: As a first step in learning to write, according to the building-block model, children are introduced to grammar so that they can understand the language. They are then drilled in small units of language such as words and spelling. They next progress to sentences, then to paragraphs, and only then are they ready to tackle an essay. Modern theory rejects this approach, holding that students learn to write by writing. They should begin writing from the earliest grades, and they should write and read as often as possible. Any attempts to teach writing skills apart from actual writing will fail. Improvements in grammatical sophistication come from exposure and practice in using new grammatical forms, not from isolated learning *about* grammar.

The findings of experimental research have also disappointed those who hoped to prove the utility of formal grammar teaching. Dozens of carefully conducted experiments dating back to the beginning of this century have shown no connection between grammar study and either improved control over surface features such as style and mechanics or improved expression.

(For more information about these studies, consult the works by Finnegan, Hartwell, and Weaver listed in the bibliography at the end of this chapter.) The old arguments based on utility do not provide a strong case for traditional grammar instruction.

Studying Grammar Is Valuable and Important

If we can rid ourselves of some of the old assumptions about goals and methods, however, we can make a case for teaching grammar—properly defined—that is unassailable.

Grammar Instruction as a Means to Better Language Skills

Whatever the controversy about teaching conscious grammatical knowledge, there is certainly no controversy about the value of students' increasing their subconscious grammatical knowledge. Teachers who disagree about methods of teaching grammar fully *agree* that students should gain a working command of grammar. All teachers want their students to speak and write fluent, effective, and grammatical English. Moreover, they want them to extend their grammatical sophistication, to have at their disposal a wide range of grammatical constructions. How, we may ask, can this knowledge best be achieved? What should teachers and parents do?

In the terms that we have studied, increased grammatical sophistication means acquiring more phrase-structure and transformational rules and applying them in productive ways. As student writers mature, for example, their syntactic repertoires grow to include adverbial clauses, participial phrases, and appositives. They learn to make choices about moving adverbials and selecting active or passive voice for reasons of emphasis and style. Much of this increased grammatical knowledge comes from exposure and practice: They learn through reading, and they refine what they learn through writing. Parents and teachers play an important role by fostering that experience. Competent writing will come naturally and fluently to children if they write frequently in school, as a part of their daily work in all subjects, not just in order to produce occasional English "essays."

More direct methods can also be useful, provided they are tied to actual writing. While isolated teaching about grammar (such as in this book) has little impact on writing skills, teaching that is intimately tied with writing can produce results. As the section "Instruction in Applied Grammar" on pages 257–260 demonstrates, new grammatical constructions can be modeled and imitated in various ways so as to extend students' grammatical repertoires. Some instructional methods, it seems, can indeed lead to wider subconscious knowledge of grammar.

Subconscious knowledge, however, is not the only target of our instruction. Conscious knowledge does have a place in at least certain usage skills, and these can be affected by direct instruction. Whereas most spelling and punctuation decisions are automatic (subconscious) matters to us, ingrained as a result of our reading and writing experience, we all make certain other decisions about our writing in a deliberate (conscious) way. In examining my own writing practice, for example, I can easily think of several examples. When I write an *i-t-s*, I consciously remember a rule about which one gets the apostrophe (*it's* is the contraction for *it is*; *its* is the possessive of *it*). In punctuating a relative clause, I sometimes need to consider whether the clause is restrictive or nonrestrictive (the latter is separated from the main clause by commas). When I write *affect* and *effect* I have to think consciously about which one is which (you can have an *effect*, *affect* the outcome, or *effect* a change).

Like all other writers, I have a whole fund of conscious stylistic notions that I apply whenever I write or edit my writing. When I write a series of phrases, I check that they are in parallel form (for instance, not mixing noun phrases with verb phrases or clauses, as in: *She likes sports, science, does crossword puzzles, and she reads mysteries*). I consciously avoid words I consider pretentious (*utilize* instead of *use*), and I try to delete unnecessary phrases to make my writing more direct. I am sure I acquired these conscious principles about writing not just from experience but also from direct school instruction and from reading articles and books about writing.

Schools can and should teach those elements of mechanics and style that are matters of conscious knowledge. The research shows, however, that such teaching is ineffective if it is conducted apart from a writing context. A lesson on punctuating relative clauses, taught by itself to a junior high school class, will simply not work. On the other hand, if that class is engaged in a large-group editing session, discussing ways to help a student improve a draft of an essay, questions about punctuation will arise naturally. Students will retain information about usage only when they are motivated—when they feel a need to learn that information and believe it will benefit them. Creating a receptive attitude and a commitment to writing is perhaps the most important task of the writing teacher.

Inasmuch as a case can be made for certain teaching about usage, is there anything to be said in favor of teaching syntax itself? Is conscious grammatical knowledge of any value? Is it desirable for students to be able to recognize nouns and verbs or to know a gerund when they write one?

One quite common argument for learning grammar is that it gives students a means for talking about their writing. Developing an analytical attitude to writing is a worthwhile goal, and we surely want students to understand how they have written, to think critically about what they have done, and to consider other choices that might have presented themselves. Conscious grammatical knowledge allows for this analysis and provides a vocabulary for communicating about it. This benefit seems reasonable, although research studies have not been able to demonstrate it conclusively. On the contrary, some argue that grammar study does not improve any aspect of writing and that it can actually have a negative effect by using time that could be spent more productively with actual reading and writing. Those who argue for grammar study based on its benefits for other academic skills continue to find themselves in a defensive and beleaguered position.

Grammar Instruction for Its Own Sake

By far the strongest argument for teaching grammar is for its own sake, and not for its impact on other skills. According to this important argument, grammar is worth learning because it has a value in and of itself.

To argue that a subject has an intrinsic value is a curious type of argument, since it is not subject to outside proof. It is impossible, for example, to prove or disprove the merits of studying the fine arts or higher mathematics. Most students will not become artists or musicians nor will many ever encounter practical applications for trigonometry or Boolean algebra, and yet most of us believe in the value of these studies. Our arguments are based on notions of value that have nothing to do with immediate utility, nothing to do with developing marketable skills or increasing our incomes. Instead we see these subjects as important areas of knowledge, connected in important ways with the meaning of being human, with beauty, and even with the nature of truth itself. Our minds, we feel, are more fully developed, our knowledge more richly completed, through our contact with these studies. It is an argument based on insight, subjective experience, aesthetics, and certain philosophical assumptions, rather than on practical consequences. Nonetheless it is an argument that is not to be dismissed out of hand.

The same arguments support the teaching of grammar. I hope that, having completed the study of this book, you now *know* the value of grammar. I hope you have found a beauty and even a pleasure, perhaps a deeply satisfying one, in understanding the remarkably elegant structure of our language. I hope you have found it a revelation as the operating principles of the English language unfolded before you and as you were struck by the clarity of what was at first quite unclear. Many millions of people have known these experiences and remain convinced of grammar's importance. They love the language, and their study of grammar has played an important role in fostering that love.

Besides conferring aesthetic rewards, the study of grammar also provides important knowledge about ourselves. The use of language is the most central of all the faculties of the human mind. All mental activity that makes us distinctly human presupposes language. Human minds are uniquely adapted to learning language, and the structures of language and of our minds are attuned. Because language is so complex and because such large areas of our brains are devoted to language (as neurological studies show), no other field of study can give us equivalent insight into the nature and structure of our minds. Like the study of philosophy, history, biology, sociology, and psychology, the study of grammar teaches us important lessons about ourselves. Self-knowledge is the central concern of a liberal and humanistic education. It is its own reward. We need look no further to justify its existence.

Methods of Teaching Grammar

The methods for teaching grammar to a class of college students are not those most appropriate for teaching grammar to primary and secondary students, and teachers must use wisdom and discretion in formulating their plans of instruction. They must also consider their goals carefully. Different methods are appropriate when teaching applied grammar (grammatical knowledge that students apply in their reading and writing) and when teaching grammar for its own sake.

Instruction in Applied Grammar

Applied grammar is best taught by teaching reading and writing. As students become more experienced and fluent readers and writers, their subconscious grammatical knowledge improves as well. Conscious knowledge about grammar has comparatively little impact on subconscious grammatical skills. Consequently, it is important for language-arts instructors on all levels to be trained in methods of teaching reading and writing. It is to those fields that we must look for information about methods for developing applied grammatical skills.

While these methods are largely indirect, they can also include some more direct methods for increasing grammatical sophistication. *Modeling exercises* can introduce students to new syntactic constructions, and they can teach stylistic lessons as well. As an example, the following activities can successfully introduce high school students to the use of participial modifiers.

As part of a unit in which students are writing descriptive essays, they may take time out to complete this exercise.

A TYPICAL MODELING EXERCISE

In each blank space, supply an active participle (-*ing* phrase) to modify the preceding noun, as in these examples:

> a. The angry demonstrators, *shaking their fists at the police*, advanced on the courthouse.
>
> b. *Stuffing their faces with mangos and rice*, the beggar children ate like savages.

Now use your imagination to invent similar modifiers for these sentences:

1. The pirates, _____-ing_____, boarded the Spanish frigate.

2. _____-ing_____, she crossed the finish line of the the marathon after four agonizing hours.

3. _____-ing_____ and _____-ing_____, the orator on the soapbox drew only smiles from the passing crowd.

An exercise like this requires very little if any formal instruction about participles and how they are formed. Grammatical terminology is not necessary for its success; it will work just as well if the participles are called simply *i-n-g phrases* (although there is no reason not to provide the standard name for them). With a little practice, students catch on to the nature of active participles, and they begin very quickly to supply their own examples.

An exercise such as this works best if it is treated as a game and made as entertaining as possible. In a discussion after students have written the exercise, the teacher can solicit a variety of their responses, with special praise going to the cleverer and more colorful examples. The class can also be shown examples of participles in the work of professional writers. A follow-up exercise can ask students to add participles to sentences for which no blank spaces are provided, such as this one:

> The mother ape confronted the human intruder.

Questions can be asked to encourage creativity in this exercise and to open students' minds to stylistic possibilities: Can more than one participle be supplied? In what places? Can participles modify *the intruder* as well as *the mother ape*? A discussion of dangling participles can arise naturally from this exercise; the class can consider whether a problem exists with a sentence such as *The mother ape confronted the human intruder, shaking her hairy fist.*

For such exercises to have a lasting effect, students must have the immediate opportunity to apply what they have learned to their own writing. As a follow-up to the modeling exercise on participles, students can revise a descriptive passage they have previously written so that it includes several participial modifiers. Furthermore, since they are engaged in a stylistic experiment, they can attempt to include as many participles as possible and then analyze the result. At what point do the participles become intrusive? Which ones work and which ones don't? Can the passage be revised again so that it contains only a few effective participles?

The point of such exercises is not to encourage the proliferation of participles for their own sake but to introduce students to new possibilities for effective writing and to increase their awareness of style. Like all attempts to teach applied grammar, these exercises are effective because they involve students in actual writing. No amount of isolated instruction *about* participles can have an equivalent effect. In addition to active participles, many other constructions, including passive participles, appositives, absolutes, gerunds, and relative clauses, can be introduced in similar ways.

It is important to see the difference between such exercises and traditional drills, which lack any direct connection with actual writing and frequently bore students besides. Exercises, for example, where students are asked to underline and label participles and other modifiers or verbals from a list of sentences or where they are told to find and correct dangling participles in a list of sentences or even where they are told simply to invent a few sentences containing participles may do more harm than good. Whatever information they provide is unlikely to be retained; students are more likely to be alienated than stimulated by such drills; and valuable time that could have been spent constructively has been wasted.

Modeling exercises are just one of many effective methods of developing a stylistic and grammatical range in student writing. Another is through *sentence combining*. Many grammatical constructions such as participles, gerunds, adverbial clauses, and relative clauses derive from embedded clauses (one S-clause embedded in another). Sentence-combining exercises cause students to broaden their syntactic repertoires by exploring various possibilities for embedding, as in the following example:

A TYPICAL SENTENCE-COMBINING EXERCISE

Combine the following clauses in as many ways as possible:

The dwarves approached the dragon's lair.
The dwarves quaked with fear.
The dwarves put on a brave front.

In the discussion that follows, students may propose combinations such as these:

> Quaking with fear but putting on a brave front, the dwarves approached the dragon's lair.

> Although they put on a brave front, the dwarves quaked with fear as they approached the dragon's lair.

> Having approached the dragon's lair, the dwarves put on a brave front to hide their quaking with fear.

> The dwarves who approached the dragon's lair quaked with fear but still put on a brave front.

Students can also be encouraged to vary or embellish the given clauses:

> Their bodies quaking inwardly with fear but outwardly showing only bravery, the intrepid dwarves approached their terrible goal, the lair of the dragon.

As variations are proposed, they can be written on the board, and the class can be encouraged to revise or add to them.

Notice the many different types of grammatical constructions used in these examples. The names of the constructions can be used in describing them, but sentence combining works equally well without grammatical labeling. More important is discussion about the results: Which sentences work well? Do they have different effects? Which ones might we revise? In addition to single-sentence exercises, longer sentence-combining exercises are also effective. For example, students can be given a dozen or more clauses and asked to combine them into a paragraph or brief essay.

Sentence-combining exercises encourage students to extend their range by attempting new and diverse constructions, and the discussion afterward can bring the stylistic consequences of the various options into focus. It is important for students to have fun with these combinations. Creativity should be encouraged, even if it sometimes results in overwriting (as in the last example) or even in errors (errors are inevitable whenever students attempt to practice unfamiliar skills). Freedom to experiment and to take risks without fear of penalty is essential to the progress of language-learners at all levels.

Modeled exercises and sentence combining are two related types of exercises that can teach applied grammar. Variations can be adapted for different grade levels, and many other activities are equally valuable. As useful as they are, however, these exercises should be only supplements to a program of writing instruction, never its central focus. Writing itself should continue to be the principal activity of the writing classroom.

Direct Instruction in Grammar

There is no point in teaching grammar if students do not understand it or, worse, if they detest it. Two primary goals of grammar teaching are for students to gain insight into the workings of the English language and to gain a love for it as well. Grammar instruction that fails to accomplish these goals is worse than useless.

Unfortunately, grammar as it is often taught is so much stale drill and memorization, a subject which pleases a few and antagonizes many. Countless adults have unpleasant memories about school English largely because of grammar. (Like most others in my profession, whenever I am asked by new acquaintances what I do, I steel myself for their reaction to "English teacher": They suddenly become visibly wary and make some nervous joke about watching their grammar.)

It should not be so. There is no reason why grammar should not be made clear enough for students to understand nor any reason why it shouldn't be interesting and fun as well. How well grammar is taught depends on the wisdom and skill of the teacher.

Our teaching is unlikely to be perfect, however, or to succeed with every student, and beginning teachers should not be crushed by their lack of perfection. Still, they should set their sights high. If grammar were taught ideally in an ideal world, it would be quite different from the way it is often taught today. Textbooks would be up to date, based on modern discoveries about our language, not discredited traditions. Teachers would teach principles of transformational grammar suitably adapted for each grade level. Information would be accurate and clear, students would be involved participants in the discovery of grammatical principles, and they would find the experience rewarding.

The world we live in, regrettably, is not ideal, but it does not have to be terrible either. Even with the constraints imposed upon teachers by the realities of their situations, they can still make grammar instruction worthwhile if they adhere to the following general guidelines:

1. Teachers should involve students in discovering grammar. The operational method of this book has been a search for the principles of our grammar, and the book's organization has been from simpler to more complex concepts. We have encountered data in the form of English sentences, and we attempted to discover the structure of these sentences and the way they have been formed. Grammar-as-discovery is the best teaching method in the schools as well as in college courses. Students should not simply be told about grammar; they should do grammar for themselves. Teachers can adapt similar methods of discovery to the abilities and needs of any grade level.

2. Teachers should make it clear. The analysis within this book is appropriate for college students; not all of it would be clear to high-school-age or younger students. Teachers must keep grammatical analyses sufficiently simple so that they can be understood by their students. The introductory analyses in Chapter 2 of this book could easily be adapted to an eighth-grade classroom, but the considerably more detailed analyses of infinitives in Chapter 15 would be inappropriate. Nevertheless, eighth graders are still capable of recognizing infinitives and discovering insights into how they work. An eighth-grade teacher can ask a class to analyze a pair of sentences such as *Harry is eager to please* and *Harry is easy to please*. The class can make many discoveries: They will see that in the first sentence, Harry is doing the pleasing while in the second, someone else is pleasing him. A conclusion the class can draw is that infinitives have underlying subjects which do not appear in the sentence itself (the surface structure).

3. **Teachers should make it fun.** The more that teachers involve students in making discoveries for themselves (as in the preceding example about infinitives), the more likely they are to accomplish their goals. The following sample activity involves noun phrases.

Can you rearrange the following groups of five words so that each makes sense as a phrase?

a. players the basketball tall five

b. many those recipes new dessert

c. record favorite two albums my

Students will all report the same answers (*the five tall basketball players* and so on). What conclusions can they then draw about how such phrases are ordered? Do the last words in each phrase (*players, recipes, albums*) have something in common? What about the words that come second (*five, many, two*)? As this lesson continues, the class can conclude that the words fall into five categories, which we know as determiners, quantifiers, adjectives, noun modifiers, and nouns. They discover that when these words occur together in a phrase they do so in that particular order. Students can also explore whether the basic order can ever be varied. Is the phrase *the tall five basketball players* ever possible? If so, what does it mean? (Perhaps the *tall* five, as opposed to some shorter set of five basketball players?)

Such an exercise introduces the concepts of noun phrases and modifiers. It demonstrates to students that when we speak we follow certain principles that we are not consciously aware of and that it can be enjoyable to discover what they may be.

4. **Teachers should adapt and supplement the available materials.** The realities that teachers must deal with include some undeniable constraints

on their teaching. Mandated textbooks may include some of the worst features of traditional grammar. Instruction may need to be directed so that students succeed on the grammar section of a particular achievement test. Parents and administrators may place demands for certain instructional goals and methods. It would be foolhardy for teachers to ignore such realities. Fortunately, even poor textbooks provide much valid and valuable information about English grammar, and the classifications and terminology they use are usually those accepted by most linguists. Good teachers can adapt those materials to worthwhile purposes, and they can provide their own supplementary exercises and discussions as well. They can also use many innovative and nontraditional strategies, but, if so, they will find it prudent to keep parents informed of their methods and reasons. For example, a teacher may have sound pedagogical reasons for not marking every spelling or grammatical error on a student's papers, but unless parents are informed of those reasons, they may complain that the teacher is slipshod or ignorant.

5. Teachers should not lose sight of real goals. The purpose of applied grammar study is to help students develop their language skills, and the purpose of direct instruction is to provide students with an understanding and appreciation of the English language. Training in advanced linguistics is not a goal of the schools. Primary and secondary students do not need a sophisticated command of theoretical grammar. Instead, they need to understand general principles about language and to be acquainted with the major grammatical constructions of our language. Tree diagrams can be a useful tool because they can make structure clear and because students usually enjoy drawing them, but they are not an end in themselves. It is also not important for students to understand all details of sentence derivations, particularly when those details are especially complicated. If through their instruction students learn to speak, read, and write with competence and confidence; if they gain an understanding and love of the English language; and if they develop a curious and inquiring attitude toward language—then their schooling will serve them well. They will be well prepared for using language in everyday life, and they will be prepared for whatever more advanced linguistic study they undertake in the future.

A Brief Bibliography for Teachers

D'Eloia, Sarah. "The Uses—and Limits—of Grammar." *Journal of Basic Writing* 1 (1977): 1–20.

Finnegan, Edward. *Attitudes Toward English Usage*. New York: Teachers College Press, 1980.

Graves, Donald. *Writing: Teachers and Children at Work*. Exeter, N.H.: Heinemann, 1983.

Hartwell, Patrick. "Grammar, Grammars, and the Teaching of Grammar." *College English*, 47 (1985): 105–127.

Pooley, Robert C. *The Teaching of English Usage*. 2nd ed. 1946, Reprint Urbana, Ill.: NCTE, 1974.

Smith, Frank. *Understanding Reading*. 2nd ed. New York: Holt, Rinehart and Winston, 1978.

Tate, Gary, and Corbett, Edward P. J. eds. *The Writing Teacher's Sourcebook*. New York: Oxford University Press, 1981.

Veit, Richard. "1984 Visited: English Debased? Students Illiterate?" *Etc.: A Review of General Semantics* 41 (1984): 409–415.

Weaver, Constance. *Grammar for Teachers*. Urbana, Ill.: NCTE, 1979.

Index

Arrow
in phrase-structure rules (→), 17
representing transformations (⟹), 93
Articles (Art), 10, 34, 71, 241–242
definite, 35–36
as determiners, 71–73
indefinite, 35–36
As
as comparative conjunction (Cj$_{Cp}$), 236
as subordinating conjunction (Cj$_S$), 123
Asterisk (*), 7. *See also* Grammatical and
ungrammatical sentences
Auxiliary category (Aux), 150. *See also*
Auxiliary verbs
Auxiliary verbs, 149–160
emphatic, 159–160
modal, 153–155
ordering of, 157–158
in participles, 227
passive, 180–181
perfect, 156–159
progressive, 156–159
supporting, 164–167

Be
in deep structure of participles, 221
as linking verb, 31
as passive auxiliary verb, 179
as progressive auxiliary verb, 157
as supporting auxiliary in participles, 228
Benefits of grammar study, 2–3, 254–257
Braces in phrase-structure rules { }, 33

Cardinal numbers, 78
Case
nominative, 47–48
objective, 47–48
of personal pronouns, 47–48
subjective, 47–48
Child language acquisition, 252–253
Clauses, 60, 61
adjectival-complement, 69–70
adverbial, 121–125, 200
complement, 61–70, 129, 134
coordinate, 59–61, 122
dependent, 122

embedded, 64
nominal-complement, 66–69
relative, 125–143, 146–148
sentential-complement, 61–65, 190, 194
subordinate, 122
as types of phrases, 60, 127
Commands. *See* Imperative mood
Common nouns (N$_C$), 22–24, 26–27
Comparative conjunctions (Cj$_{Cp}$), 236–237
Comparative form of adjectives and
adverbs, 237
Comparison of adjectives and adverbs,
236–239
Complement-clause transformation
(T-Comp), 190
Complementizer (Cj$_{Cl}$), 61–62, 63
omission of, 65–66
supplied by transformation, 190
Complementizing conjunction. *See*
Complementizer
Complement phrases and clauses, 61–70.
See also Complement-clause
transformation
adjectival-complement clauses, 69–70, 239
adjectival-complement phrases, 70
adverbial-complement clauses, 239
differentiated from relative clauses, 134
nominal-complement clauses, 66–69
in sentences with relative clauses, 129
sentential-complement clauses, 61–65
as subordinate clauses, 125
as underlying gerunds, 218–219
as underlying infinitives, 189–190
without "that," 65–66
Compound sentences, 60
Conjoined phrases and clauses. *See*
Coordination
Conjunctions
comparative (Cj$_{Cp}$), 236–237
complementizing (Cj$_{Cl}$), 61–63
coordinating (Cj$_C$), 53, 57, 122
subordinating (Cj$_S$), 121, 123
Conscious and subconscious knowledge
of language, 3–4, 5, 97, 251
Constituents, 9

Passive transformation (continued)
  cyclic operation of, 196–197
Passive voice. *See* Passive sentences
Past participles, 220
Past tense of verbs (Past), 149–150, 157
Perfect auxiliary verbs (Perf), 157–158
Person, 47
  affecting inflection of verbs, 152
  of pronouns, 47
Personal pronouns (Pro$_P$), 45–48, 49,
    111–114. *See also* Personal-pronoun
    transformation
  derived from underlying noun phrases,
    111–114
  inflection of, 47–48
  list of, 47
  as noun phrases, 46
Personal-pronoun transformation (T-Pro$_P$),
    111–114
  conditions for applying, 116–118, 125, 220
Phrasal verbs, 96
Phrases, 9, 22, 60, 62
  clauses as types of, 60, 127
Phrase-structure rules (PS rules), 17, 26–28,
    33, 90, 97
  summary of, 245–246
Place adverbials, 79
  following linking verbs, 81–82, 83
Plural, 47. *See also* Number
  of personal pronouns, 47
Plus sign (+), for repeatable elements, 29–30
Positive form of adjectives and adverbs, 237
Possessive inflection for nouns (Poss), 74–77
Possessive interrogative determiner
  (*whose*), 178
Possessive noun phrases
  as determiners, 74–77, 240
  preceding gerunds, 218–219
  as pronouns, 240
  recursion of, 75–76
  underlying possessive pronouns, 131
  underlying possessive relative pronouns, 130
Possessive pronouns (Pro$_S$). *See also*
    Possessive-pronoun transformation
  attributive, 240

derived from possessive noun phrases,
    131, 240
  as determiners, 76–77, 240
  nominal, 240
  substantive, 240
Possessive-pronoun transformation
    (T-Pro$_S$), 131
Possessive relative clauses, 129–131
Predicate, 10–11
Prepositional phrases (PP), 37–45
  as adverbial phrases, 79–80
  ambiguity of, 43–45
  containing interrogative pronouns, 174
  containing relative pronouns, 131–134
  coordination of, 57
  in deep structures of indirect objects, 106
  degree modifiers with, 83
  recursion of, 41–42
  within noun phrases, 41–45
  within verb phrases, 37–40, 43–45
Prepositions (Prep), 37–45. *See also*
    Prepositional phrases
  contrasted with particles, 89–91
  ending sentences with, 51, 136, 251
  list of, 39
Prescriptive grammar, 51, 215, 250
Present participles, 220
Present tense of verbs (Pres), 149–150, 157
Pro-adverbs, 244
Pro-forms, 240–244. *See also* Pronouns
Pro-form transformation (T-Pro-Form), 243
Progressive auxiliary verbs (Prog), 157–159
Pronominal determiners, 240–241
Pronouns, 46
  Demonstrative (Pro$_D$), 240–241
  Indefinite (Pro$_{SME}$), 185, 242
  Intensive (Pro$_I$), 145–146
  Interrogative (Pro$_Q$), 171–174
  Personal (Pro$_P$), 45–48, 49, 111–114
  Possessive (Pro$_S$), 76–77, 131, 240
  Possessive noun phrases as, 240
  Quantifiers as, 240–241
  Reciprocal, 244
  Reflexive (Pro$_X$), 114–116, 244
  Relative (Pro$_R$), 126, 131–135